# Colonial Literature and the Native Author

Jane Stafford

# Colonial Literature and the Native Author

Indigeneity and Empire

Jane Stafford
School of English, Film, Theatre and Med
Victoria University of Wellington
Wellington, New Zealand

ISBN 978-3-319-38766-6         ISBN 978-3-319-38767-3 (eBook)
DOI 10.1007/978-3-319-38767-3

Library of Congress Control Number: 2016949047

© The Editor(s) (if applicable) and the Author(s) 2016
This work is subject to copyright. All rights are solely and exclusively licensed by the Publisher, whether the whole or part of the material is concerned, specifically the rights of translation, reprinting, reuse of illustrations, recitation, broadcasting, reproduction on microfilms or in any other physical way, and transmission or information storage and retrieval, electronic adaptation, computer software, or by similar or dissimilar methodology now known or hereafter developed.
The use of general descriptive names, registered names, trademarks, service marks, etc. in this publication does not imply, even in the absence of a specific statement, that such names are exempt from the relevant protective laws and regulations and therefore free for general use.
The publisher, the authors and the editors are safe to assume that the advice and information in this book are believed to be true and accurate at the date of publication. Neither the publisher nor the authors or the editors give a warranty, express or implied, with respect to the material contained herein or for any errors or omissions that may have been made.

Printed on acid-free paper

This Palgrave Macmillan imprint is published by Springer Nature
The registered company is Springer International Publishing AG
The registered company address is: Gewerbestrasse 11, 6330 Cham, Switzerland

*For Mark*

# Acknowledgements

I am grateful for support from a Canadian Government Faculty Award, the Marsden Fund of the Royal Society of New Zealand, the Victoria University of Wellington Research Fund, and the Victoria University of Wellington Faculty of Humanities and Social Science Research Fund. Victoria University's English Programme and the Stout Research Centre for New Zealand Studies provided knowledgeable and generous audiences at various stages of this project. The resources of the Alexander Turnbull Library, the British Library, Victoria University Library and J.C. Beaglehole Room, McMaster University Library's William Ready Division of Archives and Research Collections, the National Library of New Zealand/ Te Puna Mātauranga o Aotearoa, Toronto University Libraries, and the University of British Columbia Library have all been essential to my work. I have benefited from advice and help from Tony Ballantyne, Alex Calder, Ralph Crane, Nikki Hessell, Alan Lester, Dougal McNeill, Meenakshi Mukherjee, Stuart Murray, John O'Leary, Olivia Tweedie, Lydia Wevers, and Mark Williams.

Early versions of parts of chapters 2 and 6 appear in *Empire Calling: Administering Australasia and India*, eds. Ralph Crane, Anna Johnston, and C. Vijayasree (New Delhi: Cambridge University Press India, 2013); *Moving Worlds: A Journal of Transcultural Writings, Special Issue: 'New' New Zealand*, 8:2 (2008); and the *Journal of New Zealand Literature, Special Issue: Comparative Approaches to Indigenous Studies*, 24: 2 (2007).

# A Note on Terminology

This study rests on the idea of a commonality among a diverse group of people—linked by their membership of the British Empire and their knowledge of the English literary canon, but diverse in their cultural, ethnic, and national origins. There is no one satisfactory descriptor that encompasses all members of this group. It is true that all could be described by the term 'colonised' and I have used this in places. But its universal application seems to me to flatten and limit the plurality of positions, relationships, and responses to empire which is central to my argument. The term 'Indigenous' is applicable to Apirana Ngata, Wiremu Te Rangikaheke, George Copway, Pauline Johnson, and Chief Joe Capilano, and I have used it, though not exclusively, in these contexts and in my sub-title. In the chapter on Pauline Johnson, I have followed Carole Gerson and Veronica Strong-Boag in *Paddling her own Canoe: the Times and Texts of E. Pauline Johnson, Tekahiowake* (2000) and Johnson herself in using the term 'Indian' on occasions. 'Native', despite its mildly pejorative nineteenth-century usages, seems open to recuperation, has a general application to all my subjects, and a functional neutrality. This is the term I have used in my title and most consistently throughout my text.

I have followed Meenakshi Mukherjee's practice in *An Indian for All Seasons: the Many Lives of R.C. Dutt* (2009) in using nineteenth-century forms: 'Dutt' rather than 'Datta'; 'Bengal' and 'Bengali' rather than 'Bangla'; 'Calcutta' rather than 'Kolkata'.

I have used 'Tswana' in my text, despite the fact that Sol Plaatje uses 'Bechuana' but have left quoted material in its original state.

It is now accepted practice to use macrons, where appropriate, in Māori words. I have not imposed macrons on quoted materials that do not employ them.

Throughout I have tried to emulate Gerson and Strong, who state in the introduction to their biography of Johnson, 'When writing in our own voice, we have sought language that connotes inclusion and respect'.

## Contents

1 Introduction: 'I Adopt the Language of the Poet'  1

2 Littleness, Frivolity and Vedic Simplicity: Toru Dutt, Sarojini Naidu and Mr Gosse  25

3 'Constant Reading after Office Hours': Sol Plaatje and Literary Belonging  61

4 'The Genuine Stamp of Truth and Nature': Voicing *The History of Mary Prince*  107

5 Culture's Artificial Note: E. Pauline Johnson, Tekahionwake, and her Audiences  147

6 'Pressed Down by the Great Words of Others': Wiremu Maihi Te Rangikaheke and Apirana Ngata  185

7 Conclusion: Secret Fountains and Authentic Utterance  217

**Bibliography** 227

**Index** 243

CHAPTER 1

# Introduction: 'I Adopt the Language of the Poet'

> Once more I see my fathers' land
> Upon the beach, where oceans roar;
> Where whiten'd bones bestrew the sand,
> Of some brave warrior of yore.
> The *groves*, where once my fathers roam'd –
> The *rivers*, where the beaver dwelt –
> The *lakes*, where angry waters foam'd –
> Their *charms*, with my fathers, have fled.
>
> O! Tell me, ye 'pale faces,' tell,
> Where have my proud ancestors gone?
> Whose smoke curled up from every dale,
> To what land have their free spirits flown?
> Whose wigwams stood where cities rise;
> On whose war-paths the steam-horse flies;
> And ships, like mon-e-doos in disguise,
> Approach the shore in endless files.
> From *The Life, History, and Travels
> of Kah-Ge-Ga-Gah-Bowh
> (George Copway)*, 1847.[1]

In the English language, using the rhetorical forms of English literature, an Ojibwa reflects on mid-nineteenth-century Canada. The land before him, once his ancestors', now has, as its sole marker of Indigenous inhabitation, 'whitened bones'. The Ojibwa past can be evoked only imaginatively by a negative construction in which the speaker describes what is no longer there: groves, rivers, lakes, all linked visually by italicisation – '*groves*', '*rivers*', '*lakes*' – along with the idea of their aesthetic power, their '*charms*'. This natural habitat has retreated before the settler presence and with it the Indigenous occupiers, their wigwams and smoking fires. What is actually before the speaker are the cities, ships and trains of the modern European nation, the technologies that displace the now-doomed original inhabitants of the place. 'Where have my proud ancestors gone... To what land have their free spirits flown?', the second stanza asks. But the question here is pointedly addressed to those who now possess and control this information, the 'pale faces'. The erasure has been so complete that even the certainties of Indigenous metaphysics, the geography of the afterlife, have been lost. In the bone-littered present, the only spiritual reference is contained in metaphor: the encroaching settlers' ships are 'like mon-e-doos in disguise'.

The Ojibwa word 'mon-e-doos', with its linguistic specificity, contrasts with and acts against the conventional and generalised European rhetoric of the surrounding poem, its groves and dales. The book *Life, History, and Travels* by Copway has already introduced his readers to the mon-e-doos when he describes the world he inhabited before his conversion to Christianity:

> You will see that I served the imaginary gods of my poor blind father. I was out early and late in quest of the favors of the *Mon-e-doos* (spirits), who, it was said, were numerous – who filled the air! At early dawn I watched the rising of the *palace* of the Great Spirit – *the sun* – who, it was said, made the world!... On the mountain top, or along the valley, or the water brook, I searched for some kind of intimation from the spirits who made their residence in the noise of the water falls.[2]

Copway identifies the Great Spirit as Ke-sha-mon-e-doo. He is terrible; he 'shrouds himself in rolling white and dark clouds'; but at the same time, he is nurturing, manifest in the power, but also the bounty of the natural world:

> His benevolence I saw in the running of the streams, for the animals to quench their thirst and the fishes to live; the fruit of the earth teamed wherever I looked. Every thing I saw smilingly said Ke-sha-mon-e-doo nin-ge-oo-she-ig – *the Benevolent spirit* made me.[3]

In translating the concepts of Indigenous religion into his English text, Copway falls naturally into the language of Romanticism, which becomes the bridge between his original belief system and the Christianity of his conversion:

> I was born in *nature's wide domain!* The trees were all that sheltered my infant limbs – the blue heavens all that covered me. I am one of nature's children; I have always admired her; she shall be my glory; her features – her robes, and the wreath about her brow – the seasons – her stately oaks, and the evergreen – her hair – ringlets over the earth, all contribute to my enduring love of her; and wherever I see her, emotions of pleasure roll in my breast and swell and burst like waves on the shores of the ocean, in prayer and praise to Him, who has placed me in her hand.[4]

In a trajectory that William Wordsworth would have found entirely familiar, the language here moves easily from 'nature' to a personified and female 'Nature' to 'Him who has placed me in her hand'. Bernd Peyer describes this as a 'topical naturist-nativist tribute to the American wilderness' and notes that 'Copway seemed to personify the two predominant strands in liberal white attitudes towards Indians: romantic primitivism (the vanishing act) and benevolent reformism (the transformation act)'.[5] The literary conventions of Romanticism are made to fit exactly with Copway's narrative of Christian conversion. As the young Copway's natural religion is replaced by his new Christian belief, so the unreflecting child who inhabits the natural world, who has an instinctive grasp of its immanence, changes into the adult, marked not only by separation but also by reflection, by knowing rather than being. As Wordsworth says of his childhood,

> That time is past,
> And all its aching joys are now no more...
> Not for this
> Faint I, nor mourn, nor murmur; other gifts
> Have followed – for such loss, I would believe,
> Abundant recompense.[6]

Christianity is thus presented not as an alternative to Copway's original belief, but as its natural extension. It is his questioning of Ke-sha-mon-e-doo's 'will concerning me and the rest of the Indian race' that leads him to 'a true heaven – not in the far-setting sun, where the Indian anticipated a rest, a home for his spirit – but in the bosom of the Highest'.[7] His instinctive relationship with a harmoniously spiritualised natural world is not rejected but is found to lack the teleology of what he presents as the more complex and intellectually satisfying Christianity.

In chapter 5 of his *Life*, Copway returns to this point when he quotes from Pope's 'An Essay on Man':

> Lo! the poor Indian whose untutored mind,
> Sees God in Clouds, or hears him in the wind;
> Whose soul's proud science never taught to stray,
> Beyond the solar walk or milky way.
> Yet simple nature his hopes has given
> Beyond the cloud top'd hill a humble heaven,
> Some safer world in depths of woods embrace,
> Some Island in the watery space,
> Where slaves once more their native land behold,
> No fiends torment, nor Christian thirsts for gold.[8]

The original context of Pope's passage is that of slavery rather than of settler displacement. Pope's Indians desire a 'safer world' that replicates their now lost 'native land', a world freed from the torments of captivity and the exploitative economy that attends it. Copway uses the quotation in a description of his father's conversion. In contrast to the lyrical account he has given of his own seamless move from pagan gods to Christian God, the comparison between his father's beliefs and Christianity is more abrupt. While Pope's picture of natural religion, seeing 'God in Clouds... and hear[ing] him in the wind', might parallel the *Life's* earlier description of the Ojibwa world view, here Copway emphasises the limitations of this 'humble heaven' of the 'poor Indian'. 'A carnal heaven, indeed!' he exclaims, 'A sensual paradise! Oh! the credulous and misguided Indian... Little then did [my father] know of a *heaven revealed in the gospel*'.[9]

Copway's use of the literary language of his European education is apparent not just from the way that he plays off one literary register against another. It is also demonstrated in the way his prose *Life* is punctuated by poetic excerpts: Methodist hymns and aphorisms, English translations and versifications of Ojibwa material (both his and those of other authors), literary quotations and poetry of his own composition. All these sources connect his narrative to wider discourses: of Christianity, especially that of Methodist missionary endeavours; of ethnographic Indigenous record; of the eighteenth- and early nineteenth-century literary canon. These insertions are various but not decorative or random. The poem 'Once more I see my fathers' land' comes after an account of his travels to the cities of the north-eastern United States where the extreme effects of settler presence and Indigenous dispossession are at their most obvious. The text of Charles Wesley's hymn, 'O for a thousand tongues to sing/ My great Redeemer's praise' is quoted after his account of his father's conversion, an increase of one in the number of praising tongues. Next to the hymn's English text is the Ojibwa version, 'Oh uh pa-gish ke che ingo'dwok/ Neej uh ne she nah baig', another way in which more 'tongues' – in this context, languages – are enlisted in the work of praising the Christian God.[10] In chapter 3, the translated Ojibwa 'War Song' connects Copway both with a bloodthirsty past and with contemporary ethnographic collectors of Indigenous material. 'War Song', he states, 'was first translated for Colonel McKinney, "the *Indian's friend*," on the shores of Lake Superior'. The theme of the song is the cyclical nature of vengeance and destruction in inter-tribal warfare: '[o]ur youths grown to men, to the war [we'll] lead again,'/ And our days, like our fathers', we'll end – we'll end'.[11] Whatever its veracity as ethnological record, 'War Song' is consonant with that aspect of the dying race narrative which posits that the savage habits of the native are the cause of their demise.

Cathy Rex argues that:

> Copway, in writing his own life's story, is placing himself on both sides of the ethnologist's office: he is the object of study, urged to reveal his 'authentic' life story to a white audience thirsty for anything Indian, and he is the author of that story, gathering the data and producing a textual interpretation of it.[12]

This two-way process is at its most complex in an addition in the 1850 version of *Life, History, and Travels* where Copway, as he puts it, 'adopt[s] the language of the poet':

> I will go to my tent and lie down in despair,
> I will paint me with black, and sever my hair,
> I will sit on the shore where the hurricane blows,
> And relate to the God of the tempest my woes;

> For my kindred are gone to the mounds of the dead,
> But they died not of hunger nor wasting decay,
> For the drink of the white man hath swept them away.[13]

The context here is Copway's description of the effects of alcohol on the Ojibwa, its 'soul and body-destroying influence'. The poem he 'adopts' (perhaps this term also implies 'adapts') is 'Geehale: An Indian Lament' written by the Indian Agent and ethnologist Henry Rowe Schoolcraft in 1830. In Schoolcraft's poem the disappearance of Geehale's 'kindred' is given a different cause: 'they died not by hunger or lingering decay;/ The steel of the white man has swept them away'.[14] Copway's use of the poem and his rewriting of the final lines produce a layered effect: the voice of the Indigenous as imagined by a European administrator-ethnologist-poet is modified by an actual Indigenous author for the purposes of a Methodist temperance polemic.[15] The generalised and ventriloquised rhetoric of the dying race elegy is thus given an added sense of authority as well as a specific, pragmatic and modern focus.

The variety of Copway's sources has a significant effect on the way that his own 'dying race' poem 'Once more I see my fathers' land' is contextualised. The dying race trope – in popular discourse, always a fluid mix of the ethnographic and the metaphorical – is modified within his work's wider frame of Christian redemption and salvation, which implicitly suggests that the declining savage can be rescued from extinction by conversion and the re-birth of baptism. So the fact that Copway can see his forefathers' land devoid of the living does not mean that he is not able to work for the conversion and thereby the survival of his actual father, and by extension of his contemporaries. Yes, the pagan past has vanished. But the new world of *'heaven revealed in the gospel'* replaces it.

* * *

As Copway's deployment of literary allusion demonstrates, the British Empire was a literary as well as a political network, one which provided its participants, both coloniser and colonised, with a common literary language. This language – that of the eighteenth-century Romantic and Victorian literary canons – was inculcated by agencies as diverse as the colonial education system with its newly valorised study of English literature, colonial newspapers with their ferocious middlebrow commitment to literature and the cultural arm of the global proselytising structures of the Christian church. It was tempered by local demands and agendas, from the settler nationalisms of Canada and New Zealand to the intellectual and political stringencies of the Bengali Renaissance. Also, it existed alongside and was invigorated by local Indigenous literatures and mythologies, their forms and their contents. From the library at her home at the Six Nations' Reserve where Mohawk E. Pauline Johnson read Scott's *Ivanhoe*, Longfellow's *Hiawatha* and John Richardson's *Wacousta*, to the nascent Canterbury College in Christchurch, New Zealand where Māori Apirana Ngata was taught Anglo-Saxon, to Manicktollah Street, Calcutta, where Toru Dutt read Wordsworth with her father, to the Methodist mission to the Ojibwa which introduced George Copway to 'a high-toned literature',[16] the world these colonial subjects inhabited was not just the local. It was also the literary, the textual and thereby the global.

Colonised, Indigenous or native subjects were themselves portrayed in this literature as representational models and stereotypes of, variously, the romanticised relic, the savage and the primitive, the Christian convert or the educable Indigene. But colonised subjects were also readers of such material, and – the particular focus of this book – writers. They participated not only as subjects, consumers, but also as producers within the discourses of empire. Chadwick Allen describes the ground of Indigenous literary studies as 'a body of distinct literatures emanating from distinct cultures, brought together by the historical accident of having been written in the shared language of those who colonized the communities of their authors'.[17] This study, centred on the 'historical accident' of the British Empire, concentrates on the manner in which native authors of the Victorian period, Indigenous and non-Indigenous, understood, utilised, modified and inhabited not simply the 'shared language' of English but its literary forms and conventions. What happens, the following chapters ask, when the colonised learns to write in the literary language of empire? If the romanticised subject of colonial literature becomes at the same time the author of the text, is a new kind of writing produced, or is the native author confined to and by the models of the coloniser? Is it possible to, as Copway suggests, 'adopt the language of the poet'? Can such 'adoption' be without compromise, or will such work be, as Ngata warns in his 1896 poem '*A Scene from the Past*', 'clothed in artifice'?[18]

Critics have described the dislocation of the colonial reader; how much more dislocated the colonised reader; how seemingly impossible the position of the colonised writer. Drew Lopenzina writes of the American context:

> Native writers of the colonial period and beyond were under the constant imposition of having to forge an idiom that recognized the tightly constrained discursive parameters permitted them by print culture, while simultaneously reconstructing a positive Native presence from within those constraints and holding it out for colonial audiences to acknowledge.[19]

It is, according to Lopenzina, 'an at times conflicted, always embedded literature'.[20] Yet was there profit in this conflict? Might such 'embedding' be a rewarding focus for critical examination? Might figures such as Copway, Johnson and Ngata – colonised subjects who inhabited the literary universe of Victorian English without leaving their Indigenous or native personae behind – use those personae as a way of fashioning and enabling their literary articulations in English? Gauri Viswanathan has written of nineteenth-century India:

> The English literary text, functioning as a surrogate Englishman in his highest and most perfect state, becomes a mask for economic exploitation... the split between the material and the cultural practices of colonialism is nowhere sharper than in the progressive refinement of the rapacious, exploitative, and ruthless actor of history into the reflective subject of literature.[21]

This study, based on individual experience and specific texts, finds a far more nuanced and complex picture than Viswanathan suggests, one in which the literary canon in the colonial setting allows its colonised writers variance and adaptive re-presentation.

This writing bears a relation to, yet is distinct from the postcolonial and Indigenous literatures from the mid-twentieth century onwards, as much writing *into* or *with* as writing *back*. Often privileged both within their own community and within the structures of colonial society, with access to formal education, these authors might not necessarily be opponents of empire. In his 1877 study *The Literature of Bengal* Romesh Chunder Dutt sees 'the period of European influence' as 'the brightest period in the annals of Bengali literature... a greater revolution in thoughts and ideas; in religion and society [which] removed Bengal from the moral atmosphere of Asia, to that of Europe'.[22] Membership of the literary empire might be seen as an antidote to its political or social manifestations: Leela

Gandhi describes Manmohan Ghose as '[advancing] the cause of English literature as a gesture against the lapsed imagination of the imperial project'.[23] Sol Plaatje invokes the literature of the English radical tradition to defend the erosion of what little freedoms and liberties remained to black South Africans in the early decades of the twentieth century. Leon de Kock writes:

> Black South Africans did not fight *not* to become colonial subjects, they fought to *become* colonial subjects in the public realm, the *res publica*, in the fullest possible sense ... the paradigms of straightforward oppositionality fail to provide adequate or even rudimentary explanatory value, especially when they become so generalized as to assume the status of transhistorical allegory.[24]

These figures are little written of in current literary criticism and, if they are, they are often figured in binary terms, either as informants and collaborators, or as anticipators of postcolonial resistance. Linda Tuhiwai Smith describes '"native" intellectuals' as important for 'their abilities to reclaim, rehabilitate and articulate indigenous cultures' yet sees 'these producers and legitimators of culture [as] the group most closely aligned to the colonizers in terms of their class interests, their values and their ways of thinking'.[25] Lopenzina sees this literature as 'over-inscribed by colonial norms and expectations – a literature that has been compulsively "corrected" with the red ink' of colonial culture and ideology.[26] Indigenous literary critics seek to look through the 'corrections', the literary frames of language, genre, constructed identity and rhetorical forms, to salvage what might be residually present of Indigenous material, identifying, as Jodi A. Byrd puts it, 'a long line of continuity between the past and the present that has not been disrupted'.[27] Daniel Heath Justice describes this school of criticism as having an 'overt multiplicity of purpose': it is 'an expression of intellectual agency', 'aesthetic accomplishment', but also part of 'the struggle for sovereignty, decolonization, and the reestablishment of Indigenous values to the healing of this wounded world'.[28]

This book respects that project but its focus is not continuity and retrieval, but the literary frame itself, the adaptive, at times compromised manner in which the native author fashioned a place and a voice for themselves in the often alien world of the literary empire.

The following chapters discuss a group of writers from the long nineteenth century: Bengali Toru Dutt, the indulged and prodigiously advanced daughter of a wealthy Calcutta family, educated at home by her father, himself a poet from a family of poets; Hyderabadi Sarojini Naidu, celebrated in 1890s London for her exoticism and beauty; South African Tswana Solomon T. Plaatje, journalist and political activist, one of the founders of what became the African National Congress, whose historical novel *Mhudi* uses his knowledge of Tswana history and lore – 'stray scraps... elicited from old people'[29] – as well as the generic forms of the imperial adventure story; E. Pauline Johnson, Tekahionwake, the 'Mohawk princess' who became one of Canada's best-known poets not only through her publications but also through her theatrical performances; and Apirana Ngata, the first New Zealand Māori university graduate. It also discusses figures whose membership of the literary empire was more problematic and marginal: Bermudan Mary Prince whose 1831 *History* was co-written with Susanna Strickland under the guidance of the Anti-slavery Society's Thomas Pringle; Squamish Chief Joe Capilano, Sahp-luk, the source of Johnson's *Legends of Vancouver*; and Wiremu Maihi Te Rangikaheke, New Zealand Governor George Grey's source and collaborator.

The focus of each chapter is the way that literary form, pre-existing conventions and in some cases literary institutions and the individuals that controlled them could offer membership of empire's literary club to those who could work within its structures and meet its expectations. These conventions might also determine what was said: the sinuous and sometimes covert way that literature enables new ideas and writing positions is balanced against the deterministic and conservative operations of the English language, literary structures and conventions.

The strength of literary form, even literary form which seems quite uncongenial to the native user, is marked in this writing. Central to this is the proleptic elegy or dying race narrative which is used in some sense and to some degree by most of the authors here. As Victorian science argued that access to experience of the primitive voice must necessarily recede as those voices disappeared, so the European authors of colonial literature stepped up to provide a re-enactment of that voice, bolstered on the one hand by the authority of ethnographic scholarship, and on the other hand by the persuasive force of their own poetic. Isobel Armstrong characterises this mode as 'monumental legend', 'sincerely fraudulent... a simulacrum of mock orality in the print culture of periodical and album book where so many appeared'.[30] Schoolcraft's 'Geehale' and Colonel McKinney's 'War Song' are examples of this style. The literary moment both concedes and resists the narrative of extinction – concedes in the elegiac frame; resists in the placement of the native voice within the poem. Words, phrases, beliefs, traditional histories and narratives may all be there, but the proleptic elegy accepts that the original speaker has gone. The New Zealand poet John Liddell Kelly's 1896 sonnet exemplifies this mix of regret and acceptance:

> Steep hills, deep vales, extend here mile on mile,
> Streams tinkle sweet in ferny, far recesses,
> Where sombre bush, like Maori maiden's tresses,
> Hangs shimmering, glossy, in the Sun-god's smile.
> And yet I note, with lurking discontent,
> The dark bush dwindles, golden gorse spreads free;
> So is the vigour of the Maori spent,
> So thrives the fair-haired race from sea to sea....[31]

The Indigenous are present here merely as metaphorical embellishment of a physical landscape under threat, and, while the speaker expresses a 'lurking discontent' as to this state of affairs, the symbiosis of Māori 'spent' and the 'fair-haired race' thriving is presented as inevitable.

The justificatory purpose of a settler writer such as Liddell Kelly employing this trope of extinction seems clear. Why native authors such as Copway, Ngata or Johnson should wish to express themselves in a mode which insists upon their own disappearance is less obviously explained. The Anishinaabe novelist and critic Gerald Vizenor describes such narratives as 'terminal creeds', stereotypical structures which confine and deform those who embrace them, 'beliefs which seek to fix, to impose static definitions on the world'.[32] A character in Vizenor's 1978 novel *Darkness in Saint Louis Bearheart* warns, 'We become the terminal creeds we speak'.[33] Yet, as James Clifford asserts, 'If the victims of progress and empire are weak, they are seldom passive'. Against what has been lost to Indigenous societies, Clifford points to what has been 'invented and revived in complex, oppositional contexts' which results in 'something more ambiguous and historically complex'.[34] Indeed, David Attwell, writing of nineteenth-century black mission-educated young men, claims that 'ambiguity was a keynote which sounded in virtually every project they undertook'.[35] De Kock suggests a need to focus on 'the very *dislocations* by which such hybrid forms have come into existence'.[36]

Native authors cannot contest the authority of the new scientific discourse of the mid-nineteenth century, so do not argue with the basic assumption of the dying race myth. Participation in the literary empire hard won, they politely concede their own absence, but they do so from within the text they deploy. Their narration is thus both authentic and inauthentic, teasing and complicating the ways in which such texts were read. The native author plays the general rhetorical positions of the myth – elegy and regret, blame and inevitability – against the particular circumstances of their own group: Ngata's registration of the politics of Māori cultural survival; Johnson's more compromised conciliatory gestures towards the collective nation; Copway's trajectory from 'pagan' to Christian. Literary language and the framework of literary genre may be hard to manipulate, apart from at the level of detail, but the detail can be telling. Peter Hulme warns that, in colonial discourse, 'no smooth history emerges, but rather a series of fragments which, read speculatively, hint at a story that can be never fully recovered'.[37] But by entering the Victorian literary empire, native writers could employ a complex range of imaginative and fictional literary forms and poetic conventions, even the seemingly least accommodating. They could use their native status to underwrite the authenticity of their texts, and in so doing they display a commonality among themselves, not as native, Indigenous or colonised, but as Victorian writers. Indeed, these texts can be seen to extend the categories of both Victorian writing and being a Victorian.

Memory and memorialisation are crucial in many of these works. Their concerns often dovetail with mainstream Victorian writers such as Matthew Arnold or Tennyson where a preoccupation with modernity, change and uncertainty are central and memory, or rather the trope of memory, is used to retrieve and textually delineate a nostalgically conceived past free from such instability. The settler projects of Canada and New Zealand, with their radical transformation of the physical landscape, give this a sense of added urgency. Warren Cariou writes:

> These stories of dispossession ... remind us of what has been lost, but they also remind us that not everything is lost. After a fire, something always remains; something that must be accounted for and honoured of we are to have any idea of where we are and where we are going.[38]

The Indigenous author of the colonial period is a tangible link to a pre-contact world – both for Indigenous audiences and for European readers. A contemporary Vancouver newspaper describes Johnson as 'link[ing] the vivid present with the immemorial past'[39] by 'gathering up the last fragments of the old romances scattered about our coast and in the recesses of our inland forest...gathering up folklore from the dusty "tillicums" and weaving for us more romances that bring the smell of the pine woods even into top rooms of skyscrapers'.[40] Attwell's description of the South African context could apply generally to these authors:

> The most prominent issues of the narrative literature of the nineteenth and early twentieth centuries by black South Africans...are, arguably, the emergence of Christianity, and auto-ethnographic representations of the traditional past. These issues are really the obverse of one another, and could appear in the same text: the former traces the formation of the Christianised present, usually on the understanding that Christianity inevitably represents the future, and the latter seeks to establish continuity with a traditional past that is judged to be disappearing...Both themes, overwhelmingly, are located on an axis of *accelerated time*, suggesting that the most pressing of projects for narrative literature in this period were attempts at managing a sense of temporality spinning out of control.[41]

Perhaps it is strategic for the native author to concede that, while the culture, traditions and history they are celebrating are important, they are of the past – as in Te Rangikaheke and Grey's *Polynesian Mythology* or Toru Dutt's *Ballads and Legends of Hindustan* or Pauline Johnson's *Legends of Vancouver*.

Authority and authenticity are central claims in the work of the native author, the former springing from the latter. These writers claim access to material outside the reach of their European counterparts; they fold references to that access into their texts. Native authors assure their readers that in engaging with this unique material, they are privileged. As part of this process all of these writers dramatically inhabit their writing, indeed many of the works, especially the poetry, seem chiefly an exercise in the translation of voice – from the Indigenous language of its original and from the Indigenous literary forms of that language into the conventions of Victorian literary discourse. Settler writers may attempt this as a kind of ethnographic ventriloquism, but when the native writer does so their authority does not have to be justified. Johnson is described as:

> giv[ing] us not the common report or the studied tale, but stories inherited like family jewels, idylls that are the gift of father to child, and truths learned in forest and fen, on mountain and plain, where the wind whispers of what it has heard and the grasses gossip gaily together.[42]

Supposed authenticity of voice is often bolstered by the way that voice conveys information – of the rare, the strange and the unfathomable. The critic Thomas Richards has written of the imperial archive – empire as information, the structures and operations of empire being ways of classifying and controlling the enormous amount of new and alien fact that came the way of the colonisers.[43] Literature was part of this organisational project, colonial literature being fond of footnotes, appendices, prefaces and supplements. Native authors are particularly adept at this mode, using it often as a way of conveying their dual abilities – they have access to privileged information but also are conversant with the colonisers' modes of scholarly organisation and reference. Many if not most of the authors in this book use their writing as a way of bringing traditional material – legends, histories, customs, religious systems – into the present, containing them within Victorian forms of expression but also of organisation.

Yet despite its Indigenous content, this writing is intertwined with a command of and a license to re-process the English canon, a facility that was remarked upon by contemporaries: Oscar Wilde, reviewing Manmohan Ghose's first collection of poetry in 1890, noted 'how quick and subtle are the intellectual sympathies of the Oriental mind', seeing in his work 'the temper of Keats, the moods of Matthew Arnold'.[44] Toru Dutt quotes Wordsworth, gestures to Keats, suggests Thomas Gray, mimics Christina Rossetti and echoes Elizabeth Barrett Browning. Plaatje cites Oliver Goldsmith and Shakespeare, and emulates Rider Haggard. Naidu closely follows Symons; Johnson co-opts Kipling; Ngata adopts (or adapts) the poetry of his Anglo-Saxon classes. What few do is find themselves a direct way of being in the present, in their literary personae at least. Colonial modernism, an observable stance in writing from the late nineteenth century onwards, is largely absent in these writers – indeed, few works have a relation to the modern let alone to the modernist. Many of these writers engaged directly, as modernisers, with contemporary events and political causes in their non-literary works, in essays and journalism, and several had careers in politics – Ngata as a Member of Parliament and cabinet minister; Naidu, post-independence, as a leading member of the Indian Congress Party; Plaatje as a founder of the South African Native National Congress. But in their literary works they revert to the past – even if they suggest implicitly that the past is a way of responding to the present.

This is not a biographical study. But it does consider the context and background of the writers and their writing. Although the term 'colonised' could be deployed in a very general sense to all of them, differentiations of class and status within each particular society, many of which had hierarchies which were recognised and utilised by the colonising authorities, are important. Some careers were marked by economic hardship. Sol Plaatje's efforts at fundraising, for himself and for the organisations he was part of, were all-consuming. Pauline Johnson's marginal position in both the Six Nations' hierarchy and in Canadian European society – 'Mohawk according to federal law but, since her mother was English, never in tribal law'[45] – meant that she had an economically precarious career and died reliant on the charity of her supporters. For both, journalism was crucially important – that of the mainstream and of the native press. Toru Dutt and Sarojini Naidu, on the other hand, were from backgrounds which were educated, wealthy and Anglophile. Neither had to view her writing in economic terms. Both travelled and were part of the literary and intellectual culture of the imperial centre. Both were able to access publishers and reviewers for their work, whereas Plaatje's novel *Mhudi* had to wait more than a decade before its limited publication by a local missionary press.

Institutions – the protection of institutions and the consequences of their absence – were important for all these writers. The press, in all its colonial variety – local, settler and Indigenous – as well as at the imperial centre, was vital. So too were the various structures and functions of Christianity: for Copway, conscripted to the missionary arm of Methodism; for the Dutt family, converts whose Anglicanism formed part of their social as well as spiritual identity; for Plaatje, who was taken up by the Christian Socialist Brotherhood movement on his visits to England. The colonial education system, whether David Lester Richardson's Hindu College, James Thornton's Te Aute College or the Brantford Collegiate Institute in Ontario, was a crucial conduit. English governesses were at a premium in the households of wealthy and/or Anglophile families throughout empire – Dutt, Naidu and Johnson all experienced this form of education. And the Victorian self-help movement and its stress on self-improvement – as Plaatje put it, 'reading after office hours'[46] – were as significant to the colonised writer as they were to the English working-class autodidact of the same period. European teachers, patrons, employers, editors and friends could act as important conduits: Edmund Gosse, the gatekeeper of literary London, reviewer of Toru Dutt; Arthur Symons, mentor of Sarojini Naidu; Thomas Pringle and Susanna Strickland, Anti-Slavery Society facilitators of Mary Prince's *History*; George Grey, co-author with and employer of Te Rangikaheke; John Macmillan Brown, Ngata's English literature professor. These figures held positions of power in their particular cultural spheres which they could use to further the status of the native author and their work; however, such patronage was often accompanied by expectations as to how that client should behave, write or perform.

Indeed, for all these authors being a writer and entering the literary empire involved some aspect of performance – performing not themselves but what they represented or were seen to represent generally in terms of a scripted re-enactment of the past. Susan Castillo suggests that:

> Performance, in the sense of actual stage performance and in the sense of performativity, that is to say in the iterative construction of group and individual identities though dialogic interaction whether in print or in actual embodied performance, is by its very nature the site in which colonial difference is enacted.[47]

This enactment of difference is by necessity artful – constructed and complex, simultaneously assertive and unstable. To perform the authentic is, after all, a contradiction in terms. Clifford writes that in the twentieth century, 'identities no longer presuppose continuous cultures or traditions. Everywhere individuals and groups improvise local performances from (re) collected pasts, drawing on foreign media, symbols, languages... culture is contested, temporal, and emergent'.[48] The authors in this book suggest this process begins earlier. Laura L. Mielke, in the colonial American context, notes the 'creative, adaptive, and iterative energies of Indian and white peoples alike from the very earliest encounters'.[49] In her study of nineteenth-century Indians and the imperial centre, Antoinette Burton suggests that 'cultural identities are negotiable, contingent, and ever shifting, largely because they are products not of inheritance or origins alone but of the *politics* at the micro- and the macro-levels, in the most elastic sense of the word'.[50] And indeed all authors discussed here engage in what Attwell has describes as 'modernity's capacity to provide scope for creative self-fashioning'.[51]

Johnson literally performed as a 'Mohawk princess' not just within her text but on theatrical stages around Canada. Ngata's poem is the record not of the past but of a performance of the past – in his subsequent career he was a preserver but also in some senses an inventor of Indigenous tradition. The Christchurch *Press* reports him giving a recitation of his poem 'supported by a group of stalwart spearmen' at a performance of 'characteristic Maori entertainments' – *tableaux vivants*, Māori games, poi dances, and songs.[52] Sarojini Naidu performed her role of Indian poetess and inspirer of poets in the drawing rooms of *fin de siècle* literary London and later, on her return to India, wrote to her London admirers of Hyderabad as a fairy tale word of orientalist fancy. Toru Dutt was posthumously conscripted into a similar role by her promoter Gosse. While he was in London, Plaatje took part of a 'Zulu Chief' and sang a War Song in 'The Cradle of the World' at the Philharmonic Hall in London.[53] Joseph Roach's association of performance and memory in the American colonial setting, 'out of which blossoms the most florid nostalgia for authenticity and origin', is relevant here.[54] Disallowed in the present, these figures moved into the realm of performance, of the unreal and the invented, which needed to be enacted again and again through repeated display to register their presence and their substance.

\*\*\*

There is one author in this book who to an extent disrupts these categories. Biographically, she is elusive in a way the others are not: there is no picture, sketch or photograph of her, no firm birth date, only an approximation, perhaps around 1788. There is no date of death – she vanishes after her last recorded appearance in 1833. Even her name, Mary Prince, sounds fabricated, arbitrarily bestowed rather than integral or familial. Her work relies not on the evocation of an archaic collective past but on its ability to attest to an unacceptable present, as documented by means of individual witness.

Does *The History of Mary Prince* fit with the other works to be discussed here; is Prince a member of the literary empire of the early nineteenth century? The slave narrative, autobiography written with the purpose of exposing the horror of slavery, had, by 1831 when Prince's work appeared, acquired an almost formulaic rigidity. Authority and authenticity were its fundamental principles – the authority of experience and the authenticity of documentary detail. All slave narratives are founded on information, and are often accompanied by prefaces, supplements, appendices, testimonials and letters from experts, all attesting to the truth of what is said. While the other authors in this study overtly engage in a range of sophisticated play with the literary canon, it was a crucial requirement of the slave narrative that it present itself as totally unliterary – 'artless' is the term often approvingly applied by reviewers, 'the genuine voice of truth and nature'.[55] The voice that is contained in the work must be presented as being textualised seemingly by accident. So the works are characterised by elaborate explanatory structures as to the circumstances of their production. Prince's work is openly collaborative, written with Susanna Strickland – 'taken down from Mary's own lips by a lady' as the preface explains[56] – under the editorial eye of Thomas Pringle. It thus offers a useful parallel with Te Rangikaheke's relationship with George Grey and Chief Capilano's with Pauline Johnson, where the owner of the direct experience finds expression through the words – and the cultural frame – of their amanuensis. Authorship is indirect. The details of Prince's experience as a slave are framed and controlled by Strickland's Evangelical Christianity and moral delicacy, just as Grey censors the more sexually explicit aspects of Te Rangikaheke's material, and Johnson orients Capilano's narratives towards upholding the European values of motherhood and domesticity.

One difference between Prince and the other authors discussed here is that the latter group, irrespective of locale, practise in their writing a form of careful self-protection. They are not personally exposed; they do not confront; they perform in terms of a carapaced stereotype not themselves, the literary work a costume to put on and off. If they critique it is done cautiously and inferentially. With Prince this is not the case. Her work is directly confrontational, in keeping with the genre it occupies. When she arrived at the offices of the Anti-Slavery Society in London in 1828, having fled from her owners, the odious Mr and Mrs Wood, she displayed the scars on her body as undeniable testimony to her story's truth. A consequence of her *History's* publication was two law suits involving Pringle in whose household Prince had found protection. In the first case, Prince appeared as a witness and was described by *The Times* as 'a negress of very ordinary features' whom, an article in *Blackwood's Magazine* claimed, Pringle had 'taken from the wash-tub to the closet for the purpose of collecting the filthy statement of her lies and immorality, and impressing it on the minds of his own family'.[57]

A court appearance is a performance, certainly, but not the controlled, formalised and willed performance of Ngata or Johnson or Plaatje.

What Prince has in common with the other authors in this book is her inhabitation of what Tony Ballantyne has characterised as the webs of empire.[58] The strands of web that encircle her are those of colonisation and the institution of slavery, the structures and operations of the Christian church, its global missionary interventions and its Evangelical humanitarian agendas, and the imperial discourses of economics, gender and race, all operating from and between what Alan Lester describes as the 'multiplicity of metropoles and peripheries in the British world', its 'networks, webs and circuits'.[59] The English language, and in particular English literature, formed the connective tissue of this web. Despite its claim to be 'artless', Prince's *History* draws from the eighteenth-century novel of sentiment, the Gothic novel, the conversion narrative, and the fiction of domestic realism. It absorbs and re-orientates the poetry of Thomas Pringle's African sojourn, of Susanna Strickland's religious conversion, as well as the didactic literature of working-class self-improvement.

Each of the authors in this book demonstrates a similar set of sources, influences, models, stances and conventions, contributing to what Lester describes as the nineteenth-century world's 'multiple meanings, projects, material practices, performances and experiences of colonial relations'.[60] The work of native author, whose membership of the literary empire is at best provisional, whose voice tilts between authority and performance, purity and eclecticism, whose sources range from the elaborate systems of Indigenous knowledge, encased and transmitted in the various forms of oral literature, to the popular works of European literary print culture, is the place where such complexity can be fully registered.

## Notes

1. *The Life, History, and Travels of Kah-Ge-Ga-Gah-Bowh (George Copway) a Young Indian Chief of the Ojebwa Nation, a Convert to the Christian Faith and a Missionary to his People for Twelve Years; With a Sketch of the Present State of the Ojebwa Nation in Regard to Christianity and Their Future Prospects; also an Appeal; with all the Names of the Chiefs now Living who have been Christianized, and the Missionaries Now Laboring Among Them; Written by Himself* (Albany: Weed and Parsons, 1847), p. 134 (Copway 1847). Copway's work had been reprinted seven times by 1848, and two revised versions, *The Life, Letters and Speeches of Kah-Ge-ga-gah-bowh, Or G. Copway* (New York: Benedict, 1850) (Copway 1850a) and *Recollections*

    *of Forest Life; Or, the Life and Travels of Kah-Ge-ga-gah-bowh, Or George Copway* (London: Gilpin, 1850) were also published. (Copway 1850b)
2. Copway, *Life, History, and Travels*, p. 8.
3. Copway, *Life, History, and Travels*, p. 9.
4. Copway, *Life, History, and Travels*, p. 16.
5. Bernd Peyer, *The Tutor'd Mind: Indian Missionary Writers in Ante-Bellum America* (Amherst: University of Massachusetts Press, 1997), pp. 265, 243. (Peyer 1997)
6. William Wordsworth, 'Lines Written a Few Miles above Tintern Abbey, on Revisiting the Banks of the Wye During a Tour, 13 July 1798', lines 84–89.
7. Copway, *Life, History, and Travels*, pp. 9–10.
8. Copway, *Life, History, and Travels*, p. 62. See Alexander Pope, 'Essay on Man: Epistle One', lines 99–108, *The Poems of Alexander Pope*, ed. John Butt (London: Methuen, 1968), p. 508 (Pope 1968). There are minor variations in Copway's rendering of the lines, especially the third, which in Pope's original reads 'His soul proud science never taught to stray'.
9. Copway, *Life, History, and Travels*, p. 62.
10. Copway, *Life, History, and Travels*, p. 63.
11. Copway, *Life, History, and Travels*, p. 47.
12. Cathy Rex, 'Survivance and Fluidity: George Copway's *The Life, History, and Travels of Kah-Ge-ga-gah-bowh*', *Studies in American Indian Literatures*, 18: 2 (2006): 21. (Rex 2006)
13. Copway, *Life, History, and Travels*, pp. 41–42.
14. Henry Rowe Colcraft (pseud. of Schoolcraft), 'Geehale: An Indian Lament', *Alhalla, or the Lord of Talladega: A Tale of the Creek War, With Some Selected Miscellanies, Chiefly of an Early Date* (New York: Wiley and Putnam, 1843), p. 94. (Schoolcraft 1843)
15. The poem had widespread currency. It was recorded in the canonical ballad collection, Mary O. Eddy's *Ballads and Songs from Ohio* (New York: J.J. Augustin, 1939) where it was described as having been collected from Catherine J. Rayner of Piqua, Ohio. (Eddy 1939)
16. Peyer, *The Tutor'd Mind*, p. 268. Peyer quotes Copway: 'The three most requisite things for an Indian youth to be taught are a good mechanical trade, a sound code of morality, and a high-toned literature'.
17. Chadwick Allen, *Trans-Indigenous: Methodologies for Global Native Literary Studies* (Minnesota: University of Minneapolis Press, 2012), p. xiii. (Allen 2012)
18. Apirana Ngata, 'A Scene from the Past', *Souvenir of the Maori Congress, July 1908* (Wellington: Whitcombe and Tombs, 1908), p. 5.
19. Drew Lopenzina, *Red Ink: Native Americans Picking Up the Pen in the Colonial Period* (Albany: State University of New York Press, 2012), p. 5. (Lopenzina 2012)

20. Ibid.
21. Gauri Viswanathan, *Masks of Conquest: Literary Study and British Rule in India* (London: Faber, 1990), p. 20. (Viswanathan 1990)
22. Romesh Chunder Dutt ('Arydae'), *The Literature of Bengal being an Attempt to Trace the Progress of the National Mind in its Various Aspects as Reflected in the Nation's Literature from the Earliest Times to the Present Day with Copious Extracts from the Best Writers* (Calcutta: I.C. Bose, 1877), p. 167. (Dutt 1877)
23. Leela Gandhi, *Affective Communities: Anticolonial Thought, Fin de Siècle Radicalism, and the Politics of Friendship* (Durham: Duke University Press, 2006), p. 165. (Gandhi 2006)
24. Leon de Kock, 'Sitting for the Civilisation Test: The Making(s) of a Civil Imaginary in Colonial South Africa', *Poetics Today*, 22: 2 (Summer 2001): 403. (de Kock 2001)
25. Linda Tuhiwai Smith, *Decolonizing Methodologies: Research and Indigenous Peoples* (London: Zed Books/Dunedin: Otago University Press, 1999), p. 69. (Smith 1999)
26. Lopenzina, *Red Ink*, p. xi.
27. Jodi A. Byrd, *Transit of Empire: Indigenous Critiques of Colonisation* (Minnesota: University of Minneapolis Press, 2011), p. xiv. (Byrd 2011)
28. Daniel Heath Justice, 'Current Trans/national Criticism in Indigenous Literary Studies', *American Indian Quarterly*, 35: 3 (Summer 2011): 336. (Justice 2011)
29. Solomon T. Plaatje, 'Preface to the Original Edition', *Mhudi* (Oxford: Heinemann, 1978), p. 21. (Plaatje 1978)
30. Isobel Armstrong, 'Msrepresentations: Codes of Affect and Politics in Nineteenth-century Women's Poetry', *Women's Poetry, Late Romanticism to Late Victorian: Gender and Genre, 1830–1900*, eds. Isobel Armstrong and Virginia Blain (London: Macmillan, 1999), p. 12. (Armstrong 1999)
31. John Liddell Kelly, 'Sonnet: In Maoriland' (1896), *Heather and Fern: Songs of Scotland and Maoriland* (Wellington: New Zealand Times, 1902), p. 148. Liddell Kelly ends his sonnet 'May conquering and conquered blood be blent/And breed new beauty and virility!' indicating the way in which the dying race myth could be used as a positive metaphor for miscegenation.
32. Louis Owens, '"Ecstatic Strategies": Gerald Vizenor's *Darkness in Saint Louis Bearheart*', *Narrative Chance: Postmodern Discourse on Native American Indian Literatures*, ed. Gerald Vizenor (Norman: University of Oklahoma Press, 1993), p. 144. (Owens 1993)
33. Gerald Vizenor, *Darkness in Saint Louis Bearheart* (St Paul, Minnesota: Truck Press, 1978), p. 143. (Vizenor 1978)

34. James Clifford, *The Predicament of Culture: Twentieth-century Ethnology, Literature and Art* (Cambridge, MA: Harvard University Press, 1988), p. 16. (Clifford 1988)
35. David Attwell, 'Reprisals of Modernity in Black South African "Mission" Writing', *Journal of South African Studies*, 25: 2 (June 1999): 268. (Attwell 1999)
36. Leon de Kock, *Civilising Barbarians: Missionary Narrative and African Textual Response in Nineteenth-century South Africa* (Johannesburg: University of Witwatersrand Press and Lovedale Press, 1996), p. 190. (de Kock 1996)
37. Peter Hulme, *Colonial Encounters: Europe and the Native Caribbean, 1492–1797* (London: Methuen, 1996), p. 21. (Hulme 1996)
38. Warren Cariou, 'Going to Canada', *Across Cultures, Across Borders: Canadian Aboriginal and Native American Literatures*, eds. Paul DePasquale, Renate Eigenbrod, and Emma LaRocque (Peterborough: Broadview Press, 2010), p. 21. (Cariou 2010)
39. Bernard McEvoy, Preface, *Legends of Vancouver* (Vancouver and Victoria B.C.: David Spenser, 1911). (McEvoy 1911)
40. *The Vancouver World*, 9 December 1911, p. 9.
41. Attwell, 'Reprisals of Modernity': 271–2.
42. Cutting, Box 4, file 11, E. Pauline Johnson Fonds, William Ready Division of Archives and Research Collections, McMaster University Library.
43. Thomas Richards, *The Imperial Archive: Knowledge and the Fantasy of Empire* (London: Verso, 1993). (Richards 1993)
44. Oscar Wilde, *Pall Mall Gazette*, 50 (24 May 1890): 3.
45. Carole Gerson and Veronica Strong-Boag, *Paddling her own Canoe: The Times and Texts of E. Pauline Johnson Tekahionwake* (Toronto: Toronto University Press, 2000), p. 48. (Gerson and Strong-Boag 2000)
46. Brian Willan, *Sol Plaatje: South African Nationalist 1876–1932* (Berkeley: University of California Press, 1984), p. 39, quoting 'Mr Sol T. Plaatje Honoured', *Diamond Fields Advertiser*, 1928. (Willan 1984)
47. Susan Castillo, *Colonial Encounters in New World Writing, 1500–1786* (London: Routledge, 2006), p. 16. (Castillo 2006)
48. James Clifford, *Writing Culture: The Poetics and Politics of Ethnography* (Berkeley: University of California Press, 1986), p. 19. (Clifford 1986)
49. Laura L. Mielke, Introduction, *Native Acts: Indian Performance, 1603–1832*, eds. Joshua David Bellin, and Laura L. Mielke (Lincoln: University of Nebraska Press, 2012), pp. 7–8. (Mielke 2012)
50. Antoinette Burton, *At the Heart of the Empire: Indians and the Colonial Encounter in Late Victorian Britain* (New Delhi: Munshiram Manoharlal, 1998), p. 189. (Burton 1998)
51. Attwell, 'Reprisals of Modernity': 274.

52. 'Maori Entertainment', Christchurch *Press*, 23 July 1908, p. 7.
53. Brian Willan, *Sol Plaatje, South African Nationalist, 1876–1932* (Berkeley: University of California Press, 1984), pp. 287–90.
54. Joseph Roach, *Cities of the Dead: Circum-Atlantic Performance* (New York: Columbia University Press, 1996), pp. 3–4. (Roach 1996)
55. S. Strickland, *Negro Slavery Described by a Negro; Being the Narrative of Ashton Warner, a Native of St Vincents; With an Appendix containing the Testimony of Four Christian Ministers Recently Returned from the Colonies on the System of Slavery as it Now Exists* (London: Samuel Maunder, 1831), p. 6. (Strickland 1831)
56. T.P [Thomas Pringle], Preface, *The History of Mary Prince, A West Indian Slave, Related by Herself* [1831], ed. Sarah Salih (London: Penguin, 2000), p. 3.
57. *The Times*, 22 February 1833, p. 4.
58. This concept is developed in Tony Ballantyne, *Orientalism and Race: Aryanism in the British Empire* (Basingstoke: Palgrave, 2002) (Ballantyne 2002); *Webs of Empire: Locating New Zealand's Colonial Past* (Wellington: Bridget Williams Books, 2012) (Ballantyne 2012); and Ballantyne and Antoinette Burton, *Empires and the Reach of the Global, 1870–1945* (Cambridge, MA: Harvard University Press, 2014). (Ballantyne and Burton 2014)
59. Alan Lester, 'Imperial Circuits and Networks: Geographies of the British Empire', *History Compass*, 4: 1 (January 2006): 103, 124. (Lester 2006)
60. Lester, 'Imperial Circuits and Networks': 131.

CHAPTER 2

# Littleness, Frivolity and Vedic Simplicity: Toru Dutt, Sarojini Naidu and Mr Gosse

David Lester Richardson's *Selections from the British Poets* was published in Calcutta by the Baptist Mission Press under the authority of the Committee of Public Instruction in 1840. 'Shakespeare-Richardson', as he was known, was the head of the Hindu College, a school for the sons of the Indian middle class, and he was motivated by 'the difficulty procuring a Poetical Class-book'.[1] As Gauri Viswanathan notes, 'English literature appeared as a subject in the curriculum of the colonies long before it was institutionalised in the home country.'[2] A mere five years after Macaulay's Minute on Education introduced English as the medium of instruction in Indian schools, Richardson was preparing an appropriate course of study. 'Mr Macaulay' he wrote 'favored me with several hints which, with a few exceptions, I readily availed myself'.[3] Feeling that 'the chief defect at present in the character of the people of India [is] *a want of moral elevation*', he called on the English poetic canon as lesson and remedy:

> Poetry improves us by a direct appeal to the finest sensibilities of our nature. It extends our sympathies, and purifies our thoughts. The true lover of the Muses cannot be base and mean without a perpetual struggle against his better nature...We need not make *poets* of the natives – this is not the object – poets indeed are not *made*; but we may cultivate in young minds that fine sense of the true and the beautiful to which poetry administers.[4]

It is the nature of canons to be predictable and there is nothing in Richardson's selection that surprises – Chaucer, Milton, Shakespeare,

Johnson, Beaumont and Fletcher, Southey, Campbell, James Thompson and the Romantics[5] – until, that is, the final section entitled 'British-Indian Poetry'. This is an odd term with a range of shifting denominators, then and now, not clarified by Richardson's carefully placed hyphen and rather fussy subtitle 'Specimens of British poets once or still resident in the East Indies'. Indeed, Richardson himself seems to despair of his own editorial precision when in a footnote he writes, with exasperation, of one of his inclusions:

> [t]hough Major Campbell's first published volume of poems is entitled 'Lays from the East', it contains no poems of an eastern or local cast; and I have found after some search in periodicals no more than the above little pieces of his that are of an Oriental character.[6]

The index of titles conveys the flavour of this section: 'An Evening Walk in Bengal', 'The Indian Day', 'The Dying Hindoo', 'The Mussulman's Lament over the Body of Tippoo Sultan', 'Twilight Wooing: written in India', 'Lines to a Lady who Presented the Author with some English Fruits and Flowers', 'Sonnet: on Hearing Captain James Glencairn Burns Sing (in India) his Father's Songs', which begins

> How dream-like is the sound of native song
> Heard on a foreign shore! The wanderer's ear
> Drinks wild enchantment, – swiftly fade the drear
> And cold realities that round him throng...[7]

These works, in common with colonial writing from other parts of the empire, display local conventions and popular motifs of contrast and dissonance, ownership and alienation, beauty and fearfulness, home and away. The poem beginning

> Upon the Ganges' regal stream
> The sun's bright splendours rest
> And gorgeously the noon-tide beam
> Reposes on its breast...[8]

is characteristic of a wearyingly large number of pieces about the sun sinking on the Ganges, as many perhaps as Canadian poems about the Rockies or New Zealand colonial poems about sunset on Aoraki Mt Cook.

Several of Richardson's pieces attempt to grapple with the Indian climate ('Down from his blazing car, the lord of day/ Hurls a fierce splendour through the sultry air'[9]). And – again, a common colonial trope – there are a number of comparisons between the gentility of English vegetation and the vulgarity of their Indian counterparts. There are a disproportionate number of poems about the voyage to India, as if the poet were delaying as long as possible actual arrival. There is some material, but not much, sourced from Indian mythology, which may reflect mid-century taste – a little late for the Orientalists, a little early for the Ethnographers.[10] History in these poems is that of recent events which define the English presence and coalesce its disparate parts into a communal whole. In particular, the military traditions of the pre-mutiny army are celebrated in works such as R.H. Rattray's classically framed 'Seetabuldee: on the splendid charge made on its plain, by the 6th regiment of the Bengal cavalry, November 27th, 1817' which begins:

> When Greece her lofty themes proclaim'd for verse,
> And Fame bade Genius Valour's feats rehearse;
> When God-like heroes led, in fearless pride,
> Her sons to conquest, and the world defied......[11]

Throughout the selection, the English models are adapted in a manner that verges on the plagiaristic: Richardson's own 'Lines Written on the Ruins of Rajhmahal'[12] is Shelley's 'Ozymandias' with an Indian setting; his 'Sonnet: Evening on the Banks of the Ganges'[13] beginning 'I wandered thoughtfully by Gunga's shore' is an unabashed pastiche of Wordsworth's 'Daffodils' with a dash of 'Westminster Bridge'. H.M. Parker's 'The Widow of Mysore Hill' could with very little adjustment be re-set in the Lake District:

> The way was rough the night was chill,
> Darkness was falling on the hill,
> When I heard a woman making moan;
> Bitterly, bitterly, wept she,
> Sitting upon a worn grey stone
> By a blighted Banyan tree.[14]

Change 'Banyan' to 'thorn' and the similarities to the *Lyrical Ballads* are immediately apparent. And yet there is a confident energy in both the editorial voice and the poems themselves, reflective of the society that produced them. As early as the 1820s, a visitor to Calcutta had noticed the 'journals without number, both political and literary; there are learned societies of every determination – craniological, phrenological, horticultural, literary, medical, Wernerian, and I know not how many besides'.[15] Richardson himself edited *The Bengal Magazine* whose offerings were compared, somewhat sweepingly, to

> Wild flowers – like those whose modest bloom
> Sheds light upon a desert's gloom;
> Lowly but hail'd with gladness there,
> Where nothing save themselves are fair.[16]

Richardson's footnotes to 'Specimens of British poets once or still resident in the East Indies' suggest wildly proliferating literary activity within a close community of readers and writers: Miss Emma Roberts, for instance, is referred to as 'Authoress of a poetical volume entitled "*Oriental Scenes, Dramatic Sketches*" &c. and the well-known prose sketches "*Scenes and Characteristics of Indoostan*"'.[17] Other works are denoted as by the 'Author of "Miscellaneous Verses"', by the 'Translator of the *Shah Nameh*, &c.', by the 'Author of "*India: a poem*", "*The City of the East*", &c.', by the 'Author of "*Sultry Hours*"' and by the 'Author of "*The Maniac and other Poems*" &c'.[18] There is no sense of a shortage of eligible material. Most writers are credited with a generous '&c.' or even '&c., &c.' In a defensive manner Richardson expresses the difficulty of his editorial discriminations, writing of the 'awkwardness and delicacy' and 'inward struggle and irresolution' with which he feels obliged to include nine columns of his own entirely unremarkable verse.[19]

This is a lost literature. Only two of Richardson's authors have a presence, albeit fitful and marginal, in contemporary anthologies of Indian poetry, and this is reflective of their similarly marginal position in Richards' collection. On the final page of his selection, under the rubric 'Poems by an East Indian', Richardson sets out three works by Henry Derozio;[20] and in the adjoining section, 'Poem by a Hindu', there is one poem by 'Kasiprashad Ghosh'.[21] The precise Robert Young-like delineations of race and religion of Richardson's headings ('East Indian' meaning Bengali but also perhaps a code for Derozio's mixed Indian, English and Portuguese background) mask the complexity of mid-nineteenth-century Indian cultural formation. Both men were friends of Richardson and part of the Calcutta literary world. Derozio who had died eight years earlier had been a teacher at the Hindu College – one of the poems here is a sonnet addressed to his students. Kashi Prasad Ghosh, journalist and editor of the *Hindu Intelligencer*, whose home was a meeting place for local writers, had been a student there. And it is that education which forms the tone of the two poets' offerings rather than any sectarian denominators. Indeed, it is difficult to find in their poems anything that distinguishes them from those of their 'British-Indian' companions. One of the Derozio poems, 'Ode: from the Persian of Hafiz, freely translated', is firmly part of the Orientalist-Romantic reprocessing of ancient Indian texts:

> Say, what's the rose without the smile
> Of her I deem more fair,
> And what are all the sweets of spring
> If wine be wanting there?[22]

Derozio's other poem, 'To India – My Native Land', described in parenthesis as '*Introduction to the Fakeer of Jungheera*', beginning

> 'My country! In thy days of glory past
> A beauteous halo circled thy brow,
> And worshipped as a deity thou wast –
> Where is that glory, where that reverence now?

has been read as a gesture towards the idea of nation and a national literature, but rests on the colonial trope of deploring the contrast between the colonised country's heroic past with its degraded present:

> Well – let me dive into the depths of time,
> And bring from out the ages that have rolled
> A few small fragments of those wrecks sublime.
> Which human eye may never more behold....[23]

As for the 'Poem by a Hindu', Ghosh's 'The Boatman's Song to Ganga' is of the school of Miss Roberts and Major Campbell:

> Gold river! Gold river! How gallantly now
> Our bark on thy bright breast is lifting her prow,

> In the pride of her beauty, how swiftly she flies,
> Like a white-winged spirit thro' topaz-paved skies...

\*\*\*

Richardson's *Poetical Selections* was both an anthology and a teaching text. Alexander Duff wrote in 1837:

> The study of English literature is beginning to be considered, throughout India as a necessary part of a polite education, and is often referred to as such in the native newspapers, and in common conversation....[24]

Richard's work was for many years the core of the curriculum of the government schools, alongside other canonical authors:

> Otway's *Venice preserved*, Shakespeare's *Hamlet*, *Othello* and *Macbeth*, Pope's *Iliad* by Homer, Milton's *Paradise Lost* (the first four books), Addison's *Essays*, Johnson's *Rasselas* and *The Lives of the Poets*, Paley's *Moral Philosophy*, Goldsmith's *History of England*, Bacon's *Essays*, *Novum Organon*, and *Advancement of Learning*, Malkins' *History of Greece*, Pinnock's *History of Greece*, Horace Wilson's *Universal History*, Adam Smith's *Moral Sentiments*, Abercombie's *Intellectual Powers*, and Whewall's *Moral Philosophy*.[25]

Palgrave's *Golden Treasury*, first published in 1861, a more convenient classroom resource than Richardson massive tome, became an equally significant conduit of the literary canon.[26] By 1876, Behramji Malabari could write:

> To an observant mind it can not be a secret that English, which bids fair, at no distant date, to become a world language, has so far identified herself with our dearest interests, that we not only speak and write through her medium: we have grown almost to thinking in English. Persian and Sanskrit are studied for pleasure or for fame; but the one is too light and the other too heavy for this utilitarian age.
> It is English that is becoming the current language of India – the soft insinuating English – rich in her song and her science and philosophy – the mother and moulder of the divinest human thoughts! We resort to her not only from the selfish political point of view, but from the social and intellectual point.[27]

Alumni of the Hindu College, the authors of *The Dutt Family Album*, published in 1870 in London, demonstrate the way that Indian writers in English absorbed and digested these influences. And yet there are differences, hesitations between the manner in which they offer their work and Richardson's. The Dutts are less ebullient, more cautious in their presentation. Richardson could place his British-Indian authors without apology or even comment within a compendium of the canonical British poets. Govin, Omesh, Greece and Hur Chunder Dutt, in contrast, frame their work by signalling its insufficiency. In the preface to *The Dutt Family Album* they write:

> The writers of the following pages are aware that bad poetry is intolerable, and that mediocre poetry deserves perhaps even a harsher epithet. There is a glut of both on the market. But they venture on publication, not because they think their verses good, but in the hope that their book will be regarded, in some respects, as a curiosity. They are foreigners, natives of India, of different ages, and in different walks of life, yet of one family, in whom the ties of relation have been drawn closer by the holy bond of Christian brotherhood. As foreigners educated out of England, they solicit the indulgence of British critics to poems which, on these grounds alone, it is hoped, have some title to their attention.[28]

The same cautious special pleading is evident in the book's epigraphs. The first argues the case for minor literature:

> Not oaks alone are trees, nor roses flowers;
> Much humbler wealth makes rich this world of ours. [29]

The second suggests their awareness of the danger in shifting their audience from the community of Calcutta with its networks of friendship, local learned societies and old boys' networks to the more impersonal and professional world of London:

> I liken thy outgoing, O my book,
> To the impatience of a little brook,
> Which might with flowers have lingered pleasantly,
> Yet toils to perish in the mighty sea.[30]

Hand in hand with these protestations of the minor and the mediocre nature of their work, the Dutts proffer a new distinguishing literary category, that of curiosity, as compensation. There is, indeed, little in their collection to differentiate it from the 'British-Indians' in Richardson's earlier volume. The only significant new theme is the family's Christian conversion – otherwise there are the same descriptions of the Ganges at dusk, the same tribute pieces to the Romantic poets, the same re-presentation of Indian tradition in the voice of Victorian medievalism, the same reflections on contrast and distance though 'home', significantly, is now is India and 'here' is England. It is their poetic personae – Indian, native, familial, foreign, Christian – and the fact that their work is offered, albeit apologetically, to literary London rather than provincial Calcutta, that is its claim to exceptionalism, its title to the critics' attention. Just as Richardson's denominations – 'British-Indian', 'East Indian', 'Hindu' – suggested differences which the poetry itself does not reflect, so the Dutts look to distinguish themselves not by their writing but by the variety of labels they as authors can claim – that which constitutes their 'curiosity'.

Who will now own these writers? Which national literature will now accommodate them? Not the British which has always looked at colonial literary effusions with condescension. Not the postcolonial, unless they be characterised as villains or dupes. Contemporary Indian critics might grudgingly include Derozio, Ghosh and the Dutts in the occasional anthology – 'less than genius and somewhat more than mediocrity', as one editor puts it.[31] Rosinka Chaudhuri complains that 'critics have so far been unable to find an adequate vocabulary to deal positively with the colonial interaction as it took place in the poetry of the Dutts'. But in claiming that they were 'part of the process of evolution towards the creation of a middle-class Indians, who, while making use of British education, would ultimately effect a practical resistance to British rule',[32] she assumes that proper scrutiny will reveal a link between their work and proto-nationalism, something which it is very hard to argue on the basis of such poems as 'On an Old Romaunt', 'Sonnet on the Flyleaf of Alford's New Testament', 'William Wordsworth's Poems' or 'To Lord Canning, during the Mutiny' ('Though a thousand pens condemned thee, mine still should write thy praise').[33]

Richardson's collection was not conceived in terms of Britishness, Indian-ness or even empire – all by no means self-evident terms in 1840. His guiding principles were canonical – a canon based on moral as well as aesthetic values. Miss Roberts and Kasi Prasad Ghosh are included alongside Chaucer and Milton because their works are good in a moral sense as well as good in a critical sense. Indeed, to suggest any discrimination between the two realms would be to Richardson and his readers incomprehensible. And, if a literary work is judged by its moral status, then of course apprentice poets should use great writers as their models – and reprocess, re-express and adapt their positions to share their sensibility. The use by both Richardson's British-Indians and the Dutts of the Romantic canon is thus not derivative or imitative – its very clumsiness is a clear signal of joint membership in a common enterprise which transcends nationalisms, the inculcation of, as Richardson following Keats expresses it, that 'fine sense of the true and the beautiful to which poetry administers'.[34]

Richardson filters this moral framework through the Hindu College's secular and utilitarian mode of teaching. For the Dutts, the organisational structure of their writing is one of explicit Christian belief fortified by conversion, an identity of conceptual belonging which their preface plays against their geographical outsider status – 'foreigners educated out of England'. This is the ground of both the resolution and the uncertainty which inform their collection – strangers to their hoped-for audience, but at the same time members of the international Victorian Christian community. And in adopting Christianity, the Dutts are able to situate their work within another frame of reference, that of the modern. This is part of the 'curiosity' they advertise, breaking out of the manufactured 'archaic' structures within which 'the native' was conventionally consigned. At the same time they inhabit the English language rather than choosing to stay within the community of the Bengali language as did many of their fellow writers. The modern is the ground of all these authors, British-Indian and Indian alike. However limited and derivative their means of expression, these poems are registrations of encounters with the new: with cultural and geographical strangeness; with the alien view, Indian and British; with an unfamiliar literature, Sanskrit or Lake poet; with the enabling and inhibiting classificatory scholarship and science of the Victorian world; with the inhabitation of difference, actual or imaginative, lived or read.

***

In 1876 the London literary critic Edmund Gosse received in the post what he described as 'a thin and sallow packet with a wonderful Indian postmark on it'. It contained, he later recounted, 'a most unattractive orange pamphlet of verse, printed at Bhowarupore, [a] shabby little book of some 200 pages, without preface or introduction, [which] seemed specially designed by its particular providence to find its way hastily into the wastepaper basket'.[35]

The book, *A Sheaf Gleaned in French Fields*,[36] was a collection of translations into English of French works by Toru and Aru Dutt, the daughters of one of *The Dutt Family Album's* authors, Govin Chunder Dutt. By 1881, when Gosse wrote his introductory memoir to Toru's second work, both sisters had died of tuberculosis, a fact which enables Gosse to configure Toru as an Indian Brontë, a 'fragile exotic blossom of song' in 'the brief May-day of her existence'.[37] Gosse admires Dutt's work, yet he has reservations. He is uncomfortable with the way that her translations try, as he puts it, 'vainly, though heroically, to compete with European literature on its own ground'.[38] 'She was born to write' Gosse tells us, and 'despairing of an audience in her own language [the Bengali Renaissance was obviously not part of Gosse's literary world view], she began to adopt ours as a medium for her thought'. But being 'not entirely conversant in English' her first book sounds as if she is 'chanting to herself a music that is discordant in an English ear'. To Gosse, Dutt is admirable but alien. She lacks 'a mellow sweetness...to perfect her as an English poet', and her failure is due to what he calls the 'inequality of [her] equipment...a thing inevitable to her isolation'.[39]

Of Dutt's second book, *Ancient Ballads and Legends of Hindustan*, Gosse is far more approving. Here, he says, '[t]he poetess seems to be chanting to herself those songs of her mother's race to which she has always turned with tears of pleasure...No modern Oriental has given us so strange an insight into the conscience of the Asiatic'. He commends what he calls the poems' 'Vedic solemnity and simplicity of temper', and notes approvingly '[they] are singularly devoid of that littleness and frivolity which seems, if we may judge by a slight experience, to be the bane of modern India'.[40]

In 1881, when he wrote his memoir of Dutt, Gosse was 32. He had not yet quite reached the stage when, according to his friends, it would become 'necessary to form a society for the Protection of Edmund Gosse, to intercept begging letters and consign to the flames presentation copies of poems'.[41] But he was already a force within the British literary establishment. The archetypal 'man of letters', he was busy fashioning himself as cultural commissar of the newly emerging field of English literary criticism, a field as yet unprofessionalised by the universities which were still resistant to making English literature part of the curriculum.⁴² The poet Arthur Symons wrote of Gosse at this time that he

> [h]olds a middle station between the older and the younger schools of criticism. He is neither a respectable and accomplished fossil, nor a wild and whirling Catherine-wheel. He lacks, indeed, the positive manner and enthusiasm which respectively characterize the two schools. His habitual moderation makes him, certainly, something of an outsider. With all his respect for the past and his curiosity as to the future, he keeps just far enough away from the literary arena of the present not to be soiled by its dust. He seems to lean from the window while the battle of the books is being fought out in the streets. He gently encourages both sides; but the younger men feel that he would like them to win.⁴³

Gosse the middlebrow self-improver was the gatekeeper, the administrator of the still-evolving literary canon of late Victorianism. In this role he encouraged and promoted new talent such as W.B. Yeats and Symons, argued for re-assessment of neglected writers of the past such as John Donne and introduced the English reading public to the strange and the exotic with his championing of Scandinavian literature, particularly the work of Ibsen. For the strange and exotic of empire, Gosse's feelings were ambivalent. His biographer Anne Thwaite talks of his anti-imperialism: 'The colonies were more interested in cricket than Swinburne, he feared [saying] "They add absolutely nothing to that which makes life valuable to me."'⁴⁴ But it is clear that in the literary context, he has a firm idea of what constitutes Indian-ness and what constitutes an Indian writer. The avid orientalism of his memoir of Dutt exemplifies the manner in which by the end of the nineteenth century the literary conventions of empire – that is, the way that the various parts of empire could be written about – had calcified. Marcus Clarke, in his 1901 preface to the poems of the Australian writer Adam Lindsay Gordon, wrote that, while 'Europe is the home of knightly songs, of bright deeds and clear morning thought' and America is the place of modernity and movement, 'rapid, glittering, insatiable', 'Asia sinks beneath the weighty recollections of her past magnificence, as the Suttee sinks, jewel-burdened, upon the corpse of dead grandeur, destructive even in its death'.⁴⁵ Derozio writing in the 1820s had expressed something of the same trope. Fifty years later there was an implicit Darwinian ranking given to nations in terms of their ability to engage with the modern. Yet this judgement was not without ambivalence. W.B. Yeats speaks of the charm of the archaic in the face of the paleness of modern existence, the 'out-worn heart in a time outworn'. 'Of old the world on dreaming fed' he laments, 'Grey truth is now her painted toy'.[46] But the Indian archaic could also denote decadence and excess. Thus Gosse's approval of Dutt's 'Vedic solemnity and simplicity of temper' – her work is ancient, but restrained in a vaguely Protestant way that Gosse, lapsed though he was, might find congenial. And in avoiding modern India's 'littleness and frivolity', it made no inconvenient proto-nationalist claims on the present.

Richardson's 1840 *Selections* was designed to be the foundation stone of an Indian English curriculum. By the 1870s when Toru Dutt was writing, this curriculum was well established and had moved beyond the confines of the Hindu College. The first government school for girls, the Bethune School, was founded in 1849, and was immediately locked into wider Victorian concerns about the education of women: 'early commentators were preoccupied with this issue and devoted a significant portion of their writings to it'.[47] Girls' education was inextricably linked to fears of social change, the threat of conversion and issues of national identity, but these ideals were set against an association of English and English culture with the aspirations of the middle class. The Native Ladies' Normal School (later renamed the Banga Mahila Bidyalaya) was founded by Keshub Chunder Sen of the Brahmo Samaj movement, and, despite its nationalist associations, it was an English-medium school which encouraged the girls to speak in English at all times, knowledge of the language being increasingly seen as a mark of social accomplishment. It was noted in 1874 that 'the senior girls had become very proficient in English', reading prose by Addison and Goldsmith, and such poems as Wordsworth's 'Ode to Duty', Campbell's 'The Mother' and Byron's 'Farewell to England'.[48] Not all middle-class girls went to school. Home education by English governess was popular, especially but not exclusively in Christian families. Keshub Chunder Sen, on an English tour in 1870, wrote:

> At the present moment a thousand Hindu homes are open to receive and welcome English governesses – well-trained, accomplished English ladies, capable of doing good to their Indian sisters, both by instruction and by personal example. And what sort of education do we expect and wish from you? An unsectarian, liberal, sound, useful education.[49]

Toru and Aru Dutt were educated partly by their father: 'He always appears to us to be the study companion of his daughter', wrote Clarisse Bader in the introduction to Dutt's French novel *Journal de Mademoiselle D'Arvers*.[50] Toru remembered 'Babu Shib Chunder Bannerjea, an elderly man of exemplary Christian piety and character' sharing this role: 'We used to read Milton with him', Toru remembered, 'We read Paradise Lost over and over so many times that we had the first book and part of the second book by heart'.[51] In a new edition of *A Sheaf Gleaned in French Fields* published in 1878 after his children's deaths their father wrote: 'Excepting for a few months in France, Aru and Toru were never put to school, but they sedulously attended the lectures for women in Cambridge during our stay in England'.[52] Their visit to Europe lasted from 1869 to 1873. From Nice Toru wrote to her English friend Mary Martin, 'We do not go to the school now, we have left it, and we read French with Madame Schwayer, Papa's French teacher'.[53] During their stay in London Romesh Chunder Dutt, a cousin, observed that 'Literary work and religious studies were still the sole occupation of Govin Chunder Dutt and his family',[54] but Toru records the presence of 'Mr Girard, the French teacher', 'Mrs Macfarren, our singing governess' and Mrs Lawless 'a lady of birth' who came each day between 10:00 am and 3:30 pm.[55] On her return to Calcutta, and after Aru's death in 1874, Toru's studies continued with her father, assisted by the resources of his own library and the Calcutta Public Library 'of which Papa is a shareholder'.[56] Toru published in the periodicals that Richardson had supported forty years earlier, writing an essay for *The Bengal Magazine* on the Réunion poet Leconte de Lisle in which she praised his freedom from the 'faults generally attributed to all Asiatic or half-caste poets writing in the language of Europe...weakness, languor, conventionalism, and imitation'.[57] Paradoxically, the family were now more isolated than they had been in London where they had been at the centre of a web of Anglo-Indian social networks. Dutt wrote Mary Martin:

> We do not go much into society now. The Bengali reunions are always for men. Wives and daughters and all women-kind are confined to the house, under lock and key, *à la lettre*! and Europeans are generally supercilious and look down on Bengalis. I have not been to one dinner party or any party at all since we left Europe. And then I do not know any people here except for our kith and kin, and some of them I do not know.[58]

With her father's help she attempted to get *A Sheaf Gleaned in French Fields* published: 'Calcutta publishers are a very timid class of people', she complained, 'not at all enterprising, and they are besides more given to the sales of books than publishing new ones'.[59] One might understand the reluctance of a Calcutta publisher faced with a collection of English translations from the French by an Indian child-prodigy, although it is an indication of the eclectic nature of Bengali literary culture that Toru not only found a publisher but was widely, knowledgeably and enthusiastically reviewed: 'fragrant with the aroma of true poetry', wrote *The Bengal Magazine*, 'done with so much spirit and vivacity', the poems 'would do credit to any highly educated English lady; that they are the productions of a young Bengali lady, not twenty years old, is to us a marvel'.[60] But it was her second, posthumously published work *Ancient Ballads and Legends of Hindustan* which appealed both to the local and to the London audience, from Edmund Gosse to the teachers of the Native Ladies' Institution, founded in 1882, who used it as text book.

\*\*\*

*Ancient Ballads and Legends of Hindustan* was a work written by Toru as part of Govin Dutt's programme of home study. Meenakshi Mukherjee is sceptical about the often-repeated story of her working directly with the Sanskrit texts. Mukherjee cites a letter in which Dutt writes, 'Papa says as there is no good opportunity to learn German now, we better take up Sanskrit', which suggests only a passing acquaintance with the language, and points out that Dutt would have studied for only ten months.[61] Mary Martin sent Dutt a 'grammar marker', 'in cross-stitch on thin perforated cardboard, with the words "Here I fell asleep"' and Dutt replied: 'I think I shall give up Sanskrit. It is very difficult, and the grammatical rules are legion, and so minute'.[62]

There were many current translations of the classic texts both in Bengali and in English, which would have been available to her, and the stories she chose are among the most popular, ones she was likely to have heard as well as read: most are from the *Ramayana* and the *Mahabharata*; two are from the *Vishnu Purana*, and one is described as a 'Bengali folk tale'. Toru talks about hearing 'my dear mother singing in the evening, the old songs of our country'.[63] Her cousin Romesh

Chunder Dutt, in his 1900 translation of the *Ramayana* and the *Mahabharata*, wrote:

> The Hindu scarcely lives, man or woman, high or low, educated or ignorant, whose earliest recollections do not cling round the story and the characters of the great Epics. The almost illiterate oil-manufacturer or confectioner of Bengal spells out some modern translation of the *Maha-bharata* to while away his leisure hour. The tall and stalwart peasantry of the North-West know of the five Pandav brothers, and of their friend the righteous Krishna. The people of Bombay and Madras cherish with equal ardour the story of the righteous war.[64]

Toru Dutt's intended audience seems to be English. There is a deliberation and a self-consciousness in the way she adapts and presents her sources, the way she inserts comments and amends details at will, directing the unsatisfied reader back to originals if they desire amplification or further narrative, while at the same time maintaining her own work's separateness from its sources. At one point she asks:

> What is the sequel of the tale?
> How died the king? – Oh man,
> A prophet's words can never fail –
> Go, read the Ramayan.[65]

Her diction is taken from the Romantic ballad and its later Victorian manifestations – simple language, short lines, regular rhyme and a slightly faux-child voice. Unlike her cousin, she does not attempt to reproduce what Romesh calls the 'musical movement' of the Sanskrit original, with its 'Sloka' two-line verses of sixteen syllables each, a task which he confessed caused him 'considerable trouble and anxiety'.[66] Romesh may commend the 'simple and easy flow of narrative' and the 'unadorned simplicity' of the Sanskrit original,[67] but his convoluted translations only demonstrate the freedom that Toru's use of plot rather than poetic diction and textual detail gives her. Romesh's translation of Lakshman's description of Rama in Book VI of the *Ramayana*, is ponderous and wordy:

> Cast aside thy causeless terror; in the sky or earth below,
> In the nether regions, Rama knows no peer or equal foe,
> He shall slay the seer of jungle, he shall voice no dastard cry,
> 'Tis some trick of wily Rakshas in this forest dark and high![68]

Toru's version of the same passage combines powerful visual imagery with simple but emphatic diction redolent of oral performance, exploiting the exciting nature of her material without lapsing into the arch archaisms of the Victorian epic:

> The lion and the grisly bear
> Cower when they see his royal look,
> Sun-staring eagles of the air
> His glance of anger cannot brook,
> Pythons and cobras at his tread
> To their most secret coverts glide,
> Bowed to the dust each serpent head,
> Erect before in hooded pride.[69]

There is more than a hint of the hymn tradition here. The tractability of this voice means that, where necessary, Toru can make her material less exotic, less Indian and more general in its message. The *Mahabharata* story of Savitri, the princess who chooses to marry her beloved despite his death being foretold, and who negotiates with Yama the God of Death for his return to life, was a popular tale of Hindu wifely devotion. Toru adjusts its emphasis, and turns it into a more universally applicable lesson concerning fate, acceptance and proper behaviour in general:

> Can man's device the doom repeal?
> Unequal seems to be the strife
> Between Humanity and Fate;
> None have on earth what they desire;
> Death come to all or soon or late;
> And peace is but a wandering fire;
> Expediency leads wild astray;
> The Right must be our guiding star;
> Duty our watchword, come what may....[70]

Toru renames Yama 'Death' but follows her source in his description:

> Upon his head he wore a crown
> That shimmered in the doubtful light;
> His vestment scarlet reached low down,
> His waist a golden girdle dight.

> His skin was bronze; his face
> Irradiate, and yet severe;
> His eyes has much of love and grace,
> But glowed so bright they filed with fear.[71]

But, while his surroundings are localised and specific ('the ghost-like trees, Sals, tamarisks, and South-Sea pines,/ And palm whose plumes wave in the breeze'[72]), the attendant details have the more generalised flavour of Victorian medievalism. There are 'trumpets blown from castle towers', 'gardens gay, and hedgerows trim', 'woods primeval, where reside/ The holy hermits'; the experience as a whole is 'a dream from elfland blown' under the aegis of the 'Almighty will'.[73] The three wishes which Savitri extracts from Death – that her father-in-law's blindness be cured and his kingdom restored, that her own father should have sons, and finally that her husband be restored to life – reflect the Hindu values of filial duty and the importance of lineage. But they also have the flavour of a European fairy story – the virtuous heroine rewarded, the discriminating but selfless choice of magic wishes. When Savitri realises that she may, with her final wish, get her husband back, the words Toru uses, 'She took the clue, felt Death was Love', echo the conclusion of Elizabeth Barrett Browning's first 'Sonnet from the Portuguese':

> *Guess now who holds thee?* – *Death,* I said, But, there,
> The silver answer rang, – *Not Death, but Love.*[74]

Similarly, Toru's version of the Bengali folk tale 'Jogadhya Uma' begins in tones taken straight from Christina Rossetti's 'Goblin Market':

> 'Shell-bracelets ho! 'Shell-bracelets ho!
> Fair maids and matrons come and buy!'[75]

And it continues in the tones of English pastoral:

> ...And lo! The manse,
> Humble but neat with open door!....
> Huge straw ricks, log huts full of grain,
> Sleek cattle, flowers, a tinkling bell,
> Spoke in language sweet and plain,
> 'Here smiling Peace and Plenty dwell.'[76]

There are more overt interventions. In the original version of 'The Royal Acetic and the Hind' in the *Vishnu Purana*, the story of Bharata the hermit-king who falls in love with a fawn is a lesson in the effect of vain and unstable passion. In subsequent lives the king must recuperate his position by working his way through various levels of reincarnation. The story ends with a philosophical dialogue between the erstwhile king, now a Raja's palanquin bearer, and the Raja on the nature of the self.[77] Toru Dutt's version deals only with the love of king and fawn, and she takes issue with her source's treatment of the narrative. She rejects

> [w]hat the Brahman sage would fain imply
> As the concluding moral of his tale,
> That for the hermit-king it was a sin
> To love his nursling.[78]

'What!' asks Dutt, 'A sin to love! a sin to pity!' The king's mistake, she maintains, was not in loving the fawn but in going into the forest as a hermit in the first place:

> [c]asting off all love
> By his retirement to the forest-shades;
> For that was to abandon duties high,
> And, like a recreant soldier, leave the post
> Where God had placed him as a sentinel....

The *Vishnu Purana*'s deeply Hindu narrative is modified, its sentimental detail – or what could be reinterpreted by a Westernised Victorian reader as sentimental detail – is extracted, and the piece as a whole is subjected to a Christian scrutiny which reverses the original story's moral intent. A 'pious chronicle, writ of old/ By Brahman sage' is all very well, Toru tells her reader, but 'we who happier live/ Under the holiest dispensation' know better.

This is a novel form of translation, where the translator does not just change the fundamental direction of the original, but acknowledges and justifies her changes within the text. In much the same way, the *Vishnu Purana* story of Prehlad, whose love of Vishnu challenges his royal father's omnipotence, in *Ancient Ballads* becomes a very Victorian tale of secular education and its limitations. Toru's Prehlad engages with and finds wanting 'all sciences' – astronomy, geography, logic, politics, war and medicine.[79] In the original, Prehlad's father is enraged by his son's adherence to Vishnu; in *Ancient Ballads*, reflecting Victorian discussions of belief and doubt, it is Prehlad's need for 'the gods' in general which is the cause of his father's rage. Prehlad is imprisoned for this defiance, and there his adherence to 'the gods' changes to adherence to 'one God':

> I have in my dungeon dark
> Learnt more of truth than e'er I knew,
> There is one God – One only, – mark!
> To Him is all our service due.[80]

The original story of devotion to Vishnu becomes a narrative of Christian conversion where the subject rejects both the appeals of science and modernity and the Hindu pantheon.

*Ancient Ballads and Legends of Hindustan* is thus not a translation or even a partial translation of the original texts; rather it is a *reading* of selected stories, filtered through an active and critical intelligence shaped by Dutt's Christianity and her awareness of European as well as Indian literary forms. And it is a *personal* reading, rooted not in her knowledge of Sanskrit or her scholarly deployment of the different texts, but in family and memory. The final poem in the sequence makes this framing overt. 'Sita' is a description not of the story of Sita and Valmiki, the supposed author of the *Ramayana*, but of Dutt's childhood encounter with it:

> Three happy children in a darkened room!
> What do they gaze on with wide-open eyes?
> A dense, dense forest, where no sunbeam pries,
> And at its centre a cleared spot. – There bloom
> Gigantic flowers on creepers that embrace
> Tall trees; there, in a quiet lucid lake
> The white swans glide... The peacock... herds of wild deer...
> There, dwells in peace, the poet-anchorite.
> But who is this fair lady? Not in vain
> She weeps, – for lo! at every tear she sheds
> Tears from three pairs of young eyes fall amain,
> And bowed in sorrow are the three young heads.
> It is an old, old story, and the lay
> Which has evoked sad Sita from the past
> Is by a mother sung.[81]

The darkened room of Dutt's childhood home in Manicktollah Street, Calcutta, is transformed into the forest where lonely Sita waits to be rescued by Rama. The three young listeners, Dutt, her brother Abju, and her sister Aru, are drawn into the imagined landscape and into sympathy with the abandoned queen by the power of the story's performance by their mother. The recitation over, 'melts the picture from their sight away'. Abju died in 1865; Aru in 1874. But both the story and, just as importantly, the memory of hearing it are still accessible to Dutt through the recuperative processes of poetic recreation.

That Dutt was aware of the limits of translation – whether in its straightforward sense of moving from one language to another, or in its more allusive sense of explaining and representing ideas between cultures – is demonstrated in a sonnet, dedicated to her father, at the conclusion of *A Sheaf Gleaned in French Fields*:

> The flowers look loveliest in their native soil
> Amid their kindred branches; plucked, they fade,
> And lose the colours Nature on them laid,
> Though bound in garlands with assiduous toil.
> Pleasant it was, afar from all turmoil,
> To wander through the valley, now in shade
> And now in sunshine, where these blossoms made
> A Paradise, and gather in my spoil.
> But better than myself no man can know
> How tarnished have become their tender hues
> E'en in the gathering, and how dimmed their glow!
> Wouldst thou again new life in them infuse,
> Thou who hast seen them where they brightly blow?
> Ask Memory. She shall help my stammering Muse.[82]

Vibrant originals fade when plucked, no matter how elaborately they are rearranged. The author is conscious of how far her translations fall short of the originals, and sees memory as the key to not simply preserving them, but giving them, in their new context, a new relevance.

\*\*\*

Edmund Gosse exercised his role as literary gatekeeper in the variety of periodicals and publications to which he contributed. But his judgements, advice and prescriptive relationships were also acted out in person, in the drawing rooms of London literary society, not least in his Sunday afternoons At Home. Another young Indian 'poetess', Sarojini Chattopadhyaya, later Naidu, who spent three years in Britain between 1895 and 1898, attended regularly, later describing Gosse as her 'literary godfather',[83] a 'brilliant and fascinating, slightly malicious and wholly dominating personality that was the true centre of literary life in London when I was a girl'.[84] Naidu describes the scene:

> William Watson, with his sublime, starry genius, [John]Davidson with his wild, riotous, dazzling superabundant brilliance, [Francis]Thompson with his rich, gorgeous, spiritual ecstasy of poesy, Yeats with his exquisite dreams of music, Norman Gale, redolent of spring in the meadows and autumn in the orchard, Arthur Symons, the marvellous boy, with his passionate nature and fiery eyes, all gathered together in the house of that dearest and lovingest of friends and rarest and most gifted of geniuses, Edmund Gosse.[85]

Writing in 1912, Gosse could no longer remember the circumstances of their first meeting, but remembered Naidu as 'marvellous in mental maturity' and 'as unlike the usual English maiden of that age as a lotus or a cactus is unlike a lily of the valley'.[86] However, the poems Naidu initially gave him to read were a disappointment, even an embarrassment. Though 'skilful in form, correct in grammar and blameless in sentiment', they were 'totally without individuality' and 'Western in feeling and in imagery'. Not only were they 'founded on reminiscences of Tennyson and Shelley', far worse – 'I am not sure' writes Gosse the unbeliever 'that they did not even breathe an atmosphere of Christian resignation'.[87]

Gosse had no doubt as to his role and responsibilities. Canon-making is, after all, about making rules. He records that he explained to Naidu what he wanted and did not want from her writing:

> I implored her to consider that from a young Indian of extreme sensibility, who had mastered not merely the language but the prosody of the West, what we wished to receive was, not a réchauffé of Anglo-Saxon sentiment in an Anglo-Saxon setting, but some revelation of the heart of India, some sincere penetrating analysis of native passion, of the principles of antique religion and of such mysterious intimations as stirred the soul of the East long before the West had begun to dream it had a soul.[88]

No more robins and skylarks, Gosse stipulates, but 'the mountains, the gardens, the temples... the vivid populations of her own voluptuous and unfamiliar province'. If she was to follow his advice Naidu would become 'a genuine Indian poet of the Deccan, not a clever machine-made imitation of the English classics'. In desiring the unfamiliar, Gosse is quite explicit in setting out what that unfamiliar will be like. Authentic 'Indian-ness' is to be achieved only by following his prescriptions – which, gratifyingly, he records her as doing with 'the docility and the rapid appreciation of genius'.[89]

Gosse's expectations were both literary and personal; Naidu was expected to act the Indian poetess as well as produce the appropriate poems. Antoinette Burton, in her study of Indians in late-Victorian Britain, suggests that:

> [i]n many respects, 'being Indian' was something to be learned by travel to Britain – a performance to be tested, a habitus to be tried out and reinvented on a regular basis, especially considering that 'India' was not considered to be a coherent national political entity in the late-Victorian period.[90]

Certainly, accounts of Naidu stress her dramatic appearance as well as her intellectual and literary skills. Arthur Symons describes her as

> [d]ressed always in clinging dresses of Eastern silk... so small, and her long black hair hung straight down her back, you might have taken her for a child. She spoke little, and in a low voice, like gentle music; and she seemed, wherever she was, to be alone... She sat in our midst, and judged us, and few knew what was passing behind that face 'like an awakening soul', to use one of her own epithets. Her eyes were like deep pools, and you seemed to fall through them into depths below depths.[91]

The twin rhetorics of eroticisation and infantilisation are apparent here. A sketch of Naidu by John Butler Yeats done at this time depicts a small, frail, ethereal figure swathed in a sari.[92] Naidu was fashioned – and, it must be said, fashioned herself – as a kind of checklist of fin de siècle preoccupations. She represents the empire of the exotic rather than the gung-ho empire of Gosse's friend Kipling.[93] She represents a Pater-esque, aestheticist concentration on the idea of beauty and the intensity of the sensuous experience, both in her person and in her poetry. She writes to Gosse of 'this definite, dramatic world of so varied and so fiery beauty: colour, music, perfume, and vivid human faces'.[94] Despite the very obvious influences she picks up from the fin de siècle poets',[95] her poetry is seen by her English admirers as being archaically sourced, authentic, natural and instinctive. It is expressive of, as Symons puts it, 'wisdom, as of age or of the age of a race'.[96] Naidu was complicit in these representations, writing to Symons, 'Do you know I have some very beautiful poems floating in the air and if the gods are kind I shall cast my soul like a net and capture them'.[97] To Gosse she evokes what she describes as 'my Eastern birth-right of mysticism, the ever-strengthening tendency and yearning to merge myself and become a portion of the Abstract Universal Essence'.[98]

Naidu's performance of Indian-ness connects with the fashionable contemporary enthusiasm for alternative religions sourced from the East, especially Theosophy and Vedanta. W.B. Yeats shared rooms with Symons in 1896 and was a regular at the Gosses' At Homes – Naidu writes of 'those deep Druid eyes of his'.[99] Yeats' collections *Crossways*, *The Rose* and *The Wanderings of Oisin*, central documents of the Celtic Revival, were imbued with an awareness of Indian philosophy and religion. Gosse's close friend Andrew Lang published his anthropological study *Myth, Ritual and Religion* in 1887. But by the end of the century, the authenticity and consequent authority of a poetic work was no longer attested to by its scholarly footnotes and the author's knowledge of the Sanskrit original but rather by the extent to which it was felt to convey the *feel* of the authentic. Naidu's links with the poets she met at the Gosses' At Homes, especially her friendship with Symons, meant that her poetic expression was cast in the style of the fin de siècle, where the authority of feeling and sensation rather than the authority of knowledge predominated. George Holbrook Jackson, writing in 1913, looked back on the decadence of the 1890s, defining it as '1) Perversity, 2) Artificiality, 3) Egoism and 4) Curiosity... it is a demand for wider ranges, new emotional and spiritual territories, fresh woods and pastures new for the soul'.[100] The lyric was at the centre of this poetic practice. In his 1904 *Studies in Prose and Verse*, Symons describes the lyric as 'an embodied ecstasy, and an ecstasy so profoundly personal that it loses the accidental qualities of personality, and becomes a part of the universal consciousness'.[101]

This universalising could, however, be generated from a particular stock of symbolism. Symons uses Yeats as an example of this process: 'Mr Yeats has chosen his symbolism out of Irish mythology, which gives him the advantage of an elaborate poetic background, new to modern poetry'.[102] Paradoxically, a new form of poetry is achieved by returning to archaic sources but the use of these sources, says Symons, must be free of conscious craft:

> Here, at last, is poetry which has found for itself a new form, a form really modern, in its rejection of every artifice, its return to the natural chant out of which verse was evolved.[103]

This poetry of instinct, while sourced from the particular, leads to the expression of the universal: 'it expresses, with passionate quietude, the elemental desires of humanity, the desire of love, the desire of wisdom, the desire of beauty.' It is the business of the poet to make 'visible pictures out of what comes to him invisibly, in dreams, in the energetic abandonment of meditation'.[104] He or she must do so conscious of the imprecision of language, words being 'mere compromises, mere indications' and they must also 'evade the old bondage of rhetoric, the old bondage of exteriority'.[105] Beauty should be 'evoked magically' rather than simply described. Karl Beckson defines Symons' poetry as seeking 'an autonomous art that would embrace aesthetic concern with intense personal experience'.[106] Conventional description, what Symons disparagingly calls 'catalogu[ing] the trees of the forest', must give way to a 'dutiful waiting on every symbol by which the soul of things can be made visible'.[107] In this way, 'literature, bowed down by so many burdens, may at last attain liberty, and its authentic speech'. 'Authentic speech' and traditional sources are connected. Yeats writes, 'I wanted the strongest passions, passions that had nothing to do with observation, and metrical forms that seemed old enough to have been sung by men half-asleep or riding on a journey'.[108]

It is clear from this what the appeal of Naidu was to Symons. Even more than Yeats' Irish sources, her poetry's Indian settings and legendary material, expressed in terms of symbolist poetic technique, fulfilled Symons' requirements: a preference for archaic sources and forms; an elevation of the passions and emotions over the rational and the narrative; a concentration on the idea of beauty, both in the work and in the person of the author. His desire for an 'embodied ecstasy' found its realisation not only in Naidu's poetry but in Naidu herself. He writes in his *Memoirs*:

> I either fascinated or was fascinated by a strange, beautiful and exotic Eastern girl, who, alone, as our nerves often quivered in unison, in this

tenebrous years of my life between 1895 and 1896, shared what I can hardly call less than agonies of sensation, with me; in whom they were one burning rage and one consuming fire.[109]

The closeness of their writing is demonstrated by two simultaneously composed poems, Symons' 'Javanese Dancers' and Naidu's 'Indian Dancers'. Both poems describe an exotic dance; both use symbolist techniques to evoke its musicality and physicality; both are implicitly or explicitly decadent.[110] Symons describes his dancer:

> Undulantly with cat-like steps that cling;
> Smiling between her painted lids a smile,
> Motionless, unintelligible, she twines
> Her fingers into mazy lines,
> The scarves across her fingers twine the while. [111]

Naidu's dancer has

> Eyes ravished with rapture, celestially panting, what passionate bosoms aflaming with fire
> Drink deep of the hush of the hyacinth heavens that glimmer around them in fountains of light;
> O wild and entrancing the strain of keen music that cleaveth the stars like a wail of desire,
> And beautiful dancers with houri-like faces bewitch the voluptuous watches of night.
> The scents of red roses and sandalwood flutter and die in the maze of their gem-tangled hair....[112]

Symons' restrained description manages nevertheless to have an uneasy edge to it: the music is '[d]ull, shrill, continuous, disquieting'; the dancers have 'fixed eyes, monotonously still... with smiles inanimate', 'sinuous fingers, spectral hands'.

Naidu's overload of adjectivally charged imagery, on the other hand, celebrates the exotic, sometimes at the expense of sense – it is unclear what exactly either 'celestially panting' or 'the voluptuous watches of night' mean. In Symons, a sense of the artifice of the dancers with 'painted lids', 'like painted idols', contributes to the slightly sinister tone. Naidu, on the other hand, layers imagery, language and sound to convey the reality of the experience with as much colourful intensity as possible. Apart from 'passionate bosoms aflaming with fire', a phrase that was amended in the poem's publication in *The Savoy* to 'passionate spirits', Naidu is careful to remain within the limits of the decorous. Her marginal notes in her copy of 'Laurence Hope's' 1901 poetry collection *The Garden of Kama and other Love Lyrics from India* – 'pretty', 'beauty with a touch of vulgarity', 'how vulgar'[113] – indicate her sense of the limits to what has been described as her 'decadent exoticism'.[114] Symons had his critics on that account. *The Pall Mall Gazette* in 1895 wrote:

> Mr Arthur Symons is a very dirty-minded man, and his mind is reflected in the puddle of his bad verses. It may be that there are other dirty-minded men who will rejoice in the jingle that records the squalid and inexpensive amours of Mr Symons, but our faith jumps to the hope that such men are not.[115]

Naidu was aware of such critiques and aware of the danger of letting her own work be seen in a similar light. Respectability was an important part of her self-presentation.

There were other dangers. If authenticity was closely connected with the identity of the author, to detach the two was to enter dangerous territory. Was there an appreciable difference between the works of Dutt and Naidu and imitative copies such as the Indian love lyrics of 'Laurence Hope'? In his 1918 anthology *The Bengali Book of English Verse*, Theodore Douglas Dunn asked whether Indian writers could offer anything which could not be done equally well by Europeans:

> Emerson... has conjured up a whole world of eastern religious mysticism... Sir Alfred Lyall in his poem *Siva*, has looked through and beyond the sensuous imagery... In his verse the majesty and terror of an ancient faith are made to appeal from their own oriental setting. Sir Edwin Arnold... has created the true atmosphere of the east.[116]

Indian writers in English, on the other hand, Rabindranath Tagore complained, 'appear to work in some strangely neutral zone of the imagination, and to be uninfluenced by the colour and atmosphere of their environment'.[117] Their work is, paradoxically, pallid and restrained beside the confident orientalism of their English equivalents. The constraints on

## 2 LITTLENESS, FRIVOLITY AND VEDIC SIMPLICITY: TORU DUTT, SAROJINI... 51

Indian writers were clear. In 1926 Lawrence Binyon, writing of his friend Manmohan Ghose, recognised in himself an irrational prejudice:

> ...with English people I fancy that the Orientalism of a Flecker or a Lafcadio Hearn finds much readier sympathy than the romantic admiration of English that inspired Manmohan Ghose. I remember that I myself was quite annoyed with him for persisting in choosing a Greek legend, Perseus, for the subject of a long poem rather than an Indian one. How unreasonable this was! I should not have been annoyed with myself for wanting to write a poem on Savitri or Nala or Damayanti.[118]

\*\*\*

In 1898 Naidu returned to India, but remained in contact with Gosse, Symons and the London literary scene, returning to London regularly. In 1913, for example, *The Times* records her as 'entertained at complimentary dinner' at the Hotel Cecil chaired by W.B. Yeats and attended by Alice Meynell, Walter de la Mare, Ezra Pound, Robbie Ross and leading figures from the English Indian community.[119] Her first collection of poems, *The Golden Threshold*, was published in London by her friend William Heinemann in 1905 and her second, *The Bird of Time*, in 1911. From India – or more specifically from Hyderabad – she offers her London correspondents Hyderabad as an actualisation of the fantasies of poetry. Unlike London, she writes, this is not a place where literature is manufactured: there is 'no news of literary interest to send you... no intellectual life here, no ardent, vital "movement"'.[120] Instead, Hyderabad is a lived embodiment of the literary world of faery, of beauty and the senses, of the exotic and the unattainable untouched by the modern, as Naidu describes it, 'infinitely picturesque and pleasant to the artistic sense, like a representation of some old esoteric faery tale on the stage'.[121] In 1895 Yeats had written of his desire to write not 'mere phantasies but the signatures – I use the medium's term – of things invisible and ideas'.[122] Naidu's life after her return was in fact taken up with marriage, children and the beginnings of her lifelong involvement in the politics of nationalism. But to Gosse and Symons she presents herself as

> [s]inging with the birds in a wild and lonely garden set in a desert, bordered by hills, bare indeed of trees and blossoms but rich in historic legend – such a garden full of wells decorated with friezes of fishes and buds and guarded by stone lions and living peacocks – and fruit trees,

groves of citron, orange, pomegranate, and figs, glowing flowers and fragrant fruit hanging together on the branches above, receiving channels of green well-water.[123]

There is a tension here between a desire to write in terms of the actual place – a desire that becomes part of the postcolonial project, what the New Zealand poet Allen Curnow calls attention to the local and special[124] – and the continuing power of the literary conventions and perspectives of fin de siècle London through which Naidu filters her account of her locale. In 1911 she writes to William Heinemann recalling Walter Pater who, she says, 'speaks somewhere of the hawthorn being the reddest thing [that he] had ever beheld'. Naidu compares Pater's hawthorn to the 'sumptuous, multitudinous crimsons of the gulmohur flower'. This local flower is more resonant for Naidu, not just because of its superior colour – that is, the immediate sensation – but because of its capacity to point to culture and history. '[I]t stands for me', she writes:

> [a]s the symbol of a hundred passionate and splendid emotions such as the colours that a bride wears on her bridal morn and the hue of the blood that was shed on the Rajput battlefields centuries ago: a sacred flame into which the Sati princesses leapt preferring death to dishonour: O it is a wonderful flower, with a wonderful capacity for symbolism.[125]

Although the detail of this symbolic reading – both the flower and its associations – are Indian, the process Naidu uses is derived straight from the fin de siècle symbolists, and her symbolic referents – bridal morns, battlefields, and sati, not to mention the gardens full of wells decorated with friezes of fishes and buds and guarded by stone lions and living peacocks of the earlier letter – are sourced more from European orientalism than from any local context.

Indian authors were admitted to the literary empire on strict conditions. What was of interest to literary adjudicators such as Gosse was their evocation of the east conceived in wholly western terms. The Indian author could not, in his view, engage with the modern. Naidu, in contrast to the manner in which she lived her life, fashions her art in obediently archaic terms. Dutt's work is more complex. In *Ancient Ballads* she offers the English reader a version of Indian tradition processed in terms of the particular affiliations of her Indian, English and European education. With her evocation of a performance of 'Sita' by her mother she demonstrates a means by which traditional material is brought into the present by the operations of personal memory. That domestic setting is a crucial way in which she is able to articulate the complexity of her situation: Bengali yet Christian; educated in European as well as local literary traditions; a cherished, sheltered family member as well as an author with literary friendships in France and England as well as in Calcutta. Her home at Manicktollah Street, with its various and sometimes antagonistic strands, its habits of reading and education, its absences, is central to her sense of her writing self, whether described as it is in the present or remembered as it has been. *Ancient Ballads* concludes with a section entitled 'Miscellaneous Poems'.[126] One poem, 'Our Casuarina Tree', describes a tree in the garden of the family's country home, the Garden House in Baugmaree. It is entwined with a 'creeper like a huge Python', with flowers in 'crimson clusters', a grey baboon and its family, kokilas (cuckoos), beside a tank with water lilies growing in it. The setting is presented as picturesque rather than exotic – local, domestic and particular, something to be recreated from a lovingly evoked memory. But from the outset the description is infiltrated by English literary referents. There is a Keatsian 'casement...wide open thrown', Gray-like cows are wending to their pastures, 'the sea breaking on a shingle-beach' gestures to Arnold's 'Dover Beach', and the poem's argument pivots on a Wordsworthian expression of the power of childhood memory and the 'inner vision'. Are these the actions of an inept and derivative provincial poet or a conscious entanglement of global literary landscape and colonial place? The poem's conclusion openly acknowledges its literary borrowing, comparing the casuarina tree to 'those in Borrowdale', echoing lines from Wordsworth's 1803 poem 'Yew-trees': 'Fear, trembling Hope, and Death, the skeleton, /And Time the shadow'.[127] This sets the poem firmly in a generalised frame of Romantic loss and regret, as do the words of the tree itself, a 'dirge-like murmur', 'an eerie speech'. There is a distance between the speaker and her remembered garden, one that can be overcome only by the act of commemorative writing.

Despite Gosse's approving references to 'the Hindu poetess' (he seemed unable to encompass the Dutt family's Christian conversion) and the 'Vedic solemnity' of her rendition of legendary material, in this poem Dutt does something far more interesting. 'Our Casuarina Tree' filters a realist Indian locale through a range of English literary referents, and in doing so Dutt moves from the racially charged archaic – where Gosse would place her – into the global and racially neutral discourse of Victorian Romanticism, memory and modernity.

## Notes

1. David Lester Richardson, *Selections from the British Poets from the Time of Chaucer to the Present Day with Biographical and Critical Notes by David Lester Richardson, Principal of the Hindu College* (Calcutta: Baptist Mission Press, 1840), Preface, p. 3. (Richardson 1840)
2. Gauri Viswanathan, *Masks of Conquest: Literary Study and British Rule in India* (London: Faber, 1990), p. 4. (Viswanathan 1990)
3. Richardson, Preface, *Selections from the British Poets*, p. 3.
4. Richardson, Preface, *Selections from the British Poets*, pp. 14–15.
5. Richardson exercised a measure of discrimination. He writes: 'I have often taken the liberty to suppress objectionable passages (indicating the blank with stars).... It has sometimes happened that particular passages of which I could not wholly approve were so interwoven with the general texture of the poem that it was impossible to separate them without injury or confusion. In the fields of literature a weed is sometimes so closely connected with a flower that one is not to be extracted without the other', *Selections from the British Poets*, p. 18.
6. Richardson, *Selections from the British Poets*, p. 1515, footnote.
7. *Selections from the British Poets*, pp. 1474, 1479, 1518, 1483, 1500, 1495, 1492.
8. Miss Emma Roberts, 'Song', Richardson, *Selections from the British Poets*, p. 1517.
9. H.M. Parker, 'The Indian Day: Noon', Richardson, *Selections from the British Poets*, p. 1480.
10. Rosinka Chaudhuri observes that 'the craze for Eastern poetry subsided somewhat in the West in the middle years of the century, only to be resuscitated in the last quarter in the writings of Max Muller and the verse of Edwin Arnold, who used very few explanatory footnotes in his poetry. In India, by the time Madhusudan Dutt was writing in 1849, his efforts at compiling the notes became cursory in comparison, while the Dutts, in the latter half of the century, make use of epigraphs but use hardly any notes at all', *Gentlemen Poets in Colonial Bengal: Emergent Nationalism and the Orientalist Project* (Calcutta: Seagull, 2002), p. 41. (Chaudhuri 2002)
11. Richardson, *Selections from the British Poets*, p. 1476. In the note to 'Settabuldee', Richardson describes Rattray as 'perhaps the eldest of our living British poets'.
12. Richardson, *Selections from the British Poets*, p. 1490.
13. Richardson, *Selections from the British Poets*, p. 1490.
14. Richardson, *Selections from the British Poets*, p. 1484.
15. Nigel Leask, 'Towards an Anglo-Indian Poetry? The Colonial Muse in the Writings of John Leyden, Thomas Medwin and Charles D'Oyly', *Writing*

*India, 1757–1990*, ed. Bart Moore-Gilbert (Manchester: Manchester University Press, 1996), p. 53. (Leask 1996)
16. R.H. Rattray, 'Introductory Lines', *The Bengal Annual: A Literary Keepsake for 1832*, ed. David Lester Richardson (Calcutta: Samuel Smith and Co., 1834), p. xi. (Rattray 1834)
17. Richardson, *Selections from the British Poets*, p. 1518.
18. Richardson, *Selections from the British Poets*, pp. 1496, 1515, 1511, 1514, 1516, footnotes.
19. Richardson writes: 'I am fully conscious of the awkwardness and delicacy of my task, and especially as I have to make way, a few pages further on, for my own verses, which I have not done without an inward struggle and much irresolution. Had I omitted them I should have broken the unity of my plan and exposed myself to a charge of mock modesty, while in inserting them I am perhaps equally exposed to a charge of real vanity. I should have given only a single specimen, but I could not hit upon one that I was willing to be wholly judged by, and have therefore by a little variety given myself a better chance with the reader', Richardson, *Selections from the British Poets*, p. 1476, footnote.
20. 'To India – My Native Land', 'Sonnet to the Students at the Hindu College' and 'From the Persian of Hafiz (freely translated)', *Selections from the British Poets*, pp. 1519–20.
21. Richardson, *Selections from the British Poets*, 'The Boatmen's Song to Ganga', p. 1520.
22. Richardson, *Selections from the British Poets*, p. 1519. *The Bengal Magazine* includes a similar piece 'Translation of an Ode from Hafiz' written by Sir John Malcolm.
23. Derozio expresses the same thoughts in his sonnet 'The Harp of India':

> Why hang'st thou lonely on yon withered bough?
> Unstrung, for ever, must thou there remain?
> Thy music once was sweet – who hears it now?
> Why doth the breeze sigh over thee in vain? –
> Silence hath bound thee with her fatal chain;
> Neglected, mute, and desolate art thou,
> Like ruined monument on desert plain! –
> O! many a hand more worthy far than mine
> Once thy harmonious chords to sweetness gave,
> And many a wreath for them did Fame entwine
> Of flowers still blooming on the minstrel's grave:
> Those hands are cold – but if thy notes divine
> May be by mortal wakened once again,
> Harp of my country, let me strike the strain!

*Derozio, Poet of India*, ed. Rosinka Chaudhuri (New Delhi: Oxford University Press, 2008), pp. 96–7. (Derozio 2008)
24. Alexander Duff, *New Era of the English Language and English Literature in India or, an Exposition of the Late Governor General of India's Last Act, Relative to the Promotion of European Literature and Science, through the Medium of the English Language, amongst the Natives of that Populous and Extensive Province of the British Empire* (Edinburgh: John Johnstone, 1837), p. 26. (Duff 1837)
25. Viswanathan, *Masks of Conquest*, p. 54.
26. M.K. Naik writes: 'This selection influenced not only early Indo-Anglian poets but also the new poets in the Indian languages. It was required reading in the high schools of the then Bombay Presidency, and perhaps in other parts of the country as well, and proved to be a source of inspiration to the pioneers of the new poetry in languages like Marathi and Kannada', M.K. Naik, 'Echo and Voice in Indian Poetry in English', *Indian Response* [sic] *to Poetry in English: A Festschrift for V.K. Gokak*, eds. M.K. Naik et al. (Madras: Macmillan, 1970), p. 270. (Naik 1970)
27. Behramji Merwanji Malabari, *The Indian Muse in English Garb* (Bombay: The Reporters Press, 1876), p. 4. (Malabari 1876)
28. *The Dutt Family Album* (London: Longmans, Green and Co, 1870), Preface, p. vi. (*Dutt Family Album* 1870)
29. The lines are from Leigh Hunt's 'A Thought or Two on Reading Pomfret's Choice', 1823.
30. The lines are from 'To My Book' by Richard Chenevix Trench (1807–1886), Church of Ireland archbishop of Dublin.
31. Fredoon Kabraji, *This Strange Adventure: An Anthology of Poems in English by Indian 1828–1946* (*Quarterly*, Spring 1947; London: New India Publishing Co.), p. 7. (Kabraji 1947)
32. Chaudhuri, *Gentlemen Poets in Colonial Bengal*, p. 153.
33. *Dutt Family Album*, pp. 32, 21, 14–15, 102.
34. Richardson, Preface, *Selections from the British Poets*, p. 15.
35. Toru Dutt, *Ancient Ballads and Legends of Hindustan*, with an introductory memoir by Edmund W. Gosse (London: Kegan Paul, 1882), pp. viii–ix. (Dutt 1982)
36. Toru Dutt, *A Sheaf Gleaned in French Fields* (Bhowanipore: Saptahik Sambad Press, 1876). (Dutt 1876)
37. Dutt, *Ancient Ballads and Legends*, pp. xxvi, xxvii.
38. Dutt, *Ancient Ballads and Legends*, p. xxii.
39. Dutt, *Ancient Ballads and Legends*, p. xv.
40. Dutt, *Ancient Ballads and Legends*, p. xxii.

41. Ann Thwaite, *Edmund Gosse: A Literary Landscape, 1849–1928* (London: Secker and Warburg, 1984), p. 351. (Thwaite 1984). Thwaite attributes this remark to Robbie Ross.
42. By 1928 when Gosse died, T.S. Eliot could write, 'the place that Sir Edmund Gosse filled in the literary and social life of London is one that no one can ever fill again, because it is, so to speak, an office that has been abolished', Thwaite, *Gosse*, p. 1.
43. Arthur Symons, *The Memoirs of Arthur Symons: Life and Arts in the 1890s*, ed. Karl Beckson (University Park: Pennsylvania State University Press, 1977), p. 44. (Symons 1977)
44. Thwaite, *Gosse*, p. 415.
45. Marcus Clarke, Preface to New Edition of Adam Lindsay Gordon, *Sea Spray and Smoke Drift* (Melbourne: Clarson, Massina and Co., 1876), p. vi. (Clarke 1876)
46. 'The Song of the Happy Shepherd', *Crossways* [1889], *The Collected Works, volume 1: Poems*, 2nd edition, ed. Richard J. Finneran (New York: Scribner, 1997), p. 5.
47. Meredith Borthwick, *The Changing Role of Women in Bengal, 1849–1905* (Princeton: Princeton University Press, 1984), p. 28. (Borthwick 1984)
48. Borthwick, *The Changing Role of Women*, p. 86. The Native Ladies' Institution, founded in 1882, used Toru Dutt's *Ancient Ballads and Legends of Hindustan* as text book.
49. Sen's speech is quoted in Lord Beveridge, *India Called Them* (London: Allen and Unwin, 1947), p. 84. (Beveridge 1947)
50. Clarisse Bader, Introduction to the original French edition, *The Diary of Mademoiselle D'Arvers*, trans. N. Kamala (New Delhi: Penguin India, 2005), p. 6. (Bader 2005)
51. Harihar Das, *The Life and Letters of Toru Dutt* (London: Oxford University Press, 1921), p. 17–18. (Das 1921)
52. Govin Chunder Dutt, Preface, *A Sheaf Gleaned in French Fields*, second edition, (Bhowanipore: Saptahik Sambad Press, 1878), p. ix. (Dutt 1878)
53. Das, *Life and Letters of Toru Dutt*, p. 20.
54. Das, *Life and Letters of Toru Dutt*, p. 22
55. Das, *Life and Letters of Toru Dutt*, p. 39, 34, note to 34.
56. Das, *Life and Letters of Toru Dutt*, p. 68.
57. Toru Dutt, 'An Eurasian Poet', *The Bengal Magazine*, 3 (August 1874–July 1875): 189. (Dutt 1874–1875)
58. Das, *Life and Letters of Toru Dutt*, p. 141.
59. Das, *Life and Letters of Toru Dutt*, p. 119. Individual poems had already appeared in *The Bengal Magazine*.
60. *The Bengali Magazine*, 4 (August 1875–July 1876): 476.

61. Meenakshi Mukherjee, *The Perishable Empire: Essays on Indian Writing in English* (New Delhi: Oxford University Press, 2000), p. 97. (Mukherjee 2000)
62. Das, *Life and Letters of Toru Dutt*, pp. 125 and note, 183.
63. Das, *Life and Letters of Toru Dutt*, p. 7.
64. Romesh C. Dutt, 'Translator's Epilogue', *The Ramayana and The Mahabharata* (London: Dent, 1900), p. 332–3. (Dutt 1900)
65. Dutt, *Ancient Ballads and Legends*, p.106.
66. R. C. Dutt, 'Translator's Epilogue', p. 327.
67. R. C. Dutt, 'Translator's Epilogue', p. 329.
68. R. C. Dutt, *Ramayana and The Mahabharata*, p. 81.
69. Dutt, *Ancient Ballads and Legends*, p. 46.
70. Dutt, *Ancient Ballads and Legends*, p. 11. Sudeshna Banerjee talks of this period as exhibiting a 'conscious drive to redefine domestic morality in an effort to flesh out the idea of the nation at the level of the household and the family...a Brahmanical core...laced with some features derived from Victorian notions of discipline, punctuality, and domestic Hygiene', 'Spirituality and Nationalist Domesticity: Rereading the Relationship', *Calcutta Historical Journal*, 19–20 (1997–8):175. (Banerjee 1997–8)
71. Dutt, *Ancient Ballads and Legends*, pp. 27–8.
72. Dutt, *Ancient Ballads and Legends*, p. 16.
73. Dutt, *Ancient Ballads and Legends*, pp. 13, 14, 40, 12.
74. Elizabeth Barrett Browning, Sonnet I, *Sonnets from the Portuguese* (1850), lines 13–14. Barrett Browning was one of Dutt's favourite poets.
75. Dutt, *Ancient Ballads and Legends*, p. 58; c.f. 'Morning and evening/ Maids heard the goblins cry:/ 'Come buy our orchard fruits, Come buy, come buy...', Christina Rossetti, 'Goblin Market' (1862), lines 1–4.
76. Dutt, *Ancient Ballads and Legends*, p. 59.
77. *The Vishnu Purana*, translated by Horace Hyman Wilson (London: John Murray, 1840), Book 2, chapter XIII, pp. 243–319. (*Vishnu Purana* 1840)
78. Dutt, *Ancient Ballads and Legends*, p. 69.
79. Dutt, *Ancient Ballads and Legends*, p. 113.
80. Dutt, *Ancient Ballads and Legends*, p. 119.
81. Dutt, *Ancient Ballads and Legends*, pp. 122–3.
82. Dutt, *A Sheaf Gleaned in French Fields*, 'CCIX: Concluding Sonnet: À mon père', p. 231.
83. 20 July 1911, *Sarojini Naidu: Selected Letters 1890s to 1940s*, ed. Makarand Paranjape (New Delhi: Kali for Women, 1996), p. 55.
84. 2 August 1932, Naidu, *Selected Letters*, p. 281.
85. 13 January 1896, Naidu, *Selected Letters*, p. 3. Naidu goes on to mention Swinburne, William Morris, and Edward Arnold. She declares that Watson 'is the greatest and noblest of them all'.

86. Edmund Gosse, Introduction, Sarojini Naidu, *The Bird of Time: Songs of Life, Death and the Spring* (London: Heinemann, 1912), pp. 1–7. (Gosse 1912)
87. Gosse, Introduction, *The Bird of Time*, pp. 3–4.
88. Gosse, Introduction, *The Bird of Time*, pp. 4–5.
89. Gosse, Introduction, *The Bird of Time*, p. 5.
90. Antoinette Burton, *At the Heart of the Empire: Indians and the Colonial Encounter in Late-Victorian Britain* (New Delhi: Munshiram Manoharlal, 1998), p. 19. (Burton 1998)
91. Arthur Symons, Introduction, Sarojini Naidu, *The Golden Threshold* (London: William Heinemann, 1905), pp. 16, 23. (Symons 1905)
92. Frontispiece, *The Golden Threshold*. The drawing is signed 'J.B. Yeats July 1896'.
93. In 1896 Naidu writes to her future husband Govindarajulu Naidu 'A song of a Kiplingy kind, I confess rollicked thro' my head. I don't know whether it is bad – good it is not certainly – but here it is – a style utterly foreign to me', *Selected Letters*, 17 May 1896, p. 18. The poem is 'A Ballad of the Prince's Progress'. She concludes: 'What do you think of that? Not poetry certainly, but a colourful jingle'.
94. Naidu, *Selected Letters*, August 1899, p. 39.
95. See John M. Munro, 'The Poet and the Nightingale: Some Unpublished Letters from Sarojini Naidu to Arthur Symons', *Calcutta Review*, 1 (September 1969): 136. (Munro 1969)
96. Symons, Introduction, *The Golden Threshold*, p. 17.
97. Symons, Introduction, *The Golden Threshold*, p. 13.
98. Naidu, *Selected Letters*, August 1899, p. 39.
99. Naidu, *Selected Letters*, 13 January 1896, p. 141.
100. George Holbrook Jackson, *The 1890s: A Review of Art and Ideas at the Close of the Nineteenth Century* (London: Grant Richards, 1913), p. 76. (Jackson 1913)
101. A. J. Symons, *Studies in Prose and Verse* (London: J M Dent, 1904), p. 234. (Symons 1904)
102. Ibid.
103. Symons, *Studies in Prose and Verse*, p. 235.
104. Ibid.
105. A.J. Symons, *The Symbolist Movement in Literature* (London: Heinemann, 1899), pp. 5, 9. (Symons 1899)
106. Karl Beckson, *Arthur Symons: A Life* (Oxford: Clarendon, 1987), p. 52. (Beckson 1987)
107. Symons, *The Symbolist Movement*, p. 10.
108. W. B. Yeats, *Autobiographies: Reveries over Childhood and Youth and the Trembling of the Veil* (London: Macmillan, 1926), p. 154. (Yeats 1926)

109. Naidu was not the only object of Symons' enthusiasm for the exotic. This paragraph continues: 'Then there was the ravishing and wildly exotic Hungarian girl, who vibrated every emotion...', *The Memoirs of Arthur Symons: Life and Arts in the 1890s*, ed. Karl Beckson (University Park: Pennsylvania State University Press, 1977), p. 73. (Symons 1977)
110. See Edward Marx, 'Decadent Exoticism and the Woman Poet', *Women and British Aestheticism*, eds. Talia Schaffer and Kathy Alexis Psomiades (Charlottesville: University Press of Virginia, 1999), p. 143. (Marx 1999)
111. Symons, 'Javanese Dancers', *Silhouettes*, 2nd revised and enlarged edition (London: Leonard Smithers, 1896), p. 33. The first edition of *Silhouettes* was published in Paris in 1892. (Symons 1896)
112. Naidu, 'Indian Dancers', *The Golden Threshold*, p. 19.
113. Naidu exhibits mixed feelings about Hope's work. An approving marginal note reads, 'This poem would strike wondrous music on the chord of an artistically-moulded heart', Marx, 'Decadent Exoticism', pp. 152–4; 'Laurence Hope', *The Garden of Kama and other Love Lyrics from India* (London: William Heinemann, 1901), (Hope 1901). 'Laurence Hope' was a pseudonym of Adela Nicholson.
114. Marx, 'Decadent Exoticism', p. 154.
115. *Pall Mall Gazette*, 2 September, 1895, issue 9497.
116. Rabindranath Tagore, Foreword, *The Bengali Book of English Verse*, ed. Theodore Douglas Dunn (Bombay: Longmans, Green and Co, 1918), p. xxii. (Tagore 1918)
117. Tagore, Foreword, *The Bengali Book of English Verse*, p. xxi.
118. Laurence Binyon, Introduction, Manmohan Ghose, *Songs of Love and Death* (Oxford: Basil Blackwell, 1926), pp. 17–18. (Binyon 1926)
119. *The Times*, 12 November 1913, p. 4.
120. Naidu, *Selected Letters*, August 1899, p. 39.
121. Naidu, *Selected Letters*, August 1899, p. 40.
122. *The Collected Letters of W.B. Yeats*, vol. 1, 1865–1895, eds. John Kelly and Eric Domville (Oxford: Oxford University Press, 1986), p. 459. (Yeats 1986)
123. Naidu, *Selected Letters*, 4 September 1905, p. 48.
124. 'Reality must be local and special where we pick up the traces: as manifold as the signs we follow and the routes we take', Allen Curnow, Introduction to *The Penguin Book of New Zealand Verse* (Harmondsworth: Penguin, 1960), p. 17. (Curnow 1960)
125. *Naidu: Selected Letters*, 8 June 1911, pp. 53–4.
126. Dutt, *Ancient Ballads and Legends*, p. 137.
127. William Wordsworth, 'Yew-trees' (1803), *Poetical Works* (London: Henry Froude, 1895), p. 184. (Wordsworth 1895)

CHAPTER 3

# 'Constant Reading after Office Hours': Sol Plaatje and Literary Belonging

Sol Plaatje's *Native Life in South Africa Before and Since the European War and the Boer Rebellion* was begun in 1914 during a three-week sea voyage from South Africa to England. Plaatje was part of a delegation sent to protest against the South African government's 1913 Natives' Land Act, a piece of legislation designed to segregate black South Africans in narrowly defined areas and deny them the right to own or lease land outside those limits. 'Awakening on Friday morning, June 20, 1913', Plaatje wrote, 'the South African Native found himself, not actually a slave, but a pariah in the land of his birth'.[1] The delegation Plaatje was part of had little formal success. The Colonial Office declined to interfere in the new dominion's internal ordering, and at a brief pro forma meeting the Colonial Secretary Lord Harcourt, as Plaatje put it, 'made no notes and asked no questions'. A request by the delegation 'to pay their respects to his Majesty the King' was referred back to the South African Governor-General Lord Gladstone who, in consultation with prime minister and architect of the Natives' Land Act General Botha, advised that 'no useful purpose would be served if an audience is accorded to these Natives by his Majesty and...the result might be the establishment of an inconvenient precedent for the future'.[2]

Informally the group was more successful. Booked into the Buckingham Hotel in the Strand, Plaatje 'noticed that some friends repeatedly confused my address with a more august residence of that ilk'.[3] The delegation was taken up by a group of sympathisers who organised receptions, newspaper interviews and speaking engagements. *Native Life in South Africa* is dedicated to Harriette Colenso, the daughter of the former Bishop of Natal, and the bishop's daughter-in-law Sophie entertained the delegation, Plaatje in particular, on regular occasions at her family home just outside London. Georgiana Solomon, a leading member of the suffragette movement and widow of Cape Colony liberal politician Saul Solomon, and Betty Molteno, daughter of Cape Colony politician Sir John Molteno, offered hospitality and connections. Alice Werner, soon to become lecturer at London University's newly formed School of African and Oriental Studies, became a friend.

The delegation was also popular with the wider public. The Brotherhood Movement, and its associated arm, the PSA or Pleasant Sunday Afternoon Societies, provided venues, audiences and moral support. The Brotherhood had been founded in 1875 by a West Bromwich printer and Congregationalist deacon, John Blackham, impressed by the success of the American Evangelists Moodie and Sankey's 1873 mission to Britain and desirous of a Christianity which 'avoid[ed] dullness, prolixity, gloom and restraint'.[4] Consisting of social occasions of an improving nature, PSAs aimed at 'social betterment', 'a new Socialism of Christian inspiration and purpose'.[5] Both organisations stressed the connection between the individual and the collective. William Ward, the national secretary of the Brotherhood Movement, wrote:

> Religion, to be vital, must set out not only to change the heart of the individual; it must set out to change the heart of society. . . . Before you can appeal to the soul of a man you must give him conditions in which the soul can live and grow.[6]

Plaatje found many features of this movement congenial: its non-sectarian nature, its egalitarianism, its activism, its emphasis on autodidacticism and self-help, its temperance and the support it gave his cause. Laura Chrisman talks of 'the importance, for Plaatje, of Christianity as a literary tool', 'a system based upon resourceful reversal of ethical values and semantic definitions, paradox, and parable'.[7] It was specifically this kind of liberal and humanitarian Christianity that best reflected Plaatje's own agendas. *Native Life in South Africa* lists sixty Brotherhood and PSA Societies addressed by his deputation – in the majority of cases, by Plaatje himself – during their stay, as well as 'Sisterhoods, Adult Schools and several church bodies'.[8] Chapter eighteen of *Native Life in South Africa* is a discussion of the movement, and chapter twenty-four is the text of a lecture delivered to 'the "Marsh Street Men's Own" Literary Society in the Lecture Room of their Institute' in Walthamstow.[9]

Native Life in South Africa is a work difficult to classify. Part personal testimony to the conditions the Act had produced, part record of the political machinations of the post-Boer War state, part programme for reform, it invites comparison with Cobbett's *Rural Rides*, Dickens' journalism, and Mayhew's *London Labour and the London Poor*. It looks back to the descriptive yet fictionally driven style of Defoe's *Journal of the Plague Year* and forwards to the literary journalism of George Orwell – personal, fluid and authoritative. It is testimony to Plaatje's experience as a journalist in Kimberley and Mafeking, which gave him what Elleke Boehmer describes as a 'pell-mell juxtaposition of different points of reference' which served as 'one of the templates for [his] later collage style'.[10]

Native Life in South Africa is a work of non-fiction, descriptive narrative and political polemic. It contains eye-witness accounts, direct transcription of official documents, speeches and reports. And yet, at the same time, and reflecting the journalistic style of the period, it inhabits the literary universe of the English canon which Plaatje saw as an inextricable part of his political and personal philosophy, a literary universe which he necessarily employs as a means of accessing and expressing that philosophy, referencing the literature, and especially the poetry, which he had encountered, possessed and reworked.

A classic autodidact, Plaatje's formal education at a rural Berlin Missionary Society school at Pniel in the Northern Cape ended at the age of thirteen. Given the manner in which colonial educational policy developed during the nineteenth century, this was probably no disadvantage. David Johnson writes that as early as the 1830s and 1840s:

> [a]n opposition emerged between missionaries who tended to rely on religious discourse to defend the abilities of Africans, and officials and state educationalists, who drew on a scientific discourse to establish a racial hierarchy with certain definite limits set of African intellectual potential. The missionaries failed to refute the arguments of science, moderating their aspirations with regard to converting Africans into black Englishmen and aiming instead at overseeing them in a relationship of trusteeship. This meant in effect a different type of education: rather than receiving a literary education for potential equals, Africans increasingly received a vocational training which equipped them for lower forms of service....[11]

These educational theories were a feature of the late settler empire. New Zealand Māori Apirana Ngata's classical education at Te Aute College was a consequence of headmaster John Thornton's rearguard action against such policies for Māori pupils. Ngata was able to go to university, gain a law degree and enter parliament. Plaatje points to this comparison in *Native Life* when he describes meeting a New Zealand visitor at 'an Imperial indoor demonstration organized by the "Southall Men's Own"' in London:

> Mr Boote expressed his pride in finding out how shining was the native policy of New Zealand when contrasted with the native policy of South Africa. 'Why,' said Mrs Boote to us, with evident satisfaction, 'we have got Maori members of Parliament and our country is all the better for it'.[12]

For Plaatje, a move to Kimberley and employment by the Post Office put him in touch with an educated and aspirant black middle class characterised by their Christianity, their English and European literary and musical culture, and their participation, albeit circumscribed, in the political process. 'Constant reading after office hours',[13] as Plaatje put it, was the basis of his entry into this world, and English – both the language and the literature – connected him to wider networks of empire, and also of the Anglophone world generally, especially the United States, which served as a counter to the inward-looking, Dutch-speaking, Anglophobe Boer culture of his upbringing. He wrote:

> The key to knowledge is the English language. Without such a mastery of it as will give the scholar a taste for reading, the great English literature is a sealed book, and he remains one of the uneducated, living in the miserably small world of Boer ideals, or those of the untaught natives.[14]

In this he was characteristic of his social group. Patricia Morris writes of the black South African press's 'simultaneous role as proponent and opponent of the status quo' and the manner in which '[e]arly black writers, members of the missionary-educated black community in all its motley, *declassé* ambiguity, adopted the nineteenth-century liberal conception of the artist and "literature" presented in their inherited and contemporary contact with the white middle class'.[15] As Plaatje's biographer Brian Willan put it, for Plaatje '[t]he English language was less obviously a vehicle for a ruling ideology, and more the means of advancement and progress [as well as] something to be played around with'.[16]

Signalling both his own 'mastery' and his ability to 'play around', the argument of *Native Life in South Africa* is framed and referenced by literary quotation, usually in the form of an epigraph at the beginning of a chapter, sometimes as an epilogue and sometimes as an allusion within the text. These quotations relate to the particular concerns of the chapter in which they appear, and they also relate to each other, cumulatively constructing a framework which reinforces the fundamental principles underlying Plaatje's argument. *Native Life in South Africa* is thus supported not only by data, by reason, by an appeal to the principles of justice and humanity, but also by the authority of literature.

The literary epigraph has its origins in the biblical mottos or tags which introduced medieval sermons, and remained a common feature of religious tracts, biblical marginalia and glossing into the nineteenth and early twentieth century. The practice jumped from religious to fictional literature early in the development of the novel. Michael Wheeler suggests that Ann Radcliffe 'appears to have established the convention', and Walter Scott's extensive use of epigraphs in his highly popular works of fiction consolidated their use.[17] The epigraph prepares readers for the focus of the chapter that follows, alerts them to its specific concerns and may comment in some way – supportively or subversively – on that material. That is its practical, overt work. But it has a subliminal effect as well, signalling the author's mastery of the literary canon, the confidence with which they are able to survey, identify and extract what is relevant and their fellowship with the authors they deploy. The epigraph is also a signal to the reader, an invitation to active reading. One recognises the quotation, its associations and its application to the text. This action marks one's membership of the relevant reading community, conversant with the literature being referenced. John Hollander describes allusion as 'part of a portable library shared by the author and his ideal audience' in which '[i]ntention to allude recognizably is essential ... and an inadvertent allusion is a kind of solecism'.[18] The use of literary allusion implies a relationship of confidence and communality between author and audience – what Dr Johnson called a 'community of mind',[19] part of the process of building Benedict Anderson's 'imagined community'.[20] The allusion presupposes that both author and audience belong to the same reading culture and can converse, inferentially as well as directly, through that culture.

In his essay 'New Readers in the Nineteenth Century', Martyn Lyons identifies 'the specifically ardent and determined relationship' which autodidacts of the period had with their texts, 'the style of intensive reading which was peculiar to their time and needs [answering] their serious purpose and determination to succeed with meagre resources'.[21] For Plaatje, a black South African, the occasion of whose visit to England was a process of systematic exclusion from the South African polity, the 'intensive reading' which enabled his use of allusion was particularly pertinent. While *Native Life in South Africa* describes operations of the Natives' Land Act, its literary tags suggest that despite the actions of government statute and regulation, a black such as Plaatje was still a member of the literary empire. His political argument is strengthened by the continual reminder that author and reader both read the same literary texts and rely on the same literary authorities.

The choices Plaatje makes in these literary inclusions embrace but at the same time go beyond the parameters of the late-Victorian literary canon. Canonical figures such as Shakespeare, Scott, Goldsmith and Tennyson are present but minor figures and figures of popular or modish note are also referenced. Plaatje's choices include American as well as British sources, especially the writing of the black consciousness movement. Given the ethical imperatives that underlie *Native Life in South Africa*, Christianity is an obviously appropriate register, and the biblical texts Plaatje uses are those which had had traditionally been interpreted in a radical activist manner. And hymns, especially those of the non-conformist tradition, are featured.

What this principle of discriminating selection means is that *Native Life in South Africa* builds its own canon, one that expresses and reinforces its political argument. It is not a counter-canon, not an alternative selection and not a canon that subverts that of the mainstream. If it challenges political orthodoxy it does so in a manner that is itself entirely orthodox. Plaatje, through his self-directed education, through the South African cultural milieu he was part of and through the links he made in England as he was revising *Native Life in South Africa*, participates in the English tradition of radical reading and writing which William St Clair refers to as 'the development of a distinctive, reformist working-class culture'.[22] This culture, centring on such texts as the Bible, Bunyan, Milton, Shakespeare, Blake and Shelley, was part of English radical life. It was within that community – the Brotherhood Movement, the PSA societies, the Anti-slavery and Aborigines' Protection Society who hosted his delegation, the working men's associations, the non-conformist churches – that Plaatje found his most ardent support while in England. Naturally enough their texts, with their concerns for equality and justice, would be his texts, although they might need a little translation. And Plaatje was nothing if not a translator, from his professional work as an official interpreter in Kimberley and Mafeking, to his work with Professor Daniel Jones at London University constructing a Tswana orthography, to his translation of Shakespeare's plays into Tswana. Chrisman refers to Plaatje's 'commitment to the modernity, universality, and impersonality of print [and] the law of the universal equivalences of languages'.[23] He named his youngest son, born in 1912, Johann Gutenberg. This perspective, the idea of equivalence, arose naturally out of his belief in monogenic humanity, non-sectarian Christianity, and a rhetoric of empire which stressed rights and protections. Neither the English radical tradition nor Plaatje's delegation were extreme. Both saw literature as necessarily representing a set of universal values which both authorised and reflected their own agenda. Both subscribed to what Jonathan Rose has described as 'the autodidacts' mission statement: to be more than passive consumers of literature, to be active thinkers and writers'.[24] In such a schema, the desires and demands of the English working class paralleled those of the colonial subject, and could thus be expressed by employing the same literary authorities.

In *Native Life in South Africa* the mechanism of such a translation is found in the editorial arrangement, the juxtaposition of those literary allusions with the details and descriptions of the effects of the Act. Some allusions are familiar and need only to be gestured to. The Bible is a fundamental source. Jane Sales states: 'The ability to read meant the ability to read the Bible. Nothing else was available'.[25] 'When one is distressed in mind' Plaatje tells his readers 'there is no greater comforter than an appropriate scriptural quotation'.[26] Plaatje had regularly used the Song of Songs verse beginning 'I am black, but comely' in his newspaper journalism as far back as 1902 when he wrote for the *Koranta ea Becoana* in Mafeking. '[I]t became', Brian Willan says, 'a kind of personal motto of his'.[27] It is used as the epigraph to chapter one of *Native Life in South Africa*, signalling the continuity of this work with his earlier journalism. The Isaiah verses which introduce chapter two relate more directly to the Act and its instigators and demonstrates, as Bhekizizwe Peterson notes, that 'Plaatje was well versed in the biblical mode of laments':

> Woe unto them that decree unrighteous decrees, and that write grievousness which they have prescribed; To turn aside the needy from judgment, and to take away the fruit from the poor of my people, that widows may be their prey, and that they may rob the fatherless.[28]

Plaatje supplies a balder version of the biblical text in the chapter's title: 'The grim struggle between right and wrong, and the latter carries the day'. He is aware of his local as well as his international readers, aware of the culture of fundamentalist religiosity he shares with his political opponents, and aware of the leverage it affords him. In chapter five, quoting Proverbs, 'The righteous man regardeth the life of his beast, but the tender mercies of the wicked are cruel', he glosses:

> [b]ut there is a Government of professed Bible readers who, in defiance of all Scriptural precepts, pass a law which penalizes a section of the community along with their oxen, sheep, goats, horses and donkeys on account of the colour of their owners.[29]

A reference from the Book of Kings is more elliptical. Henry Ward Beecher, American Congregationalist minister, abolitionist and brother of Harriet Beecher Stowe, is quoted in the epigraph to chapter twelve: 'Naboth was right to hold on to his home. There were garnered memories that all the wealth of Ahab could not buy'.[30] The tag comes from Beecher's autobiographical *Life Thoughts* (1858) and is used there as a part of his attack on those American clergymen who defended the notorious 1850 Fugitive Slave Act which established a legal responsibility to return escaped slaves to their owners.[31] In the Book of Kings, the story of Ahab's killing of Naboth is a narrative of greed and the alienation of land, and thus more appropriate to Plaatje's argument than is Beecher's use of it.[32] Yet by filtering the story through Beecher – that is, by quoting Beecher rather than the Bible – the epigraph intensifies the force of the biblical text by associating it with the historic specificity of the American abolitionist movement. This precedent enhances the story's use in a different but sympathetic interpretive mode. The moral energies of the abolitionist movements are conscripted to Plaatje's contemporary cause.

The second body of Christian material common to both Plaatje's local and international readers was that of the hymn tradition. Hymns, of a politically activist tone, introduce chapter twenty:

> Oh! the Battle-bow is strung,
> The Banner is outflung:
> From lowlands and from valley,
> From mountain-tops, they rally...[33]

and the book's Epilogue:

> Oh, hear us for our native land,
> The land we love the most:
> Our fathers' sepulchres are here,
> And here our kindred dwell;
> Our children, too; how should we love
> Another land so well?[34]

The provenance, as well as the content, of both these hymns is significant to Plaatje's developing argument. 'Oh! the Battle-bow is strung' was written by Levi Jenkins Coppin, a black American preacher, missionary and bishop of the African Methodist Episcopal Church, who was to visit South Africa in 1919. Elleke Boehmer states that Plaatje 'largely disassociated himself from' the 'anti-white Ethiopianism' of this church.[35] In evidence that Plaatje gave to the South African Native Affairs Commission in 1904, when asked, 'What attitude do your people take towards the African Methodist Episcopal Church?', he was more even-handed, stating, 'I have not seen it do any good and it has certainly not done any harm. That is as far as I know'.[36] Coppin's words fit with Plaatje's argument, and so are included. In the same way, the epigraph to chapter twenty-four of *Native Life in South* Africa, a poem by the African American poet Otto L. Bohanan which has the refrain 'Ethiopia shall not die!' is comfortably accommodated.[37] The use of literary allusion allows a form of sampling, where a single aspect of literary work can be isolated and given a new emphasis or context without the author being committed to the wider argument of the work as a whole.

These hymns point to political action, reflecting nineteenth-century American sacred poetry's 'strong inclination to inculcate civic righteousness, based on the highest ideals of human behaviour.[38] 'Oh, hear us for our native land', also known as 'Stanzas on Freedom', was written by the American Unitarian minister and poet James Russell Lowell.[39] The lines Plaatje uses seem straightforwardly patriotic, in keeping with the discussion of the ongoing First World War in the second half of the chapter they introduce. But the context suggests the exclusions and limitations implicit in the phrase 'native land' when it is applied to South Africa. Plaatje begins the chapter by evoking the Christian community he shares with his readers. He describes going on a series of church visits – in London 'after hot cross buns at the family table of a dear old English family'; at London University Hall; at a PSA gathering and at the City Temple 'where I heard the uniformed choir artistically sing doxologies to the risen Christ'.[40] His effortless membership of each occasion is key. He is, after all, a member of the Christian communion: he recalls his infant baptism in St Martin's Church 'in the heart of the "Free" State' and 'another church on the banks of the Vaal River' where, twenty years ago, 'another missionary laid his white hands on my curly head'. In South Africa, he explains, on Easter Sunday, just as in England, congregations are attending church: 'native congregations have this day been singing in their respective houses of worship and in a variety of tongues about the risen Christ'. But not, he says, in the Dutch Reformed Church, where 'coloured members are excluded'.

The narrative thus extends the way the term 'native land' in the chapter's epigraph is read, not by extending it through metaphor but by returning it to its literal meaning. The term 'native' suggests the colonised black. And it is the *actual* land that *Native Life in South Africa* is concerned with, as well as the patriotic abstraction, land as nation. 'How should we love another land so well?' becomes plaintively ironic sung by the African congregations excluded from both land ownership and national affiliation, and characterised by hypocritical Boer church-goers as 'verdoemde schepsels', 'damned black creatures'.[41]

Both hymns speak to the radical and activist tradition of Christianity that Plaatje called on during his English mission. Like scriptural text, a hymn is a particular kind of literary allusion, one in which the reading community becomes a congregation. The hymn is 'part of popular culture, and yet also part of a religious and literary culture'.[42] To quote a hymn points to more than simply shared knowledge or belief, or a shared experience of reading a poetic text. It evokes shared performance, the actual presence of both author and reader in a shared and sanctified space. No hymn acts as an isolated allusion. J.R. Watson suggests that 'the discourse of a hymn is a shared speech, and a conversation with other hymns...each hymn is conscious of the others and relates to them'.[43] And the hymn is not a static or passive text. It demands a response. Cheslyn Jones writes, 'The hymn acts as a mirror in which the congregation can see itself.'[44] This is a ritual of affirmation and of fellowship, very much in keeping with the religious cultures

Plaatje participated in during his stay in England. Chapter eighteen of *Native Life in South Africa* ends with a description of a meeting of the Victoria Brotherhood in Monmouthshire which Plaatje's delegation visited in early 1915. 'There', writes Plaatje, the 'now familiar hymn', James Russell Lowell's 'Brotherhood Song of Liberty', is sung, accompanied by 'the more familiar tune of "Jesu, lover of my soul" (Hollingside's)':

> Men whose boast it is that ye
> Come of fathers brave and free,
> If there breathe on earth a slave,
> Are ye truly free and brave?
> If ye do not feel the chain
> When it works a brother's pain,
> Are ye not base slaves indeed –
> Slaves unworthy to be freed? [45]

The complex set of relationships here is indicative of more than simply what Boehmer describes as Plaatje's 'multiple, interwoven linguistic and literary resources'.[46] An African delegation meets a provincial congregation, sings a hymn by an American poet replete with abolitionist rhetoric to an English hymn tune, confidently identified by Plaatje by both its original title ('Jesu, lover of my soul') and its musical setting ('Hollingside's').[47] When A.E. Voss suggests that Plaatje might be seen as a 'harbinger of modernism', expressive of 'human continuity and discontinuity', an 'agent and issue of the encounter between African traditional culture and the intrusive European', suggestive of what he describes as 'the cultural tide between centre and periphery', he is thinking of such juxtapositions. [48] 'Plaatje's *Native Life in South Africa* may be seen as backward-looking' he writes, 'but formally it may be read as a modernist collage'. Yet is this the case? Plaatje's writing does not address issues of literary or cultural innovation; it relates to communities and cultures of the present. The juxtapositions are unexpected, at first glance dissonant. But there is a deliberation about Plaatje's 'collage' that is distinctly un-modernist. There is, he suggest to his readers, a coherence about his selections when read through the structures of political and social action he inhabits in both South Africa and England.

\*\*\*

In his 2004 work, *The Reading Nation in the Romantic Period*, William St Clair criticises the 'convention of presenting the processes of cultural formation as a parliament of printed texts [where] the main site of change [is] in the writing of the texts rather than in the reading of the books'. He points to the 'periodicity of reading, with its changing patterns of stacked chronological layers... so different from the periodicity of writing'.[49] In what Voss describes as *Native Life in South Africa*'s 'practice of quotation *bricolage*' there is no such separation of reading and writing. Plaatje exists in his text as both writer and reader, the range of reference he uses demonstrating St Clair's 'changing patterns of stacked chronological layers'. This means he employs a wide chronological sweep in the literature he draws on. Jonathan Rose notes, 'At the dawn of the twentieth century, when literary modernism was emerging, the self-educated had only just mastered the great English classics'. He suggests:

> Literary canons may change over time; but at any given point, the reading tastes of the British working classes consistently lagged a generation behind those of the educated middle classes, a cultural conservatism that often coexisted with political radicalism'.[50]

Plaatje's use of eighteenth- and nineteenth-century literary texts could be read as a feature of such radical conservatism. But this shared past is not simply regressive. It allows him to associate his own argument with the authority of his canonical sources; and it provides him with an established moral vocabulary for the present – one that is familiar to his readers, as well as profoundly unsettling. Plaatje's eighteenth century was, as Voss has demonstrated, not that of the enlightenment but one of social complaint, 'tempered by Romanticism and evangelicalism.'[51] As with his use of biblical and hymn allusions, his use of this material relied on a complex dance of recognition and surprise – recognition of the quotation, surprise at its context and consequent shift in meaning.

The literature of the anti-slavery movement is central to this process. An excerpt from William Cowper's 1785 poem 'The Task', which prefaces chapter seventeen of *Native Life*, demonstrates the way this re-presentation operates:

> Slaves cannot breathe in England: if their lungs
> Receive our air, that moment they are free;
> They touch our country, and their shackles fall.[52]

The lines are familiar – not just from Cowper's poem, but as a succinct, often cited though probably legally incorrect summary of the 1772 court case which established the free status of slaves imported to England. Mary Prince relied on its provisions when she arrived in London in 1828. Perhaps Plaatje's readers were expected not just to know the reference but to continue the quotation. An earlier line of 'The Task', 'We have no slaves at home – then why abroad?', would have spoken to the London mission of Plaatje and his friends, as would the six lines which follow Plaatje's excerpt:

> They touch our country and their shackles fall.
> That's noble, and bespeaks a nation proud
> And jealous of the blessing. Spread it then,
> And let it circulate through every vein
> Of all your empire; that where Britain's power
> Is felt, mankind may feel her mercy too.[53]

The lines which appear in the text are tactful and flattering to Plaatje's English readers. The unquoted lines which follow are more challenging. Plaatje, here and elsewhere, makes conscious use of abolitionist discourse sourced both from the British anti-slavery campaigns of the late eighteenth and early nineteenth century and from the American abolitionist period leading up to the Civil War. Both movements had at their rhetorical core egalitarianism and also the responsibility of all to engage. By using tropes from both periods, Plaatje is reminding his readers that issues of slavery and oppression still remain to be confronted.

Plaatje's use of Oliver Goldsmith's 1770 poem 'The Deserted Village', not as an epigraph but within the text of chapter twelve, is more extensive and central to his argument. He sets out Goldsmith's description of the lost Arcadian world of the past, 'Dear lovely bowers of innocence and ease', inviting the reader to apply the litany of Goldsmith's rural English descriptors to South Africa: the 'green', the 'shelter'd cot, the cultivated farm, /The never failing brook, the busy mill', the 'decent church that topt the neighbouring hill' are all to be implicitly translated into an African setting. Only the summary line 'These were thy charms, sweet village!' is actually adjusted on the page, Goldsmith's word 'village' being changed to 'Province'.[54] It is an important moment, in Goldsmith's as in Plaatje's version. The line moves the reader from the idyllic scenes of the past to the desolation of the present: 'These were thy charms – but all these charms are fled'. As the pastoral positives of the first section of the poem can be adapted to the African setting, so, thanks to the Natives' Land Act, Goldsmith's negative depiction of eighteenth-century rural depopulation of England can also be reassigned:

> Amidst thy bowers the tyrant's hand is seen
> And desolation saddens all thy green:
> And trembling, shrinking from the spoiler's hand,
> Far, far away, thy children leave the land.
> Ill fares the land, to hastening ills a prey,
> Where wealth accumulates and men decay.

The parallel here is too important to his work's overall argument for Plaatje to rely on the reader to make their own connections. The moral of the illustrative text is spelt out for the reader – or rather, in a complex process of imaginative transference, the reader is invited to share the way that a 'Cape Native' would read the poem. Plaatje writes:

> The Cape Native can thoroughly endorse these sentiments of Oliver Goldsmith, which, however, compared with his own present lot, are mild in the extreme; for it could not have been amid scenes of this description, and with an outlook half as bad as ours, that the same author further sings...
>
> A time there was e'er England's grief began,
> When every rood of ground maintain'd its man;
> But times are alter'd: Trade's unfeeling train
> Usurp the land and dispossess the swain....[55]

A number of literary epigraphs in *Native Life in South Africa* are in the form of proverbial sayings. Plaatje may have remembered Burns' 'Man's inhumanity to man makes countless thousands mourn', the epigraph to chapter eight, from the poem in which the lines appear, 'Man Was Made To Mourn: A Dirge'.[56] Or he may have known it, stripped of its context, as a commonplace. Did he read the work of Amos Bronson Alcott, New England Transcendentalist and father of Louisa May, or did he just know his tag 'Egotists cannot converse; they talk to themselves only', which is used as the epigraph to chapter thirteen?[57] Charles James Fox's assertion 'Of all the characters of cruelty, I consider that as the most odious which assumes the garb of mercy', used by Plaatje as the epigraph to chapter sixteen, was from Fox's 'Speech before the 'Traitorous Correspondence

Bill April 8, 1793'.[58] But it had long since detached itself from that context and entered the lexicon of sayings of the radical left. The seventeenth-century poet Charles Cotton was hardly a widely read author at the beginning of the twentieth century. He furnishes the epigraph to chapter seven:

> Ripe persecution, like the plant
> Whose nascence Mocha boasted,
> Some bitter fruit produced, whose worth
> Was never known till roasted.[59]

Plaatje would have been as likely to have encountered this in a collection of quotations, such as Henry George Bohn's 1902 *Dictionary of Quotations from the English Poets*, where it appears under the heading 'Persecution', as in his general reading.[60] As Michael Wheeler notes, in the nineteenth century,

> ...[a]nthologies of extracts and quotations from literary and religious works sold in huge quantities. These were often arranged by topic so that the reader could dip into certain sections of, say, a collection of literary quotations for the kind of support and inspiration needed at any particular time.[61]

But, as Jane Starfield has pointed out, proverbs were also an important part of Tswana culture and communication, for Plaatje 'an accumulated stock of vehicles for social negotiation and relationship that lay at the heart of Tswana forms of social organisation'.[62]

*Native Life in South Africa* displays Plaatje's familiarity with the canon, but less canonical authors are also utilised. Chapter fifteen's epigraph, 'Sorrow like this draws parted lives in one, and knits anew the rents which time has made', comes from the forgettable and forgotten *Gycia: a Tragedy in Five Acts* by Sir Lewis Morris [63] of whom George Saintsbury wrote, 'He had, sometimes, a faculty... of writing things which looked like poetry till one began to think of them a little.' 'From the obloquy of this harsh judgment', says *The Dictionary of National Biography*, 'posterity has so far resolutely declined to rescue him'.[64] Sir Edwin Arnold's popular 1892 versified biography of Buddha, *Light of Asia*, introduces *Native Life's* chapter fourteen:

> Pity and need make all flesh kin.
> There is no caste in blood

> Which runneth of one hue; nor caste in tears,
> Which trickle salt with all.[65]

While the bulk of *Native Life in South Africa* was written before his arrival in London, some additions, especially of epigraphs, seem to come from Plaatje's London reading. The epigraph to chapter five is the first two stanzas of '1914: Chant Funebre' by the Belgian musician and librettist Maurice Kufferath, published in London in October 1914 in *L'Independance Belge*, a patriotic propaganda newspaper.[66] The poem's focus is, naturally, the current conflict – 'Allemagne! Allemagne! O perfide ennemie' – but Plaatje's placement of it at the head of a chapter entitled 'Another Night with the Sufferers' refocuses Kufferath's lines from the European war to the sufferings of the black population of South Africa:

> Heureux ceux qui sont morts dans le calme des soirs,
> Avant ces jours affreux de carnage et de haine!
> Ils se sont endormis, le coeur rempli d'espoirs,
> Dans un reve d'amour et de concorde humaine!

The epigraph to chapter twenty-four likewise suggests that Plaatje's London reading took him beyond the English canon. 'The Awakening', beginning, 'Keep me in chains? I defy you./ That is a pow'r I deny you!' is by Otto L. Bohanan. The poem is accompanied by Plaatje's note: 'In the Kalahari language Bohanan means: "to be combined"'.[67] In mimicry of nineteenth-century linguistic ethnology, he is here manufacturing a link between the Harlem Renaissance poet and the concerns of *Native Life in South Africa*. Bohanan's poem had appeared in August 1914 in *The Crisis: a Record of the Darker Races*, a magazine founded by American black civil rights activist and author W.E.B. Dubois in 1910.[68] Plaatje would meet Dubois, President of the National Association for the Advancement of Colored People (NAACP), when he visited New York in 1921. *The Crisis* also furnishes *Native Life in South Africa*'s conclusion, 'Retribution' by Ida B Luckie, which appeared in the magazine in August 1916:

> Alas, My Country! Thou wilt have no need
> Of enemy to bring thee to thy doom...
> For not alone by war a nation falls.

> Though she be fair, serene as radiant morn,
> Though girt by seas, secure in armament,
> Let her but spurn the vision of the Cross;
> Tread with contemptuous feet on its command
> Of Mercy, Love and Human Brotherhood,
> And she, some fateful day, shall have no need
> Of enemy to bring her to the dust.... [69]

Plaatje justifies the poem's inclusion by explaining, 'Her mind must have been riveted on South Africa when, quite recently, Ida Luckie sang...' It is doubtful that Luckie's concerns have any relation to the arguments of *Native Life in South Africa*. Her poem warns the American people that forces other than war may be destructive of the nation, and seems in keeping with the civil rights agenda of *The Crisis* and the NAACP. But Plaatje has already schooled his readers in associative reading. As the variety of literary epigraphs and allusions suggest, a variety of registers – anti-slavery rhetoric, the arguments of the nineteenth century radicalism, the concerns of eighteenth century poets – can all become part of a single reading process. Black American writers are a specific part in this mosaic, suffering from different though equivalent forms of oppression. In *The Souls of Black Folk* (1903) Du Bois writes of 'this double-consciousness, this sense of always looking at one's self through the eyes of others, of measuring one's soul by the tape of a world that looks on in an amused contempt and pity'.[70] Plaatje shares with Du Bois membership of a world of literature and intellect derived promiscuously from western culture. Du Bois writes:

> I sit with Shakespeare and he winces not. Across the colour line I move arm in arm with Balzac and Dumas, where smiling men and welcoming women glide in gilded halls. From out the caves of evening that swing between the strong limbed earth and the tracery of stars, I summon Aristotle and Aurelius and what soul I will, and they come all graciously with no scorn nor condescension.[71]

\*\*\*

The most significant of Plaatje's literary adaptations is his use of Shakespeare. In chapter twenty-two, Plaatje takes a passage from *Romeo and Juliet* in which Benvolio tells Montague of his fight with Tybalt and gives it a startling shift in orientation:

> Oom: Who set this ancient quarrel new aboach [sic]?
> Speak, nephew, were you by when it began?
> Neef: Here were the servants of your adversary
> And yours, close fighting ere I did approach:
> I drew to part them; in the instant came
> The fiery Tielman, who swung about his head
> And breathed defiance in my ears...
> While we were interchanging, thrusts and blows
> Came more and more, and fought on part and part
> Till the Judge came, who parted either part.[72]

Shakespeare's Montague and Benvolio become 'Oom' and 'Neef', Dutch for 'uncle' and 'nephew', detaching the passage from the specificities of the play's plot and relocating it in South Africa. The substitution of 'Teilman' for 'Tybalt' reinforces that relocation, Teilman Roos being an extremist Boer politician.

In a similar manner, the specifics of recent South African history are worked into the Shakespearian text used as the epigraph to chapter twenty-three:

> Arm, arm, Burghers; we never had more cause!
> The Goths have gathered head; and with a power
> Of high-resolved men, bent to the spoil,
> They hither march amain, under conduct
> Of Manie, son to old Gerit Maritz,
> Who threats in course of his revenge, to do
> As much as ever Black Bambata did.[73]

In the original passage from *Titus Andronicus*, Aemilius warns Rome that an attack from the Goths is imminent and that, under 'Lucius, son to old Andronicus', the damage they do may compare to that of Rome's old enemy, Coriolanus. Plaatje keeps the term 'Goths', in Shakespeare literal, in his version metaphoric. But the other specifics in the passage are given South African referents: the 'Burghers' are warned of an attack not from Lucius, son of Andronicus, but from Manie Maritz, Boer general in the Second Boer War and leader of the Boer Rebellion of 1914, son of Gerrit

Maritz, leader of the early nineteenth-century Voortrekkers. His vengeance is compared not to that of Coriolanus but to 'Black Bambata' or Bambatha kaMancinza, the Zulu leader of the Zondi clan who led a revolt against taxation in Natal in 1906.[74]

Plaatje's literary ownership is nowhere more overt than in the epigraph to chapter nine where the speech of Shylock in *The Merchant of Venice* is taken over and re-presented:

> He hath disgraced me and laughed at my losses, mocked at my gains, scorned my nation, thwarted my bargains, cooled my friends, heated mine enemies; and what is his reason? I am a Kafir. Hath not a Kafir eyes? Hath not a Kafir hands, organs, dimensions, senses, affections, passions? Is he not fed with the same food, hurt with the same weapons, subject to the same diseases, healed by the same means, warmed and cooled by the same summer and winter as a white Afrikander? If you prick us, do we not bleed? If you tickle us, do we not laugh? If you poison us, do we not die? And if you wrong us, shall we not revenge? If we are like you in the rest, we will resemble you in that.

Plaatje's use of Shakespeare conveys more than that he knows the work, its detail and nuances, and can deploy it in his own argument. It suggests something sharper and perhaps more discomforting than the contemporary piety that Shakespeare is indeed universal in his application. There is a specificity about Plaatje's use of the plays and particularly the insertion of South African referents. South African events have an importance that can command and inhabit the epic stories of Shakespeare – Manie and Banbatha are on an equal footing Coriolanus, in greatness as well as in barbarity. Plaatje thus gestures to the coherence of the literary and ethical universe. Shakespeare may be universal but at the same time his heroes can be equated with and even displaced by local heroes.

Plaatje was still in England in 1916, the tercentenary of Shakespeare's death. Although the war disrupted some of the planned celebrations, Israel Gollancz's compendium *A Book of Homage to Shakespeare*, a celebration of what Edmund Gosse, one of the contributors, called 'the constellated glory of our greatest poet...our divine poet', still appeared albeit in slimmed-down form.[75] The intention of the volume was, wrote the editor, to provide a 'fitting memorial to symbolize the intellectual fraternity of mankind in the universal homage accorded to the genius of the greatest Englishman'.[76] As this statement demonstrates, it was a project with inherent contradictions, stressing both the universal purchase of the author, 'something of the touch of Nature that makes the whole world kin',[77] and his specifically English nature, made from 'the fine red dust [of] England's central shire... Of Saxon and of Norman breed, with British strain to warm'.[78] One of the standard mechanisms for demonstrating the conflation of Englishness and universality was the idea of the British Empire, and several of *A Book of Homage's* contributors use an imperial trope to focus their effusions.[79] The poet Israel Zangwill describes Shakespeare as 'Impartial bard of Britain, Roman, Gaul,/ Jew, Gentile, white or black [whose] ventures overrun/ The globe, his sovereign art embraces all'.[80] New Zealander William Pember Reeves characterises the settler empire as one in which

> As our warring, trading, reading race
> Moved surely outward to imperial space,
> Beyond the tropics to the ice-blink's hem
> The mind of Shakespeare voyaged forth with them.[81]

'It has been', claims Lionel Cust, in another offering, 'the peaceful influence of Shakespeare and the Bible which has bound the English-speaking races in one chain of family union'.[82] Sydney Lee sees Shakespeare's language as a metonym for the growth of empire:

> Territorial expansion scarcely fosters a nation's intellectual vigour more signally than a widening of its command of expressive speech, which ennobles the lips, and both clarifies and broadens thought.[83]

American critic Charles Mills Gayley enacts a form of reverse migration as 'the blood of America,/ Turning on tribute to [Shakespeare], revisits the Heart of the Race'.[84] And in the same spirit, F.R. Benson quotes a 'sage from Bengal' visiting Stratford saying, 'I have found the heart of England in Stratford-on-Avon, and it was the heart of Shakespeare; faithful, yet tolerant, and gentle as it was strong.'[85]

Plaatje's contribution to *A Book of Homage* probably came about through his friendship with Alice Werner. He is the only contributor who is not named – his chapter is called 'A South African's Homage' – but this may have been because he had some kind of editorial role in the project.[86] His contribution is in the form of a parallel text, English and Tswana.[87] In comparison with the strenuously decorated and devotional language of many of the contributors to the volume, Plaatje's piece is refreshingly straightforward, autobiographical and anecdotal. He begins:

> I had but a vague idea of Shakespeare until about 1896 when, at the age of 18, I was attracted by the Press remarks in the Kimberley paper, and went to see *Hamlet* in the Kimberley theatre. The performance made me curious to know more about Shakespeare and his works. Intelligence in Africa is still carried from mouth to mouth by means of conversations after working hours, and, reading Shakespeare's works, I always had a fresh story to tell.[88]

Plaatje is here representative of a non-institutional Shakespeare, what Jonathan Rose characterises as 'The People's Bard',[89] an approach which by 1916 was becoming outmoded and being replaced by a professionalised sense of the discipline of English studies.[90] Many of the contributors to *A Homage* boast their academic and institutional credentials: 'A Marginal Note on Shakespeare's Language and a Textual Crux in King Lear' by Otto Jespersen, 'Professor of English Philology at the University of Copenhagen and author of *Growth and Structure of the English Language*, &c', is representative of this trend.[91] It is in significant contrast, then, that Plaatje makes it clear that his formal education did not include Shakespeare; that the press was his guide in matters of culture; that his first encounter with Shakespeare was as live theatre rather than on the written page and that oral performance was not just key to his own reception of the plays but in the way that he passed the stories on to others in 'conversations after working hours'. But he stresses that this does not mean that his relationship with the bard was any the less intrinsic. Indeed, he suggests that there was a sense in which he knew Shakespeare before he was conscious of the fact, and that knowledge was coterminous with his knowledge of spoken English. He writes, 'Many of the current quotations used by educated natives to embellish their speeches, which I had always taken for English proverbs, were culled from Shakespeare's works'.[92]

This seems to bed Plaatje's familiarity with Shakespeare in his inhabitation of English cultural forms, but at the same time he claims an affinity between Shakespeare and his own Tswana culture: 'Besides being natural story-tellers', he writes, 'the Bechuana are good listeners, and legendary stories seldom fail to impress them'. Shakespeare has an everyday presence in the Tswana public sphere:

> One morning I visited the Chief's court in Mafeking, and was asked for the name of 'the white man who spoke so well'. An educated Chieftain promptly replied for me; he said William Tsikinya-Chaka (William Shake-the-Sword)... Tsikinya-Chaka became noted among some of my readers as a reliable white oracle.[93]

Those with whom he shared Shakespearian stories and Shakespearian quotations came from a culture at ease with there being a close relationship between the legendary and the everyday. Both Plaatje and his audience could see parallels between Shakespearian plots, their own folklore and their own circumstances. As David Schalkwyk and Lerothodi Lapula put it, for Plaatje, Shakespeare constitutes 'material to be used and transformed, to be translated in the way that Bottom is, rather than as an idol to be worshipped'.[94] 'I was asked more than once' Plaatje writes, 'to which of certain speculators, then operating around Kimberley, Shakespeare referred as Shylock'. Furthermore, Plaatje suggests that his own situation led him to a personal identification with characters in the plays. On finding that he and his prospective wife have difficulty in communicating, Plaatje being unfamiliar with her native Xhosa and she, though more skilful in his language of Tswana, still at a disadvantage, their courtship is conducted 'in the language of educated people – the language which Shakespeare wrote'.[95] The need the couple have for 'daily epistles' ranging from 'the bare intention of expressing the affections of my heart' to 'completely unburdening my soul' mean, says Plaatje, that 'Shakespeare's poems fed our thoughts'. And it is not just their means of expression but their situation which Plaatje presents as being Shakespearian. 'It may be depended upon', he assures his readers, that during courtship 'we both read *Romeo and Juliet*':

> My people resented the idea of my marrying a girl who spoke a language which, like the Hottentot language, had clicks in it; while her people likewise abominated the idea of giving their daughter in marriage to a fellow who spoke a language so imperfect as to be without any clicks.

Only what he describes as 'the civilised laws of Cape Colony', that is, the prescription of English as the official language, prevented 'a double tragedy in a cemetery', and enabled 'the growth of our Chuana-M'bo family which is bilingual in the vernaculars and in European languages'. The tone here is significant. Tribalism, and its concomitant prejudice and discrimination, are reduced to an issue of clicks or no clicks. Plaatje seems to show amusement over his own cultural markers. But there is also a sense that Shakespeare himself is being treated with a lightness at odds with the unrelenting reverence shown in the other contributions to *A Homage*. Plaatje feels able to enrol Shakespeare in contemporary issues – his marriage, family, the daily conduct of his life in both its Tswana and its colonial contexts. In contrast, very few of the other contributors to *A Homage* connect Shakespeare with the present, except, by inference, as a function of the universal. Even the volume's occasional references to the ongoing war invoke Shakespeare as a mechanism for transcendence rather than connecting him or his work to the progress of the war. For example, Ronald Ross's sonnet describes the trenches, but ends

> We dying, lifting bloodied eyes and dumb,
> Behold the silver star serene on high,
> That is thy spirit there, O Master Mind sublime.[96]

G.C. Moore Smith, similarly, connects Shakespeare to the conflict only by seeing him as above it:

> O sign of comfort in a sky of woe!
> Above the warring waves and shrieking wind
> Thy starry Spirit shines and whispers 'Peace'.[97]

Plaatje, on the other hand, is entirely comfortable placing Shakespeare in the everyday – and in his own everyday, which is of necessity political. Just as the literary epigraphs and extracts used in *Native Life in South Africa* contribute to Plaatje's own political argument, so, in 'A South African's Homage', Shakespeare's work underwrites Plaatje's political message.

In his 1986 work *Decolonising the Mind: the Politics of Language in African Literature,* the Kenyan critic Ngũgĩ wa Thiong'o, born in 1938, describes the way that in his own education the writers of the English canon, and especially Shakespeare, were presented to African audiences

> [a]s if they were mindless geniuses whose only consistent quality was a sense of compassion. These writers, who had their sharpest and most penetrating

observations of the European bourgeois culture, were often taught as if their only concerns were with the universal themes of love, fear, birth and death. Sometimes their greatness was presented as one more gift to the world alongside the bible and the needle. William Shakespeare and Jesus Christ had brought light to darkest Africa.[98]

For Plaatje reading Shakespeare exists in a context that, far from being universal, is modern, part of a global culture with 'rapid means of communication and facilities for travelling' which he does not entirely endorse even though he is more conversant with it than any other contributor to *A Homage*. His essay concludes by contrasting 'a cinematograph show of the Crucifixion' in which 'the only black man in the mob was Judas Iscariot' with Shakespeare's plays which 'show that nobility and valour, like depravity and cowardice, are not the monopoly of any colour'.[99] Modern media, Plaatje suggests, can be both frighteningly real and demonstrably false. He writes:

> I have since become suspicious of the veracity of the cinema and acquired a scepticism which is not diminished by a gorgeous [film] now exhibited in London which shows, side by side with the nobility of the white race, a highly coloured exaggeration of the depravity of the blacks.[100]

Although Plaatje does not name it, the film is certainly D.W. Griffith's 1915 *Birth of a Nation*, adapted from the 1905 novel *The Clansman* by Thomas J Dixon, Jr. Willan describes Plaatje attending *Birth of a Nation* in London with Georgiana Solomon 'who on at least one occasion publically harangued cinema audiences about the iniquity of the film'.[101] With Jane Cobden Unwin, Plaatje and Solomon made representations to the British Home Secretary who undertook that the film would not be shown in South Africa. Such protests were widespread: in May 1915, W.E.B. Du Bois led a protest in Boston as part of the NAACP's campaign against the film's representation of the history of the post-Civil War reconstruction. The directorial skill and technical innovation of the film were, as Plaatje says, 'gorgeous'. But associated with its crude portrayal of the southern American black population, mostly played by white actors in blackface, the film was a disturbing experience for Plaatje, one which he returned to as late as 1931, writing an article 'An inflammatory bioscope film' for the newspaper *Umteleli wa*

*Bantu*.¹⁰² Far better to have Shakespeare, text without technology, Shylock the honorary Kaffir and Othello the noble black.¹⁰³

\*\*\*

Plaatje's debt to Shakespeare is reflected in his novel *Mhudi: An Epic of South African Native Life a Hundred Years Ago*, published in 1930 but probably written at the same time as *Native Life*.¹⁰⁴ *Mhudi* has tyrannical kings, heavenly signs and portents, wayward lovers, forest idylls, ravening animals and characters seemingly dead who miraculously reappear. It is, as Tim Couzens says, 'a kind of winter's tale of loss and regeneration'.¹⁰⁵ Shakespearian literary forms – the soliloquy, the dramatic dialogue, the revenge plot, the comic interlude, the paralleling and intertwining of story lines – are a feature of its structure.¹⁰⁶ Just as Plaatje's contribution to *A Homage* suggests that Shakespearian and Tswana conventions converge, so *Mhudi* confidently asserts the epic nature of its own local history.

However, as a reader of contemporary as well as canonical literature, Plaatje was open to influences in addition to the Shakespearian. In a letter to a friend he describes the novel as 'a love story after the manner of romances; but based on historical facts ... with plenty of love, superstitions and imaginations worked in between the wars. Just like the style of Rider Haggard when he was writing about the Zulus'.¹⁰⁷ *Mhudi* has obvious similarities to Haggard's 1892 novel *Nada the Lily*, described by Haggard as 'the tale of the youth of Umslopogaas, holder of the iron Chieftainess, the axe Groanmaker, who was named Bulalio the Slaughterer, and of his love for Nada, the most beautiful of Zulu women'.¹⁰⁸ In his preface to *Nada* Haggard claims 'a purpose somewhat beyond that of setting out a wild tale of savage life'.¹⁰⁹ He intends, he writes, 'to convey in narrative form some idea of the remarkable spirit which animated these kings and their subjects, and to make [it] accessible, in a popular shape'. Veracity and popularity, manly tales and factual underpinning are associated in an entirely conventional manner. Plaatje on the other hand, in his preface, locates his motive in writing *Mhudi* variously: in his discovery 'while collecting stray scraps of tribal history ... elicited from old people' of the *casus belli* of the Matabele Wars; as a way of 'interpret[ing] to the reading public one phase of "the back of the Native mind"'; and, more pragmatically, as a way of funding the collection and publication of Tswana folk tales, 'which', writes Plaatje, 'with the spread of European ideas, are fast being forgotten'. This process will be arrested, he hopes, 'by cultivating a love for art and literature in the Vernacular'.[110] As Victoria Collis-Buthelezi notes, *Mhudi* 'is not only written to inject a black authorial presence into South African literature but to initiate a black vernacular tradition separate from it'.[111]

Haggard suggests that in writing *Nada* he encountered problems which were authorial as well as formal. 'It will be obvious' he writes, 'that such a task has presented difficulties, since he who undertakes it must for a long time forget his civilisation, and think with the mind and speak with the voice of a Zulu of the old regime'.[112] He sees this as something that will necessarily fail: 'Neither has it been possible for the writer of it to render the full force of the Zulu idiom' says Haggard's narrator, 'nor to convey a picture of the teller'.[113] Haggard is at pain to establish and sustain what he sees as an authentic tone, demonstrated both in the manner in which his characters speak and act but also in the ethnographic frame he places them within. Central to the project of colonial writing was the emulation of the ethnographically accurate native voice, a sometimes tortured compromise between Victorian poetics and the often distinctly unliterary archives of ethnographic information the author had at their disposal. The native voice is assumed to be intrinsically more poetic than the European and more archaic, either because the narrative it is placed within is set in a romantic past, or because it is seen to inhabit what Anne McClintock describes as 'archaic space'.[114] But at the same time, footnotes, appendices and careful referencing of source materials are the hallmark of this kind of writing which is closely connected with the 'dying race' topos. Haggard performs what James Clifford terms 'salvage ethnography':

> In the salvage mode, the ethnographer portrays himself as 'before the deluge', so to speak. Signs of fundamental change are apparent, but the ethnographer is able to salvage a cultural state on the verge of transformation.[115]

'But where are they now?' Haggard asks of his heroes. 'Silence has them, and the white men write them down in books'.

*Nada* is a history of a people 'already a thing of the past', and Haggard presents himself as a bridge between that lost past and the present-day reader. Unlike Plaatje, he is not able to claim direct knowledge of 'the back of the Native mind' but he is at pains to demonstrate his sources. His preface explains that some of his material comes from 'men who, for thirty or forty years, had been intimately acquainted with the Zulu people, with their history, their heroes, and their customs' whom he encountered when as a boy of seventeen he first went to South Africa; some material 'came from the lips of an old traveller in "the Zulu"'; and he also thanks acquaintances who have a comparable expertise from their time in colonial administration.[116] He acknowledges that, aside from his personal experience and contacts, all redolent of intimate access, he has used works of colonial ethnography, the 'few scarce works of reference, rarely consulted except by students'.[117] Aware of the circumscribed nature of his direct experience, he makes book scholarship sound recondite, privileged and faintly dangerous. 'Most, indeed nearly all, of the historical incidents here recorded are substantially true' he declares, managing to be assertive and equivocal at the same time ('most', 'nearly all', '*substantially* true').

Unlike Haggard, Plaatje does not have to establish his credentials — or rather, he is able to do so with far more economy, writing *from* as well as *of* 'the back of the Native mind' with an insider's access to 'tribal history' albeit in 'stray scraps... elicited from old people'. Thus in *Mhudi* there is no reference to written sources; the material being conveyed is a history which exists in collective memory. And the transference of this memory, these 'stray scraps', from oral to written form is not seen as problematic. Just as, in *A Homage*, Shakespeare is portrayed as being consistent with the cultural values of Plaatje's Tswana contemporaries, so, in *Mhudi*, the genre of the colonial novel is used to embrace and contain the rhetoric forms of early nineteenth-century life of the Baralong tribe of the Tswana people. Central to the novel is its strong sense of being the written representation of the oral. *Mhudi* uses praise songs, laments, genealogy, magical charms and incantations. But it also emphasises the importance of everyday conversation, from formal tribal councils to gossip. When Mhudi and Ra-Thaga reach Thaba Nchu 'in the land of hope and promise' (82), the reader is told:

> [t]his dramatic arrival provided a fruitful subject for fireside conversation... For months after, the women never tired of discussing their romantic story at home, while in the corn fields and while moulding clay pots in the valley. Men whiled away the evening spinning yarns about them when engaged in braying skins or sewing karosses in the shade... (83)

The careful communal consideration of events is here portrayed as natural; a part of Baralong life as potting, spinning or sewing; and a normal accompaniment to these activities. The romance plot — whether derived from Shakespeare or from Haggard — is situated within and mediated by

Baralong society, and interpreted in terms of the values of that society: 'anecdotes in the histories of the strangers were related and exaggerated with each repetition. Gossipers wagged their tongues and twisted the story about' (73). Random events are very quickly transformed into carefully structured stories, rhetorically robust and aesthetically pleasing rather than necessarily truthful, which are then publically performed and publically assessed: 'It happened in this way. A couple of years ago...' (68). By placing the events of his novel at the centre of a talkative inquisitive community with a predilection for storytelling, Plaatje is able to vary the tone of his narration, from believable fact and stolid belief to speculation and fantasy. Each episode is bracketed and intercut with an awareness of how it was received and what the community decided it meant: 'Some reported...one chatterer...Another story was to the effect that...Such were the wild stories that circulated...' (73). Far from creating the impression of uncertainty, this suggests that what has happened has been well considered.

The potency of proverbs, the condensation of this collective wisdom, is continually underlined: 'What a truthful thing is a proverb...According to an old saying...Old people say that...' (110, 112). Communications between characters and also between the narrator and reader are often conveyed in proverbial form: 'no jackal skin could possibly be sewn to a Matabele pelt'; 'the quarry of two dogs is never too strong' (113). Tim Couzens points to a 'marked increase in the number of proverbs used' at important and significant moments in the plot.[118] As proverbs provide timeless guidance and a summary of traditional wisdom, so dreams and portents offer another source of trusted information. Plaatje has an ambivalent position with regard to this material. Sometimes he apes the colonial disapproval of 'native superstitions and evil forebodings' that lead inevitably to what Mzilikazi finally sees as 'the usual folly of the Matabele being re-enacted' (170). Magicians and 'bone-throwers and their incantations' are portrayed as ignorant, craven and manipulative. On the other hand, Mhudi's decision to follow the advice of her dreams – 'I had a call in my dream which I must obey' (152) – is portrayed as part of her admirably direct and confident engagement with her world. And the novel's sense of the historical significance of the larger events it describes is underwritten by the appearance of the comet:

> Away in the distance I can see a mighty star in the skies with a long white tail stretching almost across the heavens. Wise men have always said that such a star is the harbinger of diseases of men and beasts, wars and the overthrow of

governments as well as the death of princes. Within the rays of the tail of this star, I can clearly see streams of tears and rivers of blood. (137)

But it is significant that those practices which might be associated purely with Baralong ethnography – that is, witchdoctors and bone-throwers – are generally viewed negatively, whereas those which are common to both Baralong and European traditional forms, and are Shakespearian staples, such as prophetic dreams and comets, are viewed with approval.

The novel, then, unfolds as an adaptive product of both Tswana and English literary and cultural forms – of, on the one hand, the genre of Victorian historical fiction and the colonial adventure story and, on the other hand, of the oral traditions and narratives of the Baralong. Plaatje exploits the fluidity of the colonial novel, with its access to the emotional register of the novel's metropolitan form – its realism, its courtship plot, its concentration on domestic detail, personal relationships and ethical dilemmas – which are placed alongside the epic and incipiently nationalistic aspects of the historical novel genre. The colonial novel is able to – and has to – incorporate the factual universe, what Thomas Richards calls the imperial archive,[119] into its fabric as a means of setting its scene and delineating its universe: alien customs and exotic landscapes. Fiction thus presents itself as a repository for memories of what has been lost subsequent to colonial contact and a means of preserving what has survived. In his use of the English language and of English literary forms, working in what Willan describes as the 'cultural borderland',[120] Plaatje constructs a container for Tswana history and culture that is both expressive and respectful. As his translations of Shakespeare into Tswana argued for a common ground between the two cultures, so the incorporation of Baralong history into the novel form conveys a similar sense of accommodation.

In *Nada*, Haggard's narrator is an unnamed 'White Man' who relates what he has been told by an old man named Zweete who claims to have been an actor in the history he narrates: 'This man, ancient and withered, seemed to live again in the far past. It was the past that spoke to his listener, telling of deeds long forgotten, of deeds that are no more known'.[121] An early 'typescript-with-corrections' of *Mhudi* uses a similar figure, Half-a-Crown, a 'hoary octogenarian' who, though not an actor in the events he narrates, is the child of Mhudi and her husband Ra-Thaga. Both narrators, Zweete and Half-a-Crown, thus serve as reminder that the material they relate is from a past which has almost but not quite disappeared. Haggard feels equivocal about this:

> Then the Zulus were still a nation; now that nation has been destroyed, and the chief aim of its white rulers is to root out the warlike spirit for which it was remarkable, and to replace it by a spirit of peaceful progress.[122]

'Peaceful progress' is all very well but it comes at the cost of 'the warlike spirit'. *Mhudi* has a similar sense of registering a turning point. The historic clash between the Baralong who 'led their patriarchal life under their several chiefs who owed no allegiance to any king or emperor' (25) and 'Mzilikazi, king of a ferocious tribe called the Matabele, a powerful usurper of determined character who by his sword proclaimed himself ruler over all the land' (28) coincides with the arrival of the Boers and their 'devastating machines of war' (146). *Mhudi* has an equivocal stance towards the modern. The racism of the Boer settlers, their inflexible religiosity and their bad faith are set against the emphasis in the novel on the friendship of Ra-Thaga and Phil-Jay, described in the *Dramatis Personae* at the start of the novel as 'a noble Boer' (24). The Boers may have introduced the gun into African society but they also know how to clean their cooking pots to avoid infection. The novel may celebrate the traditional harmonies of Baralong life but at the same time Plaatje shows that society as undercut by violence and instability.

At times Plaatje seems to argue that, given the incipient violence and intrigue of the Baralong and Matabele kingdoms and the encroachment of the modern, Ra-Thaga and Mhudi can only find happiness by removing themselves from history and withdrawing into a pastoral idyll. In the earlier part of the novel, at their home named Re-Nosi (We-are-alone), Ra-thaga sings:

> I long for the solitude of the woods,
> Far away from the quarrels of men,
> Their intrigues and vicissitudes;
> Away, where the air was clean,
> And the morning dew
> Made all things new;
> Where nobody was by
> Save Mhudi and I.

Speak not to me of the comforts of home,
Tell me of the valleys where the antelopes roam;
Give me my hunting sticks and snares
In the gloaming of the wilderness;
Give back the palmy days of our early felicity
Away from the hurly burly of your city,
And we'll be young again – aye:
Sweet Mhudi and I.

If this sounds a little like Brewster M. Higley's 'My Western Home', better known as 'Home on the Range' (composed in the early 1870s in Kansas and published 1873), it is entirely in keeping with Plaatje's practice of creative bricolage which he sees as in no way detracting from the veracity of the account he gives elsewhere of the values and behaviours of the Baralong and Matabele. Gail Ching-Liang Low describes the

> [a]mbivalent and contradictory movement in Haggard's version of the African pastoral. One the one hand, Africa is represented within the Judeo-Christian myth of the garden as a place where the original perfection of man can be recovered; on the other hand Africa is also presented as an anti-garden where man's presence in the landscape merely heralds impending corruption.[123]

Plaatje's landscapes oscillate between these two poles: the felicity of Mhudi and Ra-Thaga's domestic harmonies versus the instability and violence of the political worlds of Tauana and Mzilikazi. The arrival of the Boers breaks this binary by offering Mhudi and Ra-Thaga a new direction, albeit one taken under the protection of the Boers and in a Boer wagon.

*Mhudi* and *Nada* both take their titles from their eponymous heroines; both Mhudi and Nada are symbols of beauty and virtue, and have almost talismanic status in relation to their people. Nada is 'a girl of most wonderful beauty, who was named the Lily, and whose skin was whiter than are the skins of our people'.[124] Mhudi has 'a magnificent figure...brilliant black eyes...a pretty pair of dimples...a bewitching mouth and beautiful lips' (37). Initially neither had a very commanding presence in their respective plots. Nada features simply as a prize for Umslopogaas, and in an early version of Plaatje's work, Mhudi was a similarly marginal presence, 'written to disappear'. But during his visit to the United States in 1921 an American reader told Plaatje, 'Very beautiful, Mr Plaatje, but you must alter that novel of yours to bring Mhudi back'.[125]

Despite the elevation of Nada, Haggard's novel has a distinctly misogynistic tone: 'for ever, at the bottom, Umslopogaas loved war more than women' we are told, 'though this had been his fate, that women have brought sorrow to his head'. And this theme is repeated: 'Ah, Deathgrip' mourns one of the ghost wolves who befriend Umslopogaas, '...changed is the Wolf King my brother, all changed because of a woman's kiss. Now he hunts no more, no more shall Groan-Maker be aloft; it is the women's kiss he craves, not the touch of your rough tongue, it is a woman's hand he holds, not the smooth haft of horn'. 'Surely Chaka was a great king though an evil', the reader is told, 'and he showed his greatness when he forbade marriage to warriors, marriage that makes the heart soft and turns the blood to water'.[126] In contrast, Mhudi is used to demonstrate the various praiseworthy aspects of the Baralong culture to which she belongs. She excels in domestic skills and family relations: she makes berry beer, pounds corn for porridge and fashions clay pots. The centrality of women to Baralong society is expressed by Ra-Thaga who laments that, as Mhudi's mother has been killed, he must go through life without the guidance and support of a mother-in-law. But Mhudi's portrayal is also influenced by the New Woman feminism that was part of Plaatje's intellectual milieu. Plaatje's daughter Olive, to whom *Mhudi* is dedicated, was named after his friend Olive Schriener and, as noted, many of Plaatje's London acquaintances and supporters were suffragettes, or had been until the war temporarily suspended their campaign. Mhudi is beautiful but also resourceful; adept at the womanly arts but also fearlessly brave; compliant but also a source of moral guidance. At the beginning of the novel Ra-Thaga assumes that she will be the conventionally timid woman and is confounded as she confronts a lion on his behalf. Initially victims and compassionate towards the victimised throughout the novel, Mhudi and the Matabele queen Umnandi at one point voice an explicitly gendered criticism of war which relates to the historical context in which the novel is set and the conflict between Matabele and Baralong, but also speaks to Plaatje's present, that of the First World War:

> 'How wretched,' cried Mhudi sorrowfully, 'that men in whose counsels we have no share should constantly wage war, drain women's eyes of tears and saturate the earth with God's best creation – the blood of the sons of women. What will convince them of the worthlessness of this game, I wonder?'

'Nothing, my sister,' moaned Umnandi with a sigh, 'so long as there are two men left on earth there will be war.' (165)

Mhudi is at once a traditional Baralong wife and, alone in the forest with Ra-Thaga, a new kind of wife participating in the invention of a new form of marriage – companionate, equal, not part of large and complex kin-group, not subject to family regulation or traditional practices such as bride price. The collective, creative processing of events, information and opinion which the communities, both Baralong and Matabele, demonstrate is set alongside Mhudi and Ra-Thaga's willed solitude – as individuals and, after they meet and marry, as a couple. In this new setting she describes him as 'my little father, my other self, my guide, my protector, my all', as she is 'his little mother, his sister, his other self, his helpmate, his life, his everything'. 'How can I help him to become more manly!' she asks (61). But the truth is that the manly figures – Moroka, Tauana and Mzilikazi – do not fare well in *Mhudi*, either in the old world of the Mefcane, or the new world of accommodation with the settler Boers.

* * *

In the preface to *Mhudi*, Plaatje writes, 'This book should have been published over ten years ago, but circumstances beyond the control of the writer delayed its appearance' (21). These circumstances – chiefly, the lack of a publisher – and the novel's subsequent publishing history mean that *Mhudi* presents some textual problems, though their significance may have been overstated. There are variations between a typescript with hand-written corrections, presumed to be by Plaatje, and the first version of *Mhudi* published in 1930 by the Lovedale Press.[127] The Quagga Press re-publication of 1976 regularises Lovedale's spelling and, in keeping with the editorial fashion of the time, integrates its explanatory footnotes and eliminates its glosses, but is otherwise essentially the same. The Heinemann African Writers Series edition of 1978, prepared after the discovery of the typescript, goes further. In a creative and unreferenced manner, the text integrates those aspects of the typescript the editor's favour into the Quagga Press text. The Lovedale version of *Mhudi* edited out Half-a-Crown's presence, as did the Quagga Press re-publication which appeared just before the typescript was discovered. Half-a-Crown is reinstated in the Heinemann edition but it is difficult to argue, as Tim Couzens and Stephen Gray have done, that his presence is substantial or sustained. Chapter five, 'The Forest Home', begins, 'That exactly is how my father and mother met and became man and wife'(59), with no indication of who the speaker is – the previous chapter has a third-person narration; the one before is narrated by Mhudi; other chapters are in dramatic dialogue. In chapter ten, Half-a-Crown is identified ('the hoary octogenarian') and asks permission 'to digress and describe the beauty and virtues of one of King Mzilikazi's wives' (91), likening her to the Song of Songs, a favourite text of Plaatje's. In a fashion that parallels the adaptive processes of *Native Life*, Half-a-Crown changes the biblical word 'vineyards' to 'cornfields', allowing him to 'visualise her appearance in his mind's eye with accuracy'.[128] He does not reappear. It is reasonable to conclude that the narrator of chapter five who is the child of Mhudi and the narrator named as Half-a-Crown who can remember the Matabele queen Umnandi are one and the same, although this is not overtly stated. Although the typescript may have been composed earlier than the Lovedale version (and this itself is arguable), such inconsistencies suggest that it was by no means finished and final. Couzens and Gray contend that 'what the Lovedale text, in deleting the appearance of Half-a-Crown, omitted to give evidence of was that Plaatje viewed himself not so much as a novelist but as a scribe'.[129] But this does not sufficiently recognise the multivocal nature of *Mhudi's* narration: third-person narration closely identified with Ra-Thaga; Mhudi in the first person; various story-tellers narrating tales within tales; dramatic dialogue; poetry and song individually and collectively performed; and the overall sense of novel's events occurring within an oral culture of conversation, gossip, commentary and sanction. If Plaatje is a scribe, it is in the service of many more voices than just that of Half-a-Crown, and the suppression of Half-a-Crown in the Lovedale edition may be in recognition of this.

Couzens and Gray stress the importance of Half-a-Crown as part of what makes *Mhudi* distinct, but Haggard's *Nada* also has an elderly narrator with authentic access. In fact, such a figure is a common feature of Romantic and Victorian Romantic texts which present themselves as offering the reader a fragmentary glimpse of a lost past registered in oral rather than written record. Kate Trumpener writes of the bard as a figure in early nineteenth-century Scottish fiction who represents the shoring up of fragmentary and endangered cultural knowledge.[130] *Mhudi* has the same agenda: the novel, its characters, settings, plots and sub-plots act as a container for material in danger of being lost. But despite the vestigial presence of Half-a-Crown, in *Mhudi* the function of Trumpener's bard is enacted by the collective voice.

It is within those commentaries, disputes, performances and conversations that the culture of Baralong and Matabele are preserved, and perhaps will be able to effect a transition into the present.

Couzens and Gray, writing in 1978 with knowledge of the postcolonial literature of the mid- to late-twentieth century, see the Victorian poetic language of the Lovedale *Mhudi* as being externally imposed on what they are sure is Plaatje's own preference for plain diction. But it is difficult to see why this should be the case. The Victorian literary texts utilised in *Native Life* suggest that Plaatje had a wide and promiscuous knowledge of the literary canon, and a delight in its more recondite and florid offerings. In reproducing the rhetorical and the poetic modes of speech of *Mhudi's* Baralong and Matabele characters in English, as well as situating the novel in the colonial romance genre of writers such as Haggard, it is likely that he would use these models. Couzens and Gray's dark fantasy of Plaatje obediently correcting his typescript or his proofs at the instruction of printer or missionary is just that – a fantasy – as is their supposition of self-censorship in view of mission sensibilities. Plaatje had no need for such stratagems; the novel form with its expansive polyphonic and indiscriminate energy suited his purpose. And we should perhaps give the particular sub-species, the colonial ethnographic novel, a little more credit than, for example, Laura Chrisman who claims:

> Plaatje shares nothing with Haggard here except the timing of his turn to fiction.... Where there is isolation, moribundity, and absolutism in Haggard, there is dialogue, community, vitality, and relativity in Plaatje. Where there is contradiction and aporia in Haggard, there is multiplicity and ambiguity in Plaatje. Finally where there is parody or simulation of (African) culture in Haggard, there is cultural syncretism in Plaatje.[131]

Certainly Haggard – we might think properly – writes as an outsider, keen to remain as such even while stressing his expertise and cataloguing his sources. Certainly Haggard's violence is unpleasant and lingering, his notion of 'savagery' disquieting. Haggard sees his material from a distance, producing a fictional adaptation of Mary Louise Pratt's 'monarch of all I survey' school of travel writing.[132] The ethnographic material he deploys attests to his authority and learning but is also there as a means to shock his audience. In 'this polite age of melanite and torpedoes' he writes, there are 'those who think it wrong that massacres and fighting should be written of – except by special correspondents'. Readers who think it inappropriate 'that the sufferings of mankind beneath one of the world's most cruel tyrannies should form the groundwork of romance may be invited to leave this book unread'.[133] But, at the same time, his intention is, at least in part, the reproduction of authentic material – history, customs, voice – whether sourced from personal experience, ethnographic record or chats in the club with old timers. *Mhudi* takes this generic license and this appeal to veracity from Haggard and his fellow writers of colonial romance and uses them firstly as a way of containing – in a manner which would gain the widest possible audience – a record of those aspects of Baralong society he valued and felt were disappearing. And secondly he constructs a narrative which, while true to the historical record, focuses on those aspects of that record not usually part of mainstream history. Hence although the Mefecane and the rise and fall of the Matabele kingdom are recounted, it is its effect on the Baralong that *Mhudi* is most interested in; and although the time scheme of *Mhudi* encompasses what to Boer society was the defining moment in their national history, the voortrekke; this is seen as a side issue in a narrative angled entirely from the Baralong point of view.

Couzens and Gray deplore the stylistic differences between the typescript-with-corrections and *Mhudi's* Lovedale edition:

> Whoever entrusted himself with the task of getting *Mhudi* up to scratch (perhaps Plaatje himself) was one bred on Pope, Wordsworth, and Tennyson, one who would rather have his new novel drop a well-worn British cliché than an observation about the forgotten Black past. The difference is one of tone: the tone of factual authenticity rendered in English as against the tone of the Bible, Bunyan and the English hymnal.[134]

In his employment of the English language and of English literary forms, Plaatje certainly is one 'bred on Pope, Wordsworth and Tennyson', by no means as unusual or as reprehensible at the time of writing *Mhudi* as it might become later. The 'Bible, Bunyan and the English hymnal' are indeed his models, chosen, as has been argued, for complex associative reasons. What a later period might see as 'a well-worn British cliché' was simply the standard discourse for the genre – historical novel, colonial fiction – which Plaatje used. It is not that he does not want to give his readers 'an observation about the forgotten Black past' or that he is indifferent to the interplay of tone and 'factual authenticity'. It is that these cannot exist separately from the literary culture that speaks them.

## NOTES

1. Sol Plaatje, *Native Life in South Africa before and since the European War and the Boer Rebellion* (1916) (Johannesburg: Raven's Press, 1982), p. 21 (Plaatje 1982). 'Under the terms of the bill, only 7.3% of the total land surface of the Union was to be set aside for African occupation, patently inadequate to support a population that was four times the size of the white population,' Brian Willan, *Sol Plaatje: South African Nationalist 1876–1932* (Berkeley: University of California Press, 1984), p. 160. (Willan 1984)
2. Willan, *Sol Plaatje*, p. 178.
3. Willan, *Sol Plaatje*, pp. 175–6.
4. Frederic Deland Leete, *Christian Brotherhoods* (Cincinnati: Jennings and Graham, 1912), p. 279. (Leete 1912)
5. Leete, *Christian Brotherhoods*, p. 285.
6. Leete, *Christian Brotherhoods*, p. 273, quoting William Ward, *Brotherhood and Democracy* (London: PSA Publishing House, 1910).
7. Laura Chrisman, *Rereading the Imperial Romance: British Imperialism and South African Resistance in Haggard, Schreiner and Plaatje* (Oxford: Clarendon, 2000), p. 171. (Chrisman 2000)
8. Plaatje, *Native Life in South Africa*, p. 272.
9. Plaatje, *Native Life in South Africa*, pp. 262–72, 387–96.
10. Elleke Boehmer, *Empire, the National, and the Postcolonial, 1890–1920: Resistance in Interaction* (Oxford: Oxford University Press, 2002), p. 137. (Boehmer 2002)
11. David Johnson, *Shakespeare and South Africa* (Oxford: Clarendon, 1996), p. 29. (Johnson 1996)
12. Plaatje, *Native Life in South Africa*, p. 269.
13. Willan, *Sol Plaatje*, p. 39 quoting 'Mr Sol T. Plaatje honoured', *Diamond Fields Advertiser*, 1928.
14. 'Native Teachers – the want of literature', *Imvo* (29 August 1895), quoted in Willan, *Sol Plaatje*, p. 39.
15. Patricia Morris, 'The Early Black South African Newspaper and the Development of the Novel', *Journal of Commonwealth Literature*, 15: 15 (1980): 15–29. (Morris 1980)
16. Brian Willan, 'An African in *Kimberley*', *Industrialisation and Social Change in South Africa: African Class Formation, Culture, and Consciousness, 1870–1930*, eds. Shula Marks and Richard Rathbones (New York: Longman, 1982), p. 245. (Willan 1982)
17. Michael Wheeler, *The Art of Allusion in Victorian Fiction* (London: Macmillan, 1979), p. 23. (Wheeler 1979)
18. John Hollander, *The Figure of Echo: A Mode of Allusion in Milton and After* (Berkeley: University of California Press, 1981), p. 64. (Hollander 1981)

19. 'The subject of quotation being introduced, Mr. Wilkes censured it as pedantry. JOHNSON. 'No, Sir, it is a good thing; there is a community of mind in it. Classical quotation is the *parole* of literary men all over the world', James Boswell, *The Life of Samuel Johnson*, volume IV, ed. George Birbeck Hill, rev. ed. L.F. Powell (Oxford: Clarendon, 1934), p. 102. (Boswell 1934)
20. Benedict Anderson, *Imagined Communities: Reflections on the Origins and Spread of Nationalism*, rev. ed. (London: Verso, 2006). (Anderson 2006a)
21. Martyn Lyons, 'New Readers in the Nineteenth Century', *A History of Reading in the West*, eds. Guglielmo Cavallo and Roger Chartier, trans. Linda Cochrane (Amherst: University of Massachusetts Press, 1999), pp. 340–42. (Lyons 1999)
22. William St Clair, *The Reading Nation in the Romantic Period* (Cambridge: Cambridge University Press, 2004), p. 433 (St Clair 2004). See the table 16.4, p. 337, 'The radical canon, 1820s onwards'.
23. Chrisman, *Rereading the Imperial Romance*, p. 170.
24. Jonathan Rose, *The Intellectual Life of the British Working Classes* (New Haven: Yale University Press, 2001), p. 57. (Rose 2001)
25. Jane Sales, *Mission Stations and the Colonial Communities of the Eastern Cape, 1800–52* (Cape Town: A.A. Balkema, 1975), p. 42.
26. Plaatje, *Native Life in South Africa*, p. 147.
27. Willan, *Sol Plaatje*, p. 110; Plaatje, *Selected Writings*, ed. Brian Willan (Johannesburg: Witwatersrand University Press, 1996), pp. 61–4: 'I am Black, but comely, O ye daughters of Jerusalem, as the tents of Kedar, as the curtains of Solomon. Look not upon me because I am black, because the sun hath looked upon me: my mother's children were angry with me; they made me the keeper of the vineyards; but mine own vineyard have I not kept', Song of Songs, 1.5. (Plaatje 1996)
28. Bhekizizwe Peterson, 'Sol Plaatje's *Native Life in South Africa*: Melancholy Narratives, Petitioning Selves and the Ethics of Suffering', *Journal of Commonwealth Literature*, 43: 1 (2008): 84; the quotation is from Isaiah 10.1. (Peterson 2008)
29. Plaatje, *Native Life in South Africa*, p. 95.
30. Plaatje, *Native Life in South Africa*, p. 182.
31. Henry Ward Beecher, *Life Thoughts* (Boston: Phillips, Sampson, 1858) (Beecher 1858). The piece was widely reprinted in magazines such as the *Evangelical Magazine and Missionary Chronicle*. Ward Beecher was known for his powerful preaching: 'Oh for half-an-hour of my brother Henry' wrote Harriet Beecher Stowe after experiencing a London sermon, J.R. Watson, *The English Hymn: A Critical and Historical Study* (Oxford: Clarendon Press, 1999), p. 479, fn. 15. (Watson 1999)
32. 1 Kings 21ff.
33. Plaatje, *Native Life in South Africa*, p. 295.

34. Plaatje, *Native Life in South Africa*, p. 397.
35. Boehmer, *Empire, the National, and the Postcolonial*, p. 154.
36. Plaatje, *Selected Writings*, p. 93.
37. Plaatje, *Native Life in South Africa*, pp. 387–8.
38. Watson, *The English Hymn*, p. 464.
39. Plaatje mistakenly attributes its authorship to 'Wreford', presumably James Reynell Wreford (1800–91), a Birmingham non-conformist minister. Plaatje may have been relying on his memory of some of his literary citations. On p. 271, James Russell Lowell's hymn is credited to 'F. R. Lowell' – though this may have been a typesetting error.
40. Plaatje, *Native Life in South Africa*, pp. 397–8.
41. Plaatje, *Native Life in South Africa*, p. 398.
42. Watson, *The English Hymn*, p. 5.
43. Watson, *The English Hymn*, p. 19.
44. *The Study of Liturgy*, eds. Cheslyn Jones, Geoffrey Wainwright, and Edward Yarnold (London: SPCK, 1978), p. 452. (*Study of Liturgy* 1978)
45. Plaatje, *Native Life in South Africa*, p. 270.
46. Boehmer, *Empire, the National, and the Postcolonial*, p. 128.
47. 'Hollingside' was the title of the musical setting of 'Jesu lover of my soul' composed by John Bacchus Dykes (1823–1876), precentor of Durham Cathedral. He often named hymn tunes after famous people or locations in the north of England. 'Hollingside' is a 'lost place' in County Durham.
48. A.E. Voss, 'Sol Plaatje, the Eighteenth Century, and South African Cultural Memory', *English in Africa*, 21: 1, 2 (July 1994): 72–3. (Voss 1994)
49. St Clair, *The Reading Nation in the Romantic Period*, p. 435.
50. Rose, *The Intellectual Life of the British Working Classes*, pp. 126, 116.
51. Voss, 'Sol Plaatje, the Eighteenth Century, and South African Cultural Memory': 62.
52. Plaatje, *Native Life in South Africa*, p. 248.
53. William Cowper, 'The Task: Book II: The Time Piece', lines 37–42, *Poetical Works*, 4th edition, ed. H.S. Milford, (London: Oxford University Press, 1967), p. 147. (Cowper 1967)
54. Plaatje, *Native Life in South Africa*, p. 190.
55. Plaatje, *Native Life in South Africa*, p. 191.
56. Plaatje, *Native Life in South Africa*, p. 121. Burns continues:

> Many and sharp the num'rous ills
> Inwoven with our frame!
> More pointed still we make ourselves
> Regret, remorse, and shame!
> And Man, whose heav'n-erected face
> The smiles of love adorn, –

> Man's inhumanity to man
> Makes countless thousands mourn!

'Man was Made to Mourn: a Dirge', *Poetical Works*, ed. J. Logie Robertson (London: Geoffrey Cumberlege, Oxford University Press, 1950), p. 112. (Burns 1950)

57. Plaatje, *Native Life in South Africa*, p. 192.
58. Plaatje, *Native Life in South Africa*, p. 224.
59. Plaatje, *Native Life in South Africa*, p. 110.
60. Henry George Bohn, *Dictionary of Quotations from the English Poets* (London: George Bell and sons, 1902), p. 445. (Bohn 1902)
61. Wheeler, *The Art of Allusion*, p. 14.
62. Jane Starfield, 'The Lore and the Proverbs: Sol Plaatje as Historian', unpublished paper delivered at the African Studies Institute, University of Witwatersrand, 26 August 1991 (Starfield 1991); discussed in David Schalkwyk and Lerothodi Lapula, 'Solomon Plaatje, William Shakespeare, and the Translations of Culture', *Pretexts: Literary and Cultural Studies*, 9, 1 (2000): 15. (Schalkwyk and Lapula 2000)
63. Plaatje, *Native Life in South Africa*, p. 211; Sir Lewis Morris, *Gycia: a Tragedy in Five Acts* (London: Kegan Paul, Trench, 1886), p. 179.
64. Meic Stephens, 'Morris, Sir Lewis (1833–1907)', *Oxford Dictionary of National Biography*, Oxford University Press, Sept 2004; http://www.oxforddnb.com (Stephens 2004)
65. Plaatje, *Native Life in South Africa*, p. 199. The full passage in Arnold reads:

> Then the World-honored spake: 'Pity and need
> Make all flesh kin. There is no caste in blood,
> Which runneth of one hue, nor caste in tears,
> Which trickle salt with all; neither comes man
> To birth with tilka-mark stamped on the brow,
> Nor sacred thread on neck. Who doth right deed
> Is twice-born, and who doeth ill deeds vile.
> Give me to drink, my brother; when I come
> Unto my quest it shall be good for thee.'

Edwin Arnold, *The Light of Asia*, book 6 (London: Trübner and Co, 1888), pp. 179–80. (Arnold 1888)

66. Plaatje, *Native Life in South Africa*, p. 91; *L'Independance Belge*, 21 October 1914.
67. Plaatje, *Native Life in South Africa*, p. 387.

68. *The Crisis: A Record of the Darker Races* (August 1914): 171. Otto Leland Bohanan, born in Washington DC, was a black American poet and musician who died in 1932. *The Crisis* gained its name from a poem by James Russell Lowell, 'The Present Crisis'.
69. Some day, though distant it may be – with God

> A thousand years are but as yesterday –
> The germs of hate, injustice, violence,
> Like an insidious canker in the blood,
> Shall eat that nation's vitals. She shall see
> Break forth the blood-red tide of anarchy,
> Sweeping her plains, laying her cities low,
> And bearing on its seething, crimson flood
> The wreck of Government, of home, and all
> The nation's pride, its splendour and its power.
> On with relentless flow, into the seas
> Of God's eternal vengeance wide and deep.
> But, for God's grace! Oh may it hold thee fast,
> My Country, until justice shall prevail
> O'er wrong and o'er oppression's cruel power,
> And all that makes humanity to mourn.
> Ida B Luckie, 'Retribution',
> *The Crisis* (August 1916): 173.

70. W.E.B. Du Bois, *The Souls of Black Folk* (Chicago: AC McClurg, 1903), p. 3. (Du Bois 1903)
71. Du Bois, *The Souls of Black Folk*, p. 109.
72. Shakespeare's speech is as follows:

> Montague: Who set this ancient quarrel new abroach?
> Speak, nephew, were you by when it began?
> Benvolio: Here were the servants of your adversary,
> And yours, close fighting ere I did approach:
> I drew to part them: in the instant came
> The fiery Tybalt, with his sword prepared,
> Which, as he breathed defiance to my ears,
> He swung about his head and cut the winds,
> Who, nothing hurt withal, hiss'd him in scorn;
> While we were interchanging thrusts and blows,
> Came more and more, and fought on part and part,
> Till the prince came, who parted either part.
> *Romeo and Juliet*, I, 1, lines 95–106.

73. Shakespeare's speech is as follows:

> Aemilius: Arm, arm, my lords! Rome never had more cause.
> The Goths have gathered head; and with a power
> Of high-resolved men, bent to the spoil,
> They hither march amain, under conduct
> Of Lucius, son to old Andronicus,
> Who threats, in course of this revenge, to do
> As much as ever Coriolanus did.
> *Titus Andronicus*, IV, 4, lines 61–7.

74. The campaign was of such unequal match that Mahatma Gandhi, whose ambulance corps cared for wounded and dying Zulu, described it as 'no war but a man hunt', Mahatma Gandhi, *An Autobiography, or The Story of My Experiments with Truth*, trans. Mahadev Desai (Ahmedabad: Navajivan Publishing, 1927), p. 290. (Gandhi 1927)
75. *A Book of Homage to Shakespeare: To Commemorate the Three Hundredth Anniversary of Shakespeare's Death*, ed. Israel Gollancz (Oxford: Humphrey Milford; Oxford University Press, 1916), p. 52. (*Book of Homage to Shakespeare* 1916)
76. Preface, *Book of Homage*, p. vii.
77. F.R. Benson, 'A Stratfordian's Homage', *Book of Homage*, p. 39.
78. Charlotte Carmichael Stopes, 'The Making of Shakespeare', *Book of Homage*, p. 118.
79. For a discussion of this, see Coppélia Kahn, 'Remembering Shakespeare Imperially: The 1916 Tercentenary', *Shakespeare Quarterly*, 52: 4 (Winter 2001): 456–47. (Kahn 2001)
80. Israel Zangwill, 'The Two Empires', *Book of Homage*, p. 248.
81. William Pember Reeves, 'The Dream Imperial', *Book of Homage*, p. 312.
82. Lionel Cust, 'Shakespeare', *Book of Homage*, p. 102.
83. Sydney Lee, 'Shakespeare: Inventor of Language', *Book of Homage*, p. 114.
84. Charles Mills Gayley, 'Heart of the Race', *Book of Homage*, p. 341.
85. F.R. Benson, 'A Stratfordian's Homage', *Book of Homage*, p. 39.
86. Schalkwyk and Lapula, 'Solomon Plaatje, William Shakespeare, and the Translations of Culture': 10.
87. 'A South African's Homage: William Tsikinya-Chaka', *Book of Homage*, pp. 336–9. Plaatje's is not the only chapter in a language other than English. There are chapters in Romanian, French (several), German, Dutch, Swedish, Norwegian, Danish, Polish, Serbian, Finnish, Chinese, Persian, Armenian (entitled 'Armenia's Love to Shakespeare'), Spanish, Italian (several), Greek ancient and modern, Hebrew, Sanskrit, Irish/ Gaelic, Hindi, Persian,

and Burmese. Some are in the original language, some are translated and some have a parenthetical gloss. Others are by foreign scholars but in English.
88. Plaatje, 'A South African's Homage', *Book of Homage*, p. 336.
89. Rose, *The Intellectual Life of the British Working Classes*, pp. 122–5.
90. Gary Taylor, *Reinventing Shakespeare: A Cultural History from the Restoration to the Present* (London: Hogarth Press, 1990), pp. 194–6. (Taylor 1990)
91. Otto Jespersen, 'A Marginal Note on Shakespeare's Language and a Textual Crux in King Lear', *Book of Homage*, pp. 481–3.
92. Plaatje, 'A South African's Homage', *Book of Homage*, p. 336.
93. Plaatje, 'A South African's Homage', *Book of Homage*, p. 338.
94. Schalkwyk and Lapula, 'Solomon Plaatje, William Shakespeare, and the Translations of Culture': 16.
95. Plaatje, 'A South African's Homage', *Book of Homage*, p. 337.
96. Ronald Ross, 'Shakespeare, 1916', *A Book of Homage to Shakespeare*, p. 104.
97. G C Moore Smith, 'Sonnets, 1616: 1916', *Book of Homage*, p. 237.
98. Ngũgĩ wa Thiong'o, *Decolonising the Mind: the Politics of Language in African Literature* (London: James Currey, 1986), p. 91. (Ngũgĩ wa Thiong'o 1986)
99. Plaatje, 'A South African's Homage', *Book of Homage*, p. 339. Plaatje may be referring to *The Life and Passion of Jesus* (1905) or to *From the Manger to the Cross* (otherwise known as *Jesus of Nazareth*) which first appeared in 1912 and was reissued in 1916. In both films, Judas is significantly darker skinned than the other disciples, though this might be a function of his being pictured as stereotypically Jewish rather than as black. The actor who played Judas in *From the Manger to the Cross* was an Italian.
100. Plaatje, 'A South African's Homage', *Book of Homage*, p. 339.
101. Willan, *Sol Plaatje*, p. 194.
102. Willan, *Sol Plaatje*, p. 410, note 72.
103. Herbert Aptheker, *The Literary Legacy of W.E.B. Du Bois* (New York: Kraus, 1989), pp. 214–5. (Aptheker 1989)
104. Certainly *Mhudi* in some form or another was read in United States after 1920 and modifications were suggested. It is unclear whether Lovedale Press version is a revised form of the 1920 version or an earlier version. See Brian Willan, *Plaatje*, p. 349.
105. Tim Couzens, Introduction, *Mhudi* (Oxford: Heinemann, 1978), p. 9. (Couzens 1978)
106. See Stephen Gray, 'Plaatje's Shakespeare', *English in Africa*, 4, 1 (March 1977): 1–6. (Gray 1977)
107. Letter, probably to Silas Molema, 25 August 1920, quoted in Tim Couzens and Stephen Gray, 'Printers' and other Devils: the Texts of Sol Plaatje's

Mhudi', *Research in African Literatures*, 9: 2 (Autumn 1978): 201. (Couzens and Gray 1978)
108. H. Rider Haggard, *Nada the Lily* (London: Longmans, Green, 1892), p. 5. (Haggard 1892)
109. Haggard, *Nada*, p. x.
110. Plaatje, 'Preface to the Original Edition', *Mhudi*, p. 21.
111. Victoria J. Collis-Buthelezi, '"A Native Venture": Sol (Solomon Tshekisho) Plaatje Defining South African Literature', *Xcp: Cross-Cultural Poetics, Special Issue: South Africa: Literature and Social Movements*, 21–22 (2009): 120. (Collis-Buthelezi 2009)
112. Haggard, *Nada*, p. x.
113. Haggard, *Nada*, p. 4.
114. Anne McClintock, *Imperial Leather: Race, Gender and Sexuality in the Colonial Contest* (New York Routledge, 1995), p. 30. (McClintock 1995)
115. George E. Marcus, 'Contemporary Problems of Ethnography in the Modern World System', *Writing Culture: The Poetics and Politics of Ethnology*, eds. James Clifford and George E. Marcus (Berkeley: University of California Press, 1986), p. 165, note 1. (Marcus 1986)
116. Haggard wrote that Mr F.B. Fynney, late Zulu border agent who was the chief interpreter for the colony... utilized his fluent Zulu to write ethnographical pieces on the nation... which in subsequent days I made use of in *Nada the Lily* and other books', Peter Berresford Ellis, *H Rider Haggard: A Voice from the Infinite* (London: Routledge and Kegan Paul, 1987), p. 36. (Ellis 1987)
117. Haggard cites titles such as 'Among the Zulus and the Amatongas' by 'the late Mr Leslie', Bishop Callaway's 'Religious Systems of the Amazulu', Haggard, *Nada*, p. x.
118. Couzens, Introduction, *Mhudi*, p. 13.
119. Thomas Richards, *The Imperial Archive: Knowledge and the Fantasy of Empire* (London: Verso, 1993). (Richards 1993)
120. Willan, *Plaatje*, p. 352.
121. Haggard, *Nada*, p. 4.
122. Haggard, *Nada*, p. xi.
123. Gail Ching-Liang Low, *Black Skins, White Masks: Representation and Colonialism* (London: Routledge, 1996), p. 39. (Low 1996)
124. Haggard, *Nada*, p. 178.
125. Couzens and Gray, 'Printers' and Other Devils': 202. This account comes from an interview of Michael van Reenen, a neighbour and friend of Plaatje's in the 1930s, given to Brian Willan in 1977.
126. Haggard, *Nada*, p. 267.
127. A Lovedale Press reissue in 1957 made no change, and an edition in the United States followed this version.

128. Couzens and Gray describe how the 'typescript-with-corrections' of *Mhudi* was found when the 1976 Soweto Uprising necessitated the archives of the Lovedale Mission be moved to Rhodes University, Grahamtown. Its status is uncertain. Couzens and Gray write: 'It could be the first version of the novel, the 1920 version; it could be the second version, the "American version" [written in response to an American reader who told Plaatje to enlarge Mhudi's role]; or it could be a third version, with changes made to both or either of the two earlier versions... Unfortunately there is not sufficient evidence to be certain of the truth', Couzens and Gray, 'Printers' and other Devils': 198–215.
129. Couzens and Gray, 'Printers' and Other Devils': 206.
130. Katie Trumpener, *Bardic Nationalism: The Romantic Novel and the British Empire* (Princeton: Princeton University Press, 1997), p. 6. (Trumpener 1997)
131. Chrisman, *Rereading the Imperial Romance*, p. 166.
132. Mary Louise Pratt, *Imperial Eyes: Travel Writing and Transculturation* (London: Routledge, 1992), p. 197. (Pratt 1992)
133. Haggard, *Nada*, p. xii.
134. Couzens and Gray, 'Printers' and Other Devils': 210.

# CHAPTER 4

# 'The Genuine Stamp of Truth and Nature': Voicing *The History of Mary Prince*

In 1826 the Scottish poet Thomas Pringle sailed from Cape Town to England on the brig *Luna*. He was returning after six years in South Africa in some disarray, '[r]uined in circumstances and in prospects but sound in conscience and character'.[1] As a journalist, in his own words 'unbought and unafraid',[2] he had chiefly excelled in antagonising the governor Lord Charles Somerset, not a recipe for survival in the small, incestuous and potentially autocratic Cape Colony, described by his friend John Fairburn as 'a system of misrule and frantic, drunken despotism'.[3]

Pringle embarked with his wife Margaret, his sister-in-law Janet and Marossi, a young Tswana child. He also took on board with him a freight of imaginative capital as ammunition in what Catherine Hall describes as the anti-slavery movement's 'war of representation'.[4] In his African poems published on his return, the 'pictured relics of the past' that he had dwelt on in his precolonial days – 'The scented heath, the sheafy vale,/ The hills and streams of Teviotdale'[5] – are put aside. A dedicatory sonnet, 'To Sir Walter Scott' tells his mentor and model that his work is now sourced

> [f]rom deserts wild and many a pathless wood
> Of savage climes where I have wander'd long,
> Whose hills and streams are yet ungraced by song...[6]

It is a symptom of colonial literature's contradictory stance to see the colonial place as both empty and teeming with the exotic. In Pringle's case the exotic is both strange and familiar: 'The free-born Kosa' who 'still doth hold/ The fields his father gained of old' in the 'glen' in the manner of Scott's Highlanders;[7] or the Rousseau-esque 'Wild Bushman' who declaims:

> Let the proud boor possess his flocks,
> And boast his fields of grain;
> My home is 'mid the mountain rocks,
> The desert my domain.
> I plant no herbs nor pleasant fruits,
> Nor toil for savoury cheer;
> The desert yields me juicy roots,
> And herds of bounding deer.[8]

From Scott, and from Oliver Goldsmith, Pringle takes rhetorics of deprivation and loss and applies them to his new subjects. The 'Hottentot' tends 'another's flock upon the fields/ His fathers' once, where now the White Man builds/ His home'.[9] The 'poor Caffer', 'his herds by the Christian carried away', suffers under the new dispensation which configures him as 'robber', 'savage' and 'heathen'.[10] In his poems 'The Bechuana Boy', inspired by Marossi, and 'The Bushman', the central figures enact for the home reader narratives of capture and enslavement clothed in the literary language of the abolitionist empire. On his arrival in London, Pringle's embrace by the Anti-Slavery Society was hardly surprising.

Inevitably, though, cargo shifts on voyage. The lived experience becomes frozen in the written trope. Pringle's African figures may have been sourced from actual encounters,[11] yet by the time his poems docked at Gravesend they had been converted into stereotype and abstraction, in the language of poetic generality. In a sonnet entitled 'To Oppression', Pringle's vow – '[s]till to oppose and thwart with heart and hand' the 'brutalizing sway' of slavery 'till Afric's chains/ Are burst'[12] – seems uncomfortably dislocated from lived experience.

Two years after Pringle's return, Mary Prince set out on the final stage of her own journey.[13] Born a slave in Brackish Pond, Bermuda, in 1788, as a young woman she had been sold to owners in Spanish Point, made the four-week passage to Grand Quay in the Turk and Caicos Islands, returned to Bermuda, this time to Cedar Hills, packed up and boarded ship for Antigua – first to St John's, then to Date Hill – and finally had sailed from there to London. Pringle and his party were travellers;

Mary Prince and her fellow slaves were shipped as a form of cargo, as she put it, 'tied up...like hogs – moor[ed] up like cattle...lick[ed], so as hogs or cattle, or horses never were flogged', 'examined and handled...in the same manner that a butcher would a calf or a lamb he was about to purchase'[14]. On the voyage to Turk's Island, in a becalmed sea, she had almost starved, 'had it not been for the kindness of a black man called Anthony, and his wife, who had brought their own victuals, and shared them with me' (18). On her journey to London only the fellowship of a member of her church sustained her (31).

Pringle brought with him texts. Prince brought with her the bodily witness of her scars and afflictions, physical testament to her treatment, to be read, she trusted, differently in abolitionist England than in the recalcitrant West Indies. She brought with her knowledge of her legal advantage as a slave landing in England. And she brought with her a surprising capacity for independent economic activity. Her *History* is full of the canny negotiations and the peculiarly inflected relationships between slave and the slave-owning public as she took in washing, sold coffee and yams for the provision of ships, and on-sold cargo off ships. Her owner Mr Wood claimed that on her arrival in London she had 'from £36 to £40 at least, which she had saved in his service' (31).[15] 'Unwilling to eat the bread of idleness' (21) as she put it, her industriousness, and the biblical tag with which she characterises it, point to another asset she brought with her, her Christianity, which allowed her membership of what Hall describes as the 'gathered community' of the missionary public.[16] Prince and her husband had joined the Moravian Church in Antigua in 1819. In the fervour of the anti-slavery movement, with its belief, in the words of Hannah More, that 'th' immortal principle within' was unaffected by 'the casual colour of the skin',[17] she found an audience more than ready for her story. *The History of Mary Prince, a West Indian Slave, Related by Herself* with preface and 'supplement' by Pringle, in whose Islington household she was by then living, was published in 1831.

To say that Pringle imported to England literary style and Prince brought actual experience is to oversimplify, but each had what the other lacked. Pringle needed the sharp specifics of witness; Prince needed a means by which her experiences and the oral narrative that expressed them could be given the authority of a written script. Pringle wanted ammunition in the abolitionist cause, now in its final stages; Prince wanted the right to return to Antigua and to her husband as a free woman. In the *History* it was hoped that the needs of both agents would be accommodated. At the beginning of his preface, Pringle explains that Prince herself was the instigator of the project:

> The idea of writing Mary Prince's history was first suggested by herself. She wished it to be done, she said, that good people in England might hear from a slave what a slave had felt and suffered... (iii)

The title of the *History* describes it as being 'related by herself'; Pringle's preface enlarges on this, explaining that the narrative was 'taken down from Mary's own lips by a lady who happened to be at the time residing in my family as a visitor' (iii). This 'lady' was Susanna Strickland, daughter of a determinedly literary family who had been discomposed by her recent conversion to a fierce form of Congregationalism. They were to be even more discomposed when, that year, she met, in Pringle's house, John Wedderburn Dunbar Moodie, married him, and immigrated to Canada. Her account of their life there, *Roughing it in the Bush* (1852), is now a foundational text of the Canadian literary canon. But at the time its success in no way mitigated the shame her socially ambitious sisters felt at the book's revelations of the grim poverty of settler existence.

Aware of critics eager to undermine not just Prince's story but the cause to which it contributed, Pringle is careful to explain the process by which the text was produced:

> It was written out fully, with all the narrator's repetitions and prolixities, and afterwards pruned into its present shape; retaining, as far as was practicable, Mary's exact expressions and peculiar phraseology. No fact of importance has been omitted, and not a single circumstance or sentiment has been added. It is essentially her own, without any material alteration farther than was requisite to exclude redundancies and gross grammatical errors, so as to render it clearly intelligible. (iii)

Strickland's role was to take dictation, eliminate repetition, clarify meaning and correct grammatical faults. Grammar was an important tool at the amanuensis' disposal, the means by which the spoken voice could be made to conform to the niceties of polite discourse, and the reference to pruning 'prolixities' suggests that Strickland's written text was a compressed version of Prince's spoken account. But it was important to the project's intentions that a sense of the speaking individual remained – her 'exact expressions and peculiar phraseology'. In the final paragraph of the *History*, Prince states that she 'will say the truth to English people who may read this history that my good friend, Miss S –, is now writing down for me' (23). 'Saying the truth' points to her speaking voice; 'writing down' conveys the transcription of that voice. Both were necessary in producing the text.

In the process of this transcription, certain established codes were observed. Restraint rather than exaggeration was important. Strickland wrote to a friend:

> I have been writing Mr. Pringle's black Mary's life from her own dictation and for her benefit adhering to her own simple story and language without deviating to the paths of flourish and romance.[18]

It was a style that suited Strickland's own literary temperament. Writing to her friend James Bird in the same year, she told him: 'I must scold you...for dealing so much in extravagant metaphor with which you often spoil a fine passage by giving it a ludicrous cast'.[19] A demonstrated preference for 'simple story and language' over 'flourish and romance' was important to the integrity of works such as Prince's. In the *Narrative of Louis Asa-Asa, A Captured African,* included as 'a convenient supplement' to early editions of *The History of Mary Prince,* the reader is told that his account is 'given, like [Prince's], as nearly as possible in the narrator's words, with only so much correction as was necessary to connect the story, and render it grammatical' (41).[20] Strickland describes her method in the preface to another slave narrative, *Slavery described by a Negro; being the Narrative of Ashton Warner, a Native of St Vincent's,* published in the same year:

> In writing Ashton's narrative, I have adhered strictly to the simple facts, adopting, wherever it could conveniently be done, his own language, which, for a person in his condition, is remarkably expressive and appropriate.[21]

Ashton Warner, we are assured, 'is remarkably intelligent, understands our language perfectly, and can read and write well', despite the fact that he needs an amanuensis. The terms used in his narrative are, Strickland stresses, 'his own expressions; for, though uneducated, he is a very intelligent negro, and speaks remarkably good English'.[22] He can read and yet he is uneducated – meaning that he does not have the level of written expression considered appropriate for a published work. The extent of the modification that Strickland employs is demonstrated to the reader in Asa-Asa's story – and by implication in those of Prince and Warner – when he is directly quoted. 'Me no father, no mother now; me stay with you', he tells her when offered the chance to return to Africa (41). On another occasion, a servant overhears him saying, 'Me think, – me think – '. When asked what he means, he answers, 'Me think what a good thing I came to England! Here, I know what God is, and read my Bible; in my country they have no God, no Bible' (41).

This fragmented language is very different from the manner in which his written account begins, not only with simplicity but also with clarity and formal correctness:

> My father's name was Clashoquin; mine is Asa-Asa. He lived in a country called Bycla, near Egie, a large town. Egie is as large as Brighton; it was some way from the sea. I had five brothers and sisters. We all lived together with my father and mother; he kept a horse, and was respectable, but not one of the great men. My uncle was one of the great men at Egie: he could make men come and work for him: his name was Otou. He had a great deal of land and cattle. My father sometimes worked on his own land, and used to make charcoal. I was too little to work; my eldest brother used to work on the land; and we were all very happy. (42)

Ashton Warner's *Narrative*, although in a different setting and with a different narrative trajectory, begins in much the same way, defining place, family and circumstances:

> I was born in the Island of St. Vincent's, and baptized by the name of Ashton Warner, in the parish church, by the Rev. Mr. Gildon. My father and mother, at the time of my birth, were slaves on Cane Grove estate, in Bucumar Valley, then the property of Mr. Ottley. I was an infant at the breast when Mr. Ottley died; and shortly after the estate was put to sale, that the property might be divided among his family.[23]

The formulaic quality of these openings, and their contrast with Asa-Asa's directly recorded utterances, suggests the degree of regulation and reorganisation employed by Strickland. This is signalled at the conclusion of Asa-Asa's narrative where the editor warns, 'The concluding passage in inverted commas, is entirely his own' and that 'The last sentences... will seem almost too peculiar to be his own' (41). Although the whole account

## 4 'THE GENUINE STAMP OF TRUTH AND NATURE': VOICING *THE HISTORY*...

is written in the first person, the final paragraph is bracketed by quotation marks in the left-hand margin of each line, emphatically signalling that, notwithstanding the assurances that we have been hearing Asa-Asa's unmediated voice throughout, here we are experiencing something even closer to his exact, unedited words:

> I am very happy to be in England, as far as I am very well; – but I have no friend belonging to me, but God, who will take care of me as he has done already. I am very glad I have come to England, to know who God is. I should like much to see my friends again, but I do not wish to go back to them: for if I go back to my own country, I might be taken as a slave again. I would rather stay here, where I am free, than go back to my own country to be sold. I shall stay in England as long as (please God) I shall live. I wish the King of England could know all I have told you. I wish it that he may see how cruelly we are used. We had no king in our country, or he would have stopt it. I think the king of England might stop it, and this is why I wish him to know it all. I have heard say he is good; and if he is, he will stop it if he can. I am well off myself, for I am well taken care of, and have good bed and good clothes; but I wish my own people to be as comfortable. (43–4)

The structure here is not the fragmented phrasing of 'Me think – me think – '. Neither is it the factual, ordered prose of the majority of the text. Despite its reassuringly patriotic and religious pieties, this final passage presents itself as a record of what Asa-Asa feels, a record of his thoughts and his fears, free from editorial oversight.

Editors such as Strickland were required to combine a sense of authentic tone with a sense of the innate and natural dignity of the subject, to translate raw words into polite diction. Some went further and translated what the subject said into what it might signify. In *A Narrative of the Life of John Marrant of New York in North America; Giving an Account of his Conversion when only 14 years of age* (1813), the editor, W. Aldridge, explains 'I have always preserved Mr Marrant's ideas, though I could not his language.'[24] James Ramsay in his influential *An Essay on the Treatment and Conversion of African Slaves in the British Sugar Colonies* (1784) writes of his account of the slave Quashi, 'The only liberty I have taken with it, has been to give words to the sentiment that inspired it'.[25]

Philip Gould describes this licence as responding to 'the dissonance between the refinement of African feeling and the capacity of African-American language to convey it'.[26] It was a dissonance which was most marked in poetry. In his elegy 'He Compares His Humble Fortune with the Distress of Others' (1744), William Shenstone gives an early and detailed description of this process of empathetic articulation. The poet imagines a 'poor native' captured by slavers standing 'on the wild beach in mournful guise' preparing 'to quit the Libyan shores':

> On the wild beach in mournful guise he stood,
> Ere the shrill boatswain gave the hated sign;
> He dropp'd a tear unseen into the flood,
> He stole one secret moment, to repine.

The poet wishes to use his poetic powers to express the slave's plight and asks the muse to assist: to listen to the man's speech, 'such moving plaints as nature could inspire', and to convey its essence to the poet:

> ...the Muse listen'd to the plaints he made,
> Such moving plaints as Nature could inspire;
> To me the Muse his tender plea convey'd,
> But smooth'd and suited to the sounding lyre.

The poet is then able to speak for the 'poor native' in suitably poetic diction – 'smooth'd and suited to the sounding lyre' – without the contrived nature of his verse interfering with the reader's sense of the scene's authenticity. With the assistance of Shenstone and his muse, the slave speaks:

> Why am I ravish'd from my native strand?
> What savage race protects this impious gain?
> Shall foreign plagues infest this teeming land,
> And more than sea-born monsters plough the main?

The slave, being of nature, is inspired by nature; the acculturated poet by a more complex process, albeit still in the service of the 'poor native'. When the slave declaims 'Why am I ravish'd from my native strand?' the reader is meant to understand that what they are hearing is a translation not just of the native language of the slave into English, but of his presumed unsophisticated diction into poetry and metaphor. Unlike in later nineteenth-century ethnological verse, there is no suggestion that this is a direct translation of an Indigenous poetic form. Rather it is an expression of the underlying and unspoken sensibility of the 'poor native' whose depth of feeling can only be adequately – and appropriately – conveyed by the expressive codes of eighteenth-century poetic discourse. The poet congratulates himself on focusing his poetic energy on this pitiable figure rather than his own discontents:

> Let vacant bards display their boasted woes;
> Shall I the mockery of grief display;
> No; let the Muse his piercing pangs disclose,
> Who bleeds and weeps his sum of life away![27]

The crucial difference between the eighteenth-century poetry written in the abolitionist cause and the slave narrative is the latter's realism, the insistence that the reader is hearing an actual voice speak of an actual life. By the beginning of the nineteenth century, the values of poetry had shifted to make such simplicity of expression highly sympathetic. William Wordsworth in his preface to the *Lyrical Ballads* (1800) states that his intention is to meld 'metrical arrangement' with 'a selection of the real language of men in a state of vivid sensation' to illustrate 'incidents and situations from common life', especially '[l]ow and rustic life', because

> [i]n that situation, the essential passions of the heart find a better soil in which they can attain their maturity, are less under restraint, and speak a plainer and more emphatic language; because in that situation our elementary feelings exist in a state of greater simplicity and consequently may be more accurately contemplated and more forcibly communicated; because the manners of rural life germinate from those elementary feelings; and from the necessary character of rural occupations are more easily comprehended; and are more durable...[28]

This language of 'repeated experience and regular feelings' is contrasted with the vanity of authors 'who think that they are conferring honour upon themselves and their art, in proportion as they separate themselves from the sympathies of men'. In contrast to Shenstone's ventriloquised native or the poems of Pringle's African sojourn, in the *Lyrical Ballads* Wordsworth assures his readers, 'personifications of abstract ideas rarely occur'. 'I have wished' he explains 'to keep my Reader in the company of flesh and blood, persuaded that by so doing I shall interest him':

> I have at all times endeavoured to look steadily at my subject; consequently, I hope that there is in these Poems little falsehood of description, and that my ideas are expressed in language fitted to their respective importance.

The genre of the slave narrative is consistent with this manifesto, even anticipates it, 'falsehood of description' being the antithesis of its intent, and romantic simplicity central to its ethos. By definition, its subjects are 'men in a state of vivid sensation' and their experiences are expressed in 'a plainer and more emphatic language' than more educated authors might employ. Though literary, slave narratives took pains to distinguish themselves from the various contemporary manifestations of literary fashion and practice. In the popular and influential work, *The Interesting Narrative of the Life of Olaudah Equiano, or Gustavus Vassa, the African, Written by Himself* (1789), the author stresses that his work is a 'genuine Narrative'.[29] The evidence he gives for this is, paradoxically, the fact that it is 'the product of an unlettered African' and 'a work wholly devoid of literary merit' written with no thought for 'immortality or literary reputation'.[30] The author is not and does not wish to be part of the literary world or the recipient of its rewards. Reviews appended to later editions of Equiano's work agree: 'The simplicity that runs through his Narrative is singularly beautiful', writes *The Monthly Review*, 'and that beauty is heightened by the idea that it is *true*'. Author and text are conflated: 'The Narrative wears an honest face', the *Review* continues, 'and we have conceived a good opinion of the man, from the artless manner in which he has detailed the variety of adventures and vicissitudes that have fallen his lot'.[31] *The Narrative of the Enslavement of Ottobah Cugoano, a Native of Africa; published by himself, in the Year 1787* is described approvingly as an 'artless narrative'.[32] Artlessness implies authenticity. As Sara Salih observes, '[t]he slave narrator must not be perceived as emplotting, fictionalizing, or engaging in acts of textual poesis, but s/he must provide a clear, sequential, unfalsified, authentic account'.[33] Indeed, the most effective work was that which gave the sense of as little distance as possible between the individual and the written text, the speaker and the story being presented as interchangeable. 'Any reader, who wishes it', writes Strickland at the conclusion of Ashton Warner's *Narrative*, 'may see and converse with himself, by making application through the publisher'.[34] Reading the text and talking to the man are identical experiences.

At the time the *History* was published, the truth or otherwise of the details contained in Prince's and other slave narratives – of the general situation of slavery or of the particular case of the individual slave – were hotly debated. But, in this fiercely contestatory climate, there is little concern with issues of authorship and collaboration. The mechanics of the slave narratives' production are invariably set out in a straightforward manner within the text and accepted as such by the reading public. A review of Equiano's *Interesting Narrative* states:

> We entertain no doubt of the general authenticity of this very intelligent African's story; though it is not improbable that some English writer has assisted him in the compliment, or, at least, the correction of his book; for it is sufficiently well-written.[35]

The editorial involvement of someone else is not seen as contradicting Equiano's authorship. *A Narrative of the Most Remarkable Particulars in the Life of James Albert Ukawsaw Gronniosaw, an African Prince, as Related by Himself* (1772), according to its preface, 'was taken from his own Mouth and committed to Paper by the elegant Pen of a young Lady of the Town of Leominster'.[36] Vincent Carretta observes:

> The phrase 'written by himself' appears in more than 1,000 eighteenth-century titles of fiction and non-fiction, almost always of works attributed to authors whose presumed levels of education and social status were likely to make readers suspect their authenticity.[37]

There was an acknowledged fluidity in how the term was used: 'written by himself' did not rule out the assistance of an 'elegant pen'. 'Memoirs' could be 'of' someone and 'by' someone else: *The Blind African Slave, or Memoirs of Boyrereau Brinch, Nick-named Jeffrey Brace* (1810) states on its title page that it is by Benjamin F. Prentiss.[38] 'Related by' implies the cooperation of an amanuensis but does not contradict a claim to authorship. Strickland quotes Prince referring to her as her 'dear Missie and Biographer'[39] but also describes composing the text 'from [Prince's] own dictation', the two activities, biography and dictation, being consistent.[40] John Jea's (1811) work signals authorship in its title, *The Life, History, and Unparalleled Sufferings of John Jea, the African Preacher; Compiled and Written by Himself*, yet gives an account of a complex and not entirely easy collaborative relationship, where it is made clear that, while Jea might have control of his *Life*, he did not in a literal sense write it:

> My dear reader, I would now inform you, that I have stated this in the best manner I am able, for I cannot write, therefore it is not quite so correct as if I had been able to have written it myself; not being able to notice the time

and date when I left several places, in my travels from time to time, as many do when they are travelling; nor would I allow alterations to be made by the person whom I employed to print this Narrative.[41]

Literacy was not a simple, absolute state; there were gradations. Being able to read but not write was common. The literate but uneducated subject could still feel that he or she was in need of educated assistance to adequately express their story. Claims to authorship could carry their own risks. In a letter to a friend Strickland describes the composition of Prince's 'pathetic little history... now printing in the form of a pamphlet to be laid before the Houses of Parliament', saying, 'Mr. Pringle has added a very interesting appendix and I hope the work will do much good' but adding, 'Of course my name does not appear'.[42] The heated nature of the anti-slavery debate was an added disincentive to authorial acknowledgement. Pringle fought two libel cases arising from the *History*, one as plaintiff and one as defendant.[43] In a lightly fictionalised autobiographical story 'Trifles from the Burthen of Life', published in 1851, Strickland describes the kind of opprobrium that anti-slavery activists could attract:

> 'One would think,' [Mrs Dalton, a fellow immigrant *en route* to Canada] said, 'that you belong to the Anti-Slavery Society. By the by, have you read a canting tract published by that *pious* fraternity called "The History of Mary P –." It is set forth to be an authentic narrative, while I know it to be a tissue of falsehoods from beginning to end.'
> 'Did you know Mary P –?'
> 'Pshaw! – who does? It is an imaginary tale, got up for party purposes.'
> 'But I do know Mary P –, and I know that narrative to be strictly true, for I took it down myself from the woman's own lips.'
> 'You?' – and Mrs. Dalton started from the ground, as though she had been bitten by serpent.[44]

Contemporary critics have been more concerned to define the exact nature of authorship in the slave narrative genre than eighteenth- and nineteenth-century audiences were, and, in the case of *The History of Mary Prince*, have reached various and contrasting conclusions. Misao Dean, in the context of Canadian literary history, lists the *History* as one of Strickland's (or Moodie's) works without any reference to Prince.[45] On the other hand, Moira Ferguson treats Prince as the author of the *History*, albeit one who has had to contend with interference from Pringle.[46] Ferguson identifies Strickland only in a footnote as 'the transcriber of

Mary Prince's manuscript', incorrectly states that Strickland 'never seems to have mentioned the transcription', and speculates that this 'could indicate the extent to which the narrative was indeed (Pringle's disclaimers to the contrary) Mary Prince's own'.[47] Prince is, confusingly, portrayed as both 'claiming voice and agency', but at the same time as being 'pinioned in the discourse of her violators', her 'sparring voice audible only to initiates'.[48] More usefully, John Thurston describes the *History* as the product of an 'affiliative network' emerging from 'a shared moral fabric'. But he asserts that 'the shaping of Mary Prince into an intelligible, linear, grammatically correct narrative has taken this text away from Mary. It is a corporate text – Mary, Strickland, Pringle – that finally only the Anti-Slavery Society could be said to author...'.[49] Gould writes: 'Because of the power dynamics informing the collaborative production of these early autobiographies, critics tend to view them suspiciously. But, more recently, others have challenged the traditional critiques of collaborative autobiography'. He quotes Robert Desrochers, Jr. who argues that 'in assuming that whites consciously and effectively silenced the voices of the first black narrators, scholars too often limit themselves in search of a "true" black voice of irreconcilable and discernible difference'.[50] Salih has questioned 'the comforting illusion of a single black author who protested against the evils of slavery in a self-authored, mono-vocal, mono-cultural text'.[51]

Thurston is certainly correct that cultural surroundings and generic expectations influence the *History*. This is the case with all literary works. It is not possible to write without the influence of context and genre, and the context of the late stages of the anti-slavery campaign and the genre of the slave narrative certainly mould the production of the *History*. Does this '[take] the text away from Mary'? Texts still need authors and it seems sensible and useful to consider *The History of Mary Prince* as jointly authored by two women who shared a degree of common purpose and common belief, though their backgrounds and histories could hardly have been more different. Their relationship was inflected by inequalities of power – if Prince ceased to be a slave on reaching England, she quickly became a servant and entered the codes and practices of the early nineteenth-century domestic worker. Strickland's personal references to her outside the *History* seem affectionate and condescending in a manner that was quite orthodox for a mistress and servant. In a letter describing her wedding day Strickland writes, 'Black Mary, who has treated herself with a complete new suit on the occasion, went on the coach box, to see her dear

Missie and Biographer wed'.[52] But on the other hand, both women were Christian and thereby were bound by a relationship of spiritual equality. Free, English and educated, Strickland had, so the anti-slavery campaign constantly told her, an obligation of sympathy and service towards the enslaved, even if the object of that service was also doing her washing. Both women had experienced conversion as adults. Strickland, brought up in a High Anglican family, had been admitted to the Wrentham Congregational Chapel in April 1830, describing it as 'that memorable never to be forgotten day when I first received the cup of salvation from the hand of my beloved pastor'.[53] Prince had been invited to a 'Methodist meeting for prayer' when she was living in Date Hill in 1817:

> This meeting had a great impression on my mind, and led my spirit to the Moravian church; so that when I got back to town, I went and prayed to have my name put down in the Missionaries' book; and I followed the church earnestly every opportunity. (16)

Both women encountered opposition in making these choices. Strickland's 'secession' was, her sister Catherine felt, 'the cause of disunion and withdrawal of the old harmony and confidence which had hitherto existed in the family'.[54] And it marked a change in her career as a writer. She had previously gained some success producing children's books and light work for popular periodicals. Writing to Mary Russell Mitford in 1829 she describes herself as 'one of Fancy's spoiled and wayward children [who] have roamed through the beautiful but delusive regions of Romance, entirely to gratify my restless imagination', now resolving 'to give up my pursuit of fame, withdraw entirely from the scene of action, and, under another name, devote my talents to the service of my God'.[55] Prince's decision to join the Moravian church created problems which were more straightforward, baldly described in the *History*: 'I did not then tell my mistress about it; for I knew that she would not give me leave to go. But I felt I must go' (16).

Strickland's conversion to Congregationalism was accompanied by a conversion of another kind. Instances of the slave narrative genre were often framed by a personal conversion narrative in which, instead of recording progress from sinfulness to Christian belief, the amanuensis describes his or her journey from scepticism to support of the anti-slavery cause. John Newton's account of his transition from slaver to anti-slavery activist in his 1788 pamphlet *Thoughts upon the Slave Trade* was a dramatic instance of the form; less dramatically, many editors of slave narratives confessed to an early opposition or indifference to the tenets of the cause. In the *Narrative of Ashton Warner*, Strickland describes herself as having been 'one of the apathetical and deluded class' whose knowledge of slavery was gained from the press, 'chiefly from literary periodicals on the side of the planters, such as the *Quarterly Review*, *Blackwood's Magazine*, *Blackwood's Magazine*, and other publications of the same class'. The issue was not, she confesses, something to which she had given much serious thought, 'still less imagined that I was a sharer in a great national crime'. She had dismissed first-person accounts of conditions in the West Indies 'as very greatly exaggerated at the least, if not in some cases absolutely fabricated for political purposes'. While she might have accepted slavery as wrong in an abstract sense, that very abstraction, she subsequently realised, enabled her to evade the necessary questions she should have confronted. Her conversion came, she writes, from encounters with individuals. Where Pringle had seen Oppression 'face to face', what Strickland was forced to confront were Mary Prince, Asa-Asa, Ashton Warner and their fellows:

> To their simple and affecting narratives I could not listen unmoved. The voice of truth and nature prevailed over my former prejudices. I beheld slavery unfolded in all its revolting details... the authentic accounts of the real character and effects of the system.[56]

These are key words in anti-slavery discourse – 'simple', 'affecting', 'truth', 'nature', 'authentic' and 'real' – in logical and irresistible combination and conveyed by a believable 'voice'. Wordsworth had written of his intent 'to keep my Reader in the company of flesh and blood, persuaded that by so doing I shall interest him'. In the slave narrative, this agenda is given particular sharpness and force.

***

Central to all of this activity was a belief in the power and importance of print – of not just telling one's story but of recording it in written form and publishing it to the world at large. As Pringle wrote to his friend John Fairbairn, 'Nothing tells permanently so much as a book.'[57] Slave narratives validate the written and printed word, not just in the fact of their existence or accounts they give of their composition, but in the awareness the authors demonstrate within the text of the importance of reading and writing generally. Reading is purposeful, associated with religious conversion, involves duties rather than pleasure and often means reading the Bible. Being prevented from learning to read is one of the charges these narratives bring against slave owners. In the 'Testimony of the Rev. J.M. Trew on Colonial Slavery', an appendix to the *Narrative of Ashton Warner*, the Reverend writes that in the West Indies

> [a]ny general attempt to teach the slave to read should be constructed into an act little short of treason... [to] many planters, the sight of a book in a negro's hand should be viewed with much the same feelings of indignant suspicion, as the Roman Catholic priest would eye the possession of a Bible by an Irish peasant'.[58]

Slave owners realise, he writes, that '[k]nowledge is power', even though, far from inciting violence or insurrection, education 'when tempered with religious instruction' is essential in preserving the peace and securing the colonies.

While Mary Prince might need the assistance of an amanuensis, she was certainly at home in the culture of the printed word. The *History* describes how in Bermuda the granddaughter of her owner used to pass on her reading instruction:

> Directly [Betsey] had said her lessons to her grandmamma, she used to come running to me, and make me repeat them one by one after her; and in a few months I was able not only to say my letters but to spell many small words. (2)

She relates that, after she was sold to the Woods, 'Whenever I carried the children their lunch at school, I ran round and went to hear the teachers' (17). In a footnote Pringle tells us, 'She possesses a copy of Mrs Trimmer's "Charity School Spelling Book", presented to her by the Rev. Mr Curtin, the Anglican minister who baptised her' (17). Prince claims she could not attend his Sunday School because 'he would not receive me without a written note from my master, granting permission' (17). This was obviously a significant charge against the Woods, and one Mr Wood contested in the libel case he brought against Pringle. There he claims that Prince had been taught to read and that, when Rev. Curtin told her to learn the Lord's Prayer, 'she got some of her neighbours to teach her it, and paid them'.[59]

Prince's Moravian church attendance involved educational instruction. The *History* states:

> The Moravian ladies (Mrs Richter, Mrs Olufsen, and Mrs Sauter) taught me to read in the class; and I got on very fast. In this class there were all sorts of people, old and young, grey headed folks and children; but most of them were free people. After we had done spelling, we tried to read in the Bible. After the reading was over, the missionary gave out a hymn for us to sing. (17)

Pringle is cautious about overstating her abilities: 'Her religious knowledge', he writes in his supplement to the *History*, 'not withstanding the pious care of her Moravian instructors in Antigua, is still but very limited, and her views of christianity indistinct' (35). He continued her instruction in his household. The *History* states, 'My dear mistress [that is, Pringle's wife Margaret] teaches me daily to read the word of God, and takes great pains to make me understand it' (22).

In 1832 *The Anti-Slavery Reporter* debated 'the capacity of the slaves for receiving instruction' and decided that 'they were much like other human beings; some were apt, and others very stupid, and some remarkably acute' but 'there appeared in them no natural incapacity whatever for instruction'. The 'retentiveness and minuteness of their memories, and especially in the children' was particularly remarked on, and comparisons were made with the Scottish peasantry, not always to the advantage of the latter group.[60] In her story 'Trifles from the Burthen of Life', Strickland's portrayal of the central character Rachel's debate with her fellow immigrant covers the question of slave educability. Rachel states:

> I taught a black man from the island of St. Vincent to read the Bible fluently in ten weeks; was that a proof of mental incapacity? I never met with an uneducated white man, who learned to read so rapidly, or pursued his studies with the ardour that his poor, despised, soulless negro did. His motive for this exertion was a noble one (and I believe it cost him his life), the hope of carrying the glad tidings of salvation to his benighted and unfortunate countrymen, which he considered the best means of improving their condition, and rendering less burdensome their oppressive yoke.[61]

It is significant that when Prince arrived in Pringle's household she possessed at least one book, *The Charity School Spelling Book* (c.1799) by Sarah

Trimmer.[62] This popular and much reprinted work was a carefully graded text book from which working-class English children could be taught not just reading but moral lessons appropriate to their station in life – as Thomas Laqueur puts it, the lessons of 'civility and gratitude'.[63] The first volume is described in its sub-title as containing *The Alphabet, Spelling Lessons, and Short Stories of Good and Bad Boys in Words of One Syllable Only* with the companion volume containing *Stories of Good and Bad Girls*. Elementary lessons consist of reading exercises such as:

> The Girl makes the boy's shirt.
> Good Girls make their own clothes.
> Good Boys take care of their shoes
> A good Boy likes to have a clean face.
> A good Girl loves to be neat and clean.
> It is a sad sight to see dirt on the skin.[64]

At a more advanced level pupils rehearse:

> If you would be wise and good, you must learn to read your book.
> It is a good thing to learn to read well.
> If you spend all your time in play you will be a dunce.
> None but a dunce will spend all his time in play.
> Play is good when work is done, and the book learnt.[65]

Prince's experience of play was presumably limited, but she may have been influenced in the way she tells her story in the *History* by Mrs Trimmer's emphasis – in the reading exercises and in the short stories of good and bad girls – on hard work, thrift, cleanliness, domestic organisation, and personal responsibility as a way of controlling one's life and improving (within prescribed limits) one's circumstances. The necessarily simple style and plain, straightforward vocabulary of the reading lessons – *in Words of One Syllable Only* and *in Words of Two Syllables Only* – is identical to that of the *History*. And the precision with which Mrs Trimmer's works delineate the material world also resonates with Prince's narrative.

Mrs Trimmer's universe is one of consequences. Good actions have good consequences and bad actions bad consequences, as demonstrated in the story of Ruth Ward, 'one of those cross girls no one loves to be with' who pulls the legs off flies and 'has the ill luck to break her own leg, and it was so bad that it was cut off.⁶⁶ In the section 'Lessons, consisting of words not exceeding two syllables', the reader learns of

> Cicely Parker [who] is a very civil young woman; she lives servant in the house of a merchant in the city, who was once Lord Mayor of London. She is a very good servant; she works hard, and does not care how many rooms she has to scrub; she keeps all that part of the house that is under her care as neat as can be, and in her dress she is quite a pattern of neatness. She covets no fine things; no trimmed caps or bonnets, no long trains to her gown, nor is she above wearing worsted stockings, leather shoes, and a blue apron; but contrives to lay out her money so that, though she has not such high wages as some servants, she saves more money than they do.⁶⁷

In 'Short Stories of Good and Bad Girls' Polly is rewarded by being sent to a school 'where she learnt to spin and knit, and sew and work, and clean a house; and in time she was a nice neat [illeg.] girl and got a good place'.⁶⁸ Another story tells of Patty who does not care for cleanliness: 'Her face was all smut, her hair stood on end for want of a comb, her gown was all grease and rags'. The consequences can be guessed: 'In short she lost her life through dirt; for those who wish to live in such filth as she did, have no chance to get well when they are so bad as she was'.⁶⁹

This is the future world the anti-slavery movement desired for enfranchised slaves – where virtue and justice are consistent with one another, where there are social gradations but each place has its own dignity and its own rewards and where the individual can have a measure of power and freedom over their own fortune. Prince's *History* registers this world as it delineates its obverse – the chaos of slavery and its absence of orderly and just consequences.

* * *

*The History of Mary Prince* begins with a straightforward, confident and uninhibited first-person voice setting out a sequence of undisputed facts:

> I was born in Brackish-Pond in Bermuda, on a farm belonging to Mr Charles Myners. My mother was a household slave; and my father, whose name was Prince, was a sawyer belonging to Mr Trimmingham, a ship-builder at Crow-Lane. When I was an infant, old Mr Myners died, and there was a division of the slaves and other property among the family. I was bought along with my mother by old Captain Darrel, and given to his grandchild, little Miss Betsey Williams. (7)

This opening paragraph, identical in form to that of many other slave narratives, is deceptively simple: many central aspects of the *History* are being established. Its factual specificity is important: place names, personal names, genealogies, chronologies and the like all suggest the verifiable status of what follows. It is important that Prince is presented as having a family. The Anti-Slavery Society's rhetoric emphasised the destructive effect of slavery on family life, and Prince's reference to her parents plays into what Gould describes as 'the sentimental drama of the slave trade's disruption of the African home, and the moral bankruptcy of the social law compared with the natural law'.[70] The matter-of-fact description of the commodification of that family life – 'I was bought along with my mother' – suggests more than simply the vulnerability of the slave's familial bonds. Prince speaks clearly and directly to the reader, but it is made clear from the outset that this is someone who can be bought and given to a child as a possession: 'She [Betsey] used to lead me about by the hand and call me her little nigger' (1).

From the outset, the *History*'s task was to effect in the English public an imaginative identification. Its intention is 'that good people in England might hear from a slave what a slave had felt and suffered' (i). 'I have been a slave myself – I know what slaves feel', Prince says and, furthermore, 'I can tell by myself what other slaves feel, and by what they have told me' (23). She is thus both an individual and a pattern; she voices her own experience, and she is a spokesperson for others. Although it is stressed that the articulation of her *History* is a difficult operation – 'I wish', she says, 'I could find words to tell you all I then felt and suffered; [t]he great God above alone knows the thoughts of a poor slave's heart' (7) – we are continually assured of the task's emotional weight: 'the great grief that filled my heart, and the woeful thoughts that passed to and fro though my mind' (10). Her heart is the organ by which she not only feels, but also tests the truth of all assertions: 'Oh the Buckra [white] people who keep slaves think that the black people are like cattle', she laments, 'without natural affection. But my heart tells me it is far otherwise' (9). Indeed, lack of heart is, she claims, the distinguishing feature of the slave-owning public: 'slavery hardens white people's hearts towards the blacks... Oh those white people have small hearts who can only feel for themselves' (4). Slavery denies that the slave has sensibility; it is the task of the anti-slavery author to counter this belief. Hannah More tells her readers:

> Plead not, in reason's palpable abuse,
> Their sense of feeling callous and obtuse:

> From heads to hearts lies Nature's plain appeal,
> Tho' few can reason, all mankind can feel.[71]

These assertions of feeling are strategically placed and reinforced by their juxtaposition with descriptions of particular instances of cruelty. Dwight A. McBride claims that '[w]e witness... the performance of an inability to bear witness... the rhetorical gesture of unspeakability is, in part, effective because these kinds of horrific images are already part of public discourse'.[72] But in fact the *History* balances between rhetorics of incapacity and focused descriptions of particular events. In between the account of Daniel, too old to keep working, who is beaten by Mr D – and then drenched with salt water, and Ben, who is savagely punished for stealing, Prince observes:

> Oh the horrors of slavery! – How the thought of it pains my heart! But the truth ought to be told of it; and what my eyes have seen I think it is my duty to relate; for few people in England know what slavery is. I have been a slave – I have felt what a slave feels, and I know what a slave knows; and I would have all the good people in England to know it too, that they may break our chains, and set us free. (21)

'Horrors' and 'pains' are processed by 'thought', 'heart', 'truth', 'duty' and 'feeling', offered to the reader framed by the absolute authority of experience: 'I have been a slave'. This extremity of feeling is presented as not something Prince seeks, but something she is forced to bear witness to. Of the death of one fellow slave she writes, 'I could not bear to think about it; yet it was always present in my mind for many a day' (16) – again, expressions of incapacity are set side by side descriptions of exactly what has been claimed is impossible to describe.

Prince and Strickland's readers are asked to engage with the narrative as they would with a novel of sensibility: to follow the plot, but also to become one in emotional sympathy with the characters, not only Prince herself, but also Cyrus, Jack, Hetty, Anthony, Daniel, Ben, Elizabeth the cook and Mash the shoe cleaner. We feel for her because we believe – and it is demonstrated to us – that she herself feels. Markman Ellis writes of 'the two modes in the sentimental novel: on the one hand its efficiency in moulding the emotions and feelings of readers, and on the other, its insertion of matters of political controversy into the text of the novel itself'.[73] Prince's *History* follows this model, one which contains, in Ellis's words, a 'focus on youth, simplicity and "natural feeling"' and a 'preference for (or appearance of) the unpolished and the fragmentary'.[74] Ellis argues, 'The sentimental novel as a genre develops a discussion around a set of issues or themes concerned with reforming British society and manners',[75] a project in which the anti-slavery campaign saw itself taking a central role.

This novelistic mode is at times at odds with the *History's* religious frame of reference. Prince's self-portrayal as suffering victim sits, sometimes uneasily, beside Christian expressions of herself as sinner in need of forgiveness. And her active and pragmatic negotiations with those around her – from her various owners in Bermuda and Antigua to her shipboard companions to the London washerwomen to the ladies and gentlemen of the Anti-Slavery Society – are at odds with her exhibitions of pious fatalism:

> I still live in the hope that God will find a way to give me my liberty, and give me back my husband. I endeavour to keep down my fretting, and leave all to Him, for he knows what is good for me better than I know myself. Yet, I must confess, I find it a hard and heavy task to do so. (37)

There is an echo here of Mrs Trimmer's one-syllable moral lessons:

> If you are good, God will take care of you by night and by day.
> God, if he sees fit, will give you strength to work and sense to earn.
> God will do that which is best for you, and he knows what is best for all.[76]

The two rhetorics, of feeling and of religious abnegation, both central to the Anti-Slavery Society's position, chaff. While the novelistic voice endorses emotion and calls for redress, the Christian code requires acceptance. Prince's suffering, given such weight in other places in the narrative, is here, from a Christian perspective, reduced to 'fretting'.

Set against both the novelistic sensibility of her appeal and the piety of the work's Christian frame is the novel ingredient in Prince's work, the sense of the material world of the slave. This may spring from the factual, legalistic mode in which her presentation is couched. In her poem 'Appeal to the Free', published in the same year as the *History*, Strickland tried to rouse an apathetic public by asking her readers, 'Are your slumbers unbroken by visions of dread?'/ Does no spectre of misery glare on your bed?'[77] Prince's *History* moves its readers not by delivering visions or spectres, but with the particularities of the everyday. There are the specifics of geography: the carefully named places, from Brackish Pond to Hatton Garden. There are the details of work, as precise as anything in Mrs Trimmer's lessons: washing 'bed ticks' and 'bed-coverlets', baking 'supper of potatoes and milk' and a corn soup called 'blawly', picking cotton and wool, planting and hoeing sweet potatoes, Indian corn, currying the horse and 'sometimes... rid[ing] him a little' (13). There is the 'little black silk hat' her mistress Miss Pruden made for her, snatched from her head by her new owner Mrs I– who 'said in a rough voice, "You are not come here to stand up in corners and cry, you are come here to work"' (5); the five bags of clothes 'which we had used at sea, and also such as had been worn since we came on shore, for me and the cook to wash' (19). There is the work in the salt ponds and on the coral reef where the distinction is apparent between the tasks which an English reader would recognise – work similar to that of an English housewife or domestic servant or farm worker – and those which are alien and distressing. Even in the descriptions of the mundane and unexceptional, the reader is reminded that these tasks are undertaken under compulsion, and that their improper performance carries with it sanctions. 'I continued to do my work and do all I could to give satisfaction', Prince says, 'but all would not do' (19). Centrally and serially, there are the specifics of transgression and punishment rendered with a sharp particularity. We are told of 'the exact difference between the smart of a rope, the cart-whip, and the cow-skin' (6) for the faults of a cracked jar or a loose cow. Because the reader has been drawn into the furnished world of Brackish Pond or Date Hill, the rooms, the relationships, the domestic routines, it is not possible to resist also being imaginatively present at the acts of violence. As early as 1787 Ottabah Cugoana, in his *Narrative of Enslavement*, could tell his reader:

> It would be needless to give a description of the horrible scenes which we saw, and the base treatments which we met within this dreadful captive situation, as the similar case of thousands which suffer by this infernal traffic, are well known'.[78]

Prince and Strickland are aware of the danger of reader fatigue, and to counter it lay out the malign in juxtaposition with and framed by the familiar.

'Related by herself', as the title of Prince's *History* reminds us, this sharpness of detail is accompanied by a sense of a sharpness of voice.

We understand, if not the exact nuance, then something of slave society's gradations and differentiations when, in Bermuda, Prince comes upon her drunken master Mr D– beating his own daughter and remonstrates, 'Sir, this is not Turk's Island' (13). The precise naming of the place implies that even violence has its codes and prescriptions; that there are places worse than Bermuda. And the scene suggests, as many anti-slavery commentators claimed, that a society based on slavery will be abusive and degenerate in all its dealings, not just its dealings with the slave population. We are made aware of the intimate specifics that constitute slavery's codes of racial distaste when Prince quotes her mistress saying 'she would not...allow a nigger man's clothes to be washed in the same tub where hers were washed' (18); or when Prince refers to Hetty as a 'French Black' (6); or when she objects to what she calls 'a mulatto woman' – 'a saucy woman, very saucy' – being in authority over her simply 'because I was a slave and she was free' (14). We hear Prince describe the 'light words' of those watching the sale of herself and her family as '[falling] like cayenne on the fresh wounds of our hearts' (4); we hear her say of her new home at Spanish Point, 'The stones and the timber were the best things in it; they were not so hard as the hearts of the owners' (5). We have been told by Pringle, 'These strong expressions, and all of similar character in this little narrative, are given verbatim as uttered by Mary Prince' (5). We trust the detail because it is no more than that.

* * *

At least in part, this specificity is produced as an anticipatory defence against the *History's* critics and detractors. There is a legalistic flavour to what Pringle calls the 'characteristic and minute details' (37) of Prince's account. It resembles an affidavit or witness statement and has, the reader is assured, been subjected to quasi-legal scrutiny. Pringle writes in his preface:

> After [the *History*] had been thus written out, I went over the whole, carefully examining [Prince] on every fact and circumstance detailed; and in all that relates to her residence in Antigua I had the advantage of being assisted in this scrutiny by Mr. Joseph Phillips, who was a resident in that colony during the same period, and had known her there. (iii)

Gillian Whitlock says, 'Ironically, [Pringle] assures us of the truth from Mary's lips – and the certification of this truth by others more authoritative'.[79]

## 4 'THE GENUINE STAMP OF TRUTH AND NATURE': VOICING *THE HISTORY*... 131

But the basis of that authority is admittedly tenuous. Mr Phillips confesses that '[i]n regard to Mary's narrative generally', he 'cannot speak to the accuracy of the details, except in a few recent particulars'. Nevertheless, he feels able to state:

> I can with safety declare that I see no reason to question the truth of a single fact stated by her, or even to suspect her of any instance of intentional exaggeration. It bears in my judgement the genuine stamp of truth and nature. Such is my unhesitating opinion, after a residence of twenty-seven years in the West Indies. (32–3)

The phrase 'the genuine stamp of truth and nature' echoes Strickland's recognition of 'the voice of truth and nature' in the narratives she oversaw. Again, feeling is the mode of assessment. Pringle admits that Prince's account of her life in the West Indies 'must necessarily rest entirely, – since we have no collateral evidence, – upon their intrinsic claims to probability'. In admitting the criteria are subjective, Pringle then proceeds to confidently assert:

> To my judgement, the internal evidence of the truth of her narrative appears remarkably strong. The circumstances are related in a tone of natural sincerity, and are accompanied in almost every case with characteristic and minute details, which must, I conceive, carry with them full conviction to every candid mind that this negro woman has actually seen, felt, and suffered all of that she so impressively describes. (37)

Accompanied by various supplements and appendices, the *History*, as Salih says, resembles 'nothing so much as a lawyers' "bundle" with its witness statements, depositions, and corroborating evidence'.[80] Such compilations were standard practice in the genre, giving evidential credence to the narrative and enabling the more generalised arguments concerning slavery in general to be considered separately from the core work. There was a tonal differentiation between the two parts. In the *Narrative of Ashton Warner* the reader is reassured that Warner's expressions are 'neither dictated by revenge nor by an egotistical desire to recount his own sorrows' and that his account sets out 'the simple facts' rather than a 'recital of revolting cruelty...mournful narratives of human depravity'.[81] But, says Strickland, such disturbing details do have their place and should be considered by the discerning reader who is directed to 'look elsewhere' and find them 'recorded in the publications of the Anti-Slavery Society'. The autobiographical testimony sits side by side and is supplemented by the Anti-Slavery Society witness, in Ashton Warner's case the 'Testimony of Four Christian Ministers, Recently Returned from the Colonies, on the System of Slavery as It Now Exists', but is carefully sectioned from it. The various texts co-exist; they support each other but they do not merge. Just as the slave is believable only when they abjure rhetorical decoration or any ambition to publish their story, so the factual nature of their account is given more weight when it is presented as separated from any abstract or polemical exhortations, or even from any excessively emotive retelling. Pringle is aware of this expectation and of its paradoxical effect: in his supplement to Prince's *History* he reassures his readers that 'there is nothing in the revolting nature of the facts to affect their credibility' (59). In her preface to Ashton Warner's *Narrative*, Strickland confesses that initially it was the excesses of the Anti-Slavery Society's polemics that made her wary of believing them. 'Such tales', she writes, 'appeared far too shocking to be true'.[82]

This wariness may have come, at least in part, from a desire by the Anti-Slavery Society authors to establish a distinction between themselves and the sensational fiction of the period, especially the gothic novel. 'Revolting' themes, 'tales...far too shocking to be true' were this mode of fiction's ground. Jane Austen might defend the novel as a form 'in which the greatest powers of the mind are displayed, in which the most thorough knowledge of human nature, the happiest delineation of its varieties, the liveliest effusions of wit and humour, are conveyed to the world in the best-chosen language'.[83] But the plot of *Northanger Abbey* also demonstrates the dangers of 'the luxury of a raised, restless, and frightened imagination'.[84] Aspects of the novel of sensibility, less concerned with plot than with empathy, might be folded very easily into the slave narrative form, intent as it was on inspiring appropriate feeling in its readers. The intention was that the reader feel and then consider: the anti-slavery cause was founded on a process that led, via imaginative empathy, to a reasoned rejection of the institution of slavery. The gothic novel, on the other hand, is plot-driven. Although the plots contained in the works of Prince, Warner and their fellows were only too consistent with the horrors of the gothic, the very cursory attention paid by the gothic to the moral and the gothic's reliance on sensation as an end in itself, was, for the anti-slavery campaign, counter-productive. In the introduction to *Frankenstein* Mary Shelley writes:

> I have busied myself to think of a story...one which would speak to the mysterious fears of our nature, and awaken thrilling horror – one that would make the reader dread to look around, to curdle the blood and quicken the beatings of the heart.[85]

The slave narrative aims for neither the mysterious nor the thrilling; far from wanting the reader to 'dread to look around', alertness to the world and its injustices are its overt aims. The curdling of the blood and the quickened beating of the heart are of little purpose if unaccompanied by an understanding of their causes and a resolution to reform. So plainness of style and an apologetic warning about the horrific nature of what is described are the norm. The reader is invited to feel empathy. But they are also reassured that their feeling is directed towards a purpose and underwritten by fact and testimony.

\*\*\*

Although an accompanying apparatus was conventional to the slave narrative genre, the supplementary material appended to *The History of Mary Prince* is unusual in content and purpose, being related specifically to Prince's vexed relationship with her Antiguan owners, the Woods. On her behalf, and on behalf of the anonymous Strickland, Pringle sets out the documents at his disposal which counter the Woods' charges against Prince and her defenders. They are many, varied and tortuously interconnected. Participants, all with associated documentation, multiply, testimony to the interconnected web of activity and influence at the Anti-Slavery Society's command. Postscripts and footnotes compound as earlier disputes are refought: the 1829 Report of the Ladies' Society of Birmingham for the Relief of British Negro Slaves, described by Dr Coull and Mr M'Queen of Glasgow as 'an abominable falsehood' (33), is defended by Mr Phillips in a postscript to his letter supporting Prince's *History*. Describing his opponents' position as an 'impudent contradiction of notorious facts' and an 'audacious libel of my personal character', Phillips hints darkly that he 'can furnish further information respecting Dr Coull's colonial proceedings, both private and judicial, should circumstances require it' (33). Pringle weighs in, in a footnote to a postscript, with a defence of the financial dealings of the Birmingham Ladies and their representative Mr Phillips, in which he refers to their 1826 and 1830 reports, as well as the *Glasgow Courier*, the *Leicester Chronicle*, and the *Weekly Register* of Antigua whose charges are, Pringle snorts, 'COMPLETELY REFUTED in our Appendix, No. 4, to which we refer our readers'. For good measure he appends a testimonial to Mr Phillips' good character signed by two members of the Antigua House of Assembly, the collector of customs, and four Antigua merchants, and directs readers to 'others of a more recent date... sufficient to cover with confusion all his unprincipled calumniators'. And if the exhausted reader still needs documentary evidence – and at this stage this seems unlikely – Pringle directs them to '[s]ee also [Mr Phillips'] account of his own case in the Anti-Slavery Reporter, No. 74, p. 60' (footnote 20). Despite the obsessive referencing of every fact and the character references that accompany every actor, it is a difficult narrative for the uninitiated to follow.

Salih describes this material – 'layering' is the term she uses – as 'extremely dense, the texts compressed tightly together', 'a concatenation of mutually validating and interlinked documents'.[86] This suggests more coherence than the collection in fact displays. Rather, it is as if Prince's *History* acts as a trigger to enable the articulation of a multiplicity of issues, arguments, offences, corrections and amendments whose frenetic and splenetic tone is symptomatic of the culmination of the abolitionist campaign. In this documentary storm, personal ties of friendship as well as of deep animosity are evident, and the issue of public reputation is central. Mr Manning, a 'respectable West India merchant', is recorded as offering 'friendly intervention' and 'personal conference' to persuade Mr Wood 'to relent and let the bondwoman go free' (25–6). As a counter, Mr Wood presents 'the ready affirmation of some of his West Indian friends' and 'one or two plausible letters procured from Antigua' (26). There are letters from the Moravian Church's agent in London to the Moravian missionaries in Antigua and back again, from a member of the London Society of Friends to the Governor who is a small-f friend and who replies enclosing a letter from Mr Wood to his (the Governor's) secretary.

The letter is the fullest account of the Woods' case against Prince, and is set out in full with just one omission, indicated by a line of asterisks. In a footnote Pringle states: 'I omit the circumstance here mentioned, because it is too indecent to appear in a publication likely to be perused by females.' Mr Wood's charge is, Pringle asserts, 'in all probability, a vile calumny' and would not add to his case even if true. But, he says reassuringly, if this

## 4 'THE GENUINE STAMP OF TRUTH AND NATURE': VOICING THE HISTORY...

censorship raises doubts, 'Any reader who wishes it, may see the passage referred to, in the autograph letter in my possession' (footnote 19). Pringle is concerned to present himself as fair and even-handed in the exercise of his editorial role. Faced with the suggestion that the Woods are 'grossly misrepresented in [Prince's] narrative' and are in fact 'the most benevolent and kind-hearted people that can possibly live', Pringle is happy to publish supporting evidence. His informant, however,

> [h]as declined to furnish me with any written corrections of the misrepresentation she complains of, although I offered to insert her testimony in [sic] behalf of her friends if sent to me in time. And having already kept back the publication a fortnight waiting for communications of this sort, I will not delay it longer. Those who have withheld their strictures have only themselves to blame. (footnote 22)

This information is contained in a lengthy footnote which begins, 'Since the preceding pages were printed off...' There is a sense here of rapidly evolving debate, in contrast with the reflective, summative recollections of other slave autobiographies where past events are recalled and assessed with the aid of hindsight. The *History's* status as a pamphlet rather than a book is apparent. Nothing is resolved – not the case for abolition, nor Prince's case against the Woods, nor indeed the true character of Mary Prince who is variously portrayed as victim or delinquent, sorely maligned or outrageously and deceitfully exploitative. Her testimony is part of the overall anti-slavery campaign, but it also presented as having a personal urgency, sick, potentially destitute, and far from home and husband as she is said to be. Slavery must be defeated, urge Pringle and his supporters, but at the same time Mr and Mrs Wood must relent and guarantee Prince's right to return to Antigua free.

For this reason, there is an immediacy and a fluidity about the supplementary material that surrounds Prince's more static narrative. There are documents quoted in the text in full and in excerpt, documents described in the text, documents which are not in the text but are referenced, documents Pringle has wanted in the text that have failed to materialise and documents which cannot be in the text but which can, on application to the editor, be accessed elsewhere. Pringle will include all material that arrives ahead of his printing deadline, and he will tell his readers everything in exhaustive detail, except when he cannot tell them. But in such a circumstance he will show them, as long as they are not female.

In fact the suppressed details from Mr Wood's letter are revealed in a letter from Mr Phillips, given in full, which helpfully sets out to counter 'the immoral conduct ascribed to Molly by Mr Wood' by explaining with a relaxed relativism that although Prince may have had 'a connexion with a white person, a Capt.– ... such connexions are so common, I might almost say universal, in our slave colonies', they are 'so very venial as scarcely to deserve the name of immorality'. Context is all, as Mr Wood and his supporters well know. 'The tale of the slave Molly's immoralities', says Mr Phillips, 'be assured, was not intended for Antigua so much as for Stoke Newington, and Peckham, and Aldermanbury' (32).

Despite this, Whitlock points out that in this accompanying contextual material Prince is fashioned as 'virtuous, docile and domesticated'.[87] Pringle calls up evidence of Prince's good character, 'not the less valuable to her because her condition is so humble' (31). What he describes is a range of qualities that one would commend in a servant: she is 'perfectly honest and trustworthy in all respects'; of 'the utmost discretion and fidelity'; 'careful, industrious, and anxious to do her duty and to give satisfaction', albeit 'not, it is true, a very expert housemaid, nor capable of much hard work'. Indeed, he makes his use of the language of the employment reference explicit when he concludes:

> In short, we consider her on the whole as respectable and well-behaved a person in her station, as any domestic, white or black, (and we have had ample experience of both colours,) that we have ever had in our service. (35)

Pringle also reproduces a 'certificate' from Mrs Forsyth 'in whose service' Prince spent the summer of 1829 who describes her as 'honest, industrious and sober' and offers to provide 'her character in full' to '[a]ny person wishing to engage her' (34). In seeking to extract Prince from slavery, Pringle is nonetheless realistic about the kind of place she can expect to occupy in post-abolition society, English or Antiguan.

This is not to say that Pringle denies Prince the subjectivity or sensibility that the *History* has claimed for her. He has learned the lesson of Prince's complaint, 'Oh the Buckra people who keep slaves think that the black people are like cattle without natural affection' (9). Prince has, Pringle tells his readers, 'discretion and fidelity'; 'she is capable of strong attachments, and feels deep, though unobtrusive, gratitude for real kindness shown her'. She has 'natural sense' and 'quickness of observation and discrimination of character'. And as a counter to the charges of Mr Wood – suppressed by

Pringle, justified by Phillips – she is, Pringle asserts, 'remarkable for *decency* and *propriety* of conduct – and her *delicacy*, even in trifling minutiae, has been a trait of special remark by the females of my family' (35).

However, there is a distinct difference between the language Pringle uses to describe Prince and the way he describes Marossi, the Tswana child the family brought with them from South Africa in 1826. In a footnote to his poem 'The Bechuana Boy', Pringle writes of Marossi:

> ...with the gradual development of his feelings and faculties he became interesting to us in no ordinary degree. He was indeed a remarkable child. With a great flow of animal spirits and natural hilarity, he was at the same time docile, observant, reflective and always unselfishly considerate of others. He was of a singularly ingenious and affectionate disposition....[88]

By the time she entered the Pringles' household in 1829, Prince was nearly 40; Marossi was a child – 'still very young when he died, apparently not above eleven, or at most twelve years of age', says Pringle.[89] Romantic notions of childhood innocence and spiritual awareness inform Pringle's description of him. Marossi's African as opposed to Prince's Bermudan origins intensify this distinction, Africa being easier to romanticise as nature unsullied than were the slave-owning West Indies whose less savoury aspects were much in the news as the anti-slavery campaign reached its final stages. As a child Marossi is educable in a way that middle-aged Prince is not. The Pringles' intention was that he should become a missionary or a teacher 'for which he manifested both the wish and the capacity'.[90] In contrast to Prince's 'indistinct' religious knowledge, Pringle assures his correspondent that 'in proportion as [Marossi's] reason expanded, his heart became more thoroughly imbued with the genuine spirit of the gospel'.[91] He is, significantly, described as 'rather a child than a menial attendant',[92] a family member not a domestic servant, and his death, writes Pringle, 'was a very severe stroke to [the childless] Mrs P., who truly loved him as "her own"'.[93] Prince, on the other hand, is presented as a loyal but not very effective domestic. When she appeared as a witness in Pringle's case at against *Blackwood's Magazine*, *The Times* described her as 'a negress of very ordinary features' whom, *Blackwood's* article claimed, Pringle had 'taken from the wash-tub to the closet'.[94] 'Servants in England', said the *Morning Chronicle*, 'were not so transferred from their proper sphere without some object'.[95]

Marossi was the inspiration for Pringle's poem 'The Bechuana Boy'.[96] There he is pictured as a 'swarthy Stripling' with 'foot unshod and naked limb' who has escaped from enslavement by a 'relentless robber clan' of 'stout-manstealers' on 'prancing steeds'. He tells the poet that 'tears and toil have been [his] lot' and that he is 'in the world alone' apart from a pet springbok. In his note to the poem Pringle gives the specifics of their meeting – 'at Milk River in Camdeboo, in September 1825' – but makes it clear that the work is not strictly documentary. The 'incidents in the poem' are 'taken from [the boy's] own simple narrative' except where Pringle can invent something better.[97] Nor does Pringle let Marossi's individual story, real or fabricated, obscure the larger cause. With an incoherent tangle of metaphor he declaims:

> Oh! Englishmen! Thou ne'er canst know
> The injured bondman's bitter woe,
> When round his breast, like scorpions, cling
> Black thoughts that madden while they sting!

In a letter written in August 1829 Pringle expresses the hope that, in 'The Bechuana Boy',

> my aim to attain the simple language of truth and nature has not been entirely unsuccessful. *Condensation* and *simplicity* are *now* my great aims in any poetical attempts, for without these I am satisfied that nothing I may write will *live* – or deserve to live – and many of my early pieces are very deficient, especially in the former of the qualities.[98]

In 1834 Pringle sent a proof copy of the poem to Samuel Taylor Coleridge who failed to see either condensation or simplicity in the piece. He told Pringle:

> I dare say there may be several 'neaths' in my own poems – worse barbarisms, I am sure, there are! But purity of style and even *severe* propriety of words, appear to me more and more, the especial Duty of a Poet....[99]

The angelic qualities of Marossi might be easier to express than was the altogether more problematic character of Mary Prince, the conventions of poetry more easily manipulated than the bald and adversarial form of the slave narrative. But, if we seek 'the simple language of truth and nature' or condensation and simplicity, they are to be found not in 'The Bechuana

Boy' but in the *History* where 'purity of style' and 'severe propriety of words' are key. Marossi is hard to reclaim imaginatively – save perhaps through Mrs P's grief. 'The Bechuana Boy' does not contain his voice or tell his story. But the *History* does in some carefully delineated sense represent Mary Prince as it pedantically sets out the means by which it was produced, deploys its 'words of one syllable only' with forceful effect, and inhabits its genre in a way that is both familiar and disturbing. In fashioning a voice seemingly simple and straightforward, yet which can contain the complex and the horrific, and in manufacturing a collectivity out of sensibility, Christianity, and a meticulously delineated record of the everyday, the *History* introduces its readers to a mode of moral geography where they are compelled to journey back in imagination to Brackish Pond, Spanish Point and Turk's Island. There they can, in the words of Pringle's sonnet, see Oppression 'face to face', not as Pringle would have it, to meet its 'cruel eye', 'cloudy brow', and 'soul-withering glance', not in the form of man-stealers on prancing steeds, but to encounter it in a far more disturbing and familiar mode: as Captain I–, Mr D–, or Mr Woods and his querulous wife, and feel, as Prince did, 'the exact difference between the smart of a rope, the cart-whip, and the cow-skin'.

## Notes

1. Joseph Conder, 'Biographical Sketch of the Author' in Thomas Pringle, *Narrative of A Residence in South Africa*, new edition (London: Edward Moxon,1835), p. xx. (Conder 1835)
2. Jane Meiring, *Thomas Pringle: His Life and Times* (Cape Town: A .A. Balkema, 1968), p. 127. (Meiring 1968)
3. Meiring, *Thomas Pringle*, p. 128. Pringle and Fairburn are described as having 'fought their political battles in the polemical language of regency Britain', Rodney Davenport and Christopher Saunders, *South Africa: A Modern History*, 5th ed. (London: Macmillan, 2000), p. 45. (Davenport and Saunders 2000)
4. Catherine Hall, *Civilising Subjects: Metropole and Colony in the English Imagination, 1830–1867* (Chicago: University of Chicago Press, 2002), p. 107. (Hall 2002)
5. Thomas Pringle, 'The Autumnal Excursion (Addressed to a Friend)', *Ephemerides; or, Occasional Poems written in Scotland and South Africa* (London: Smith, Elder, 1828), p. 3. (Pringle 1828)
6. 'To Sir Walter Scott, Bart', *Ephemerides*, p. 84.

7. 'Amakosìna', *Ephemerides*, p. 99. In a confusion of registers, Pringle describes the way that 'through the glen the hamlets smoke;/ And children gambol round the kraal...', p. 100.
8. 'Song of the Wild Bushman', *Ephemerides*, p. 92.
9. 'Sonnet II: The Hottentot', *Ephemerides*, p. 144.
10. 'The Caffer Commando', *Ephemerides*, pp. 125–7. In later versions 'Christian' becomes 'Colonists'.
11. Damian Shaw, 'Thomas Pringle's "Bushmen": Images in Flesh and Blood', *English in Africa*, 25: 2 (October 1998): 37–61. (Shaw 1998)
12. 'To Oppression', *Ephemerides*, p. 156.
13. As Sue Thomas states, 'Very little is known of the life of Mary Prince after the publication of the third edition of... *The History of Mary Prince*' in 1833, 'New Information on Mary Prince in London', *Notes and Queries*, 58: 1 (2011): 82. (Thomas 2011)
14. Mary Prince, *The History of Mary Prince, a West Indian Slave, Related by Herself; with a Supplement by the Editor; to which is added, the Narrative of Louis Asa-Asa, a Captured African* (London: F. Westley and A.H. Davis, 1831), pp. 23, 11 (*History of Mary Prince, a West Indian Slave* 1831); subsequent page numbers parenthetically in the text.
15. Pringle contests this, saying that 'she had a one time 113 dollars in cash; but only a very small portion of that sum appears to have been brought by her to England, the rest having been partly advanced, as she states, to assist her husband, and partly lost by being lodged in unfaithful custody' (31). But the point still stands – she was active in the money economy.
16. Hall, *Civilising Subjects*, p. 292.
17. Hannah More, 'The Black Slave Trade', *Poems* (London: T. Cadell and W. Davies, 1816), p. 375. (More 1816)
18. To James and Emma Bird, late January 1831, Susanna Moodie, *Letters of a Lifetime*, eds. Carl Ballstadt, Elizabeth Hopkins, and Michael Peterman (Toronto: Toronto University Press, 1985), p. 57. (Moodie 1985)
19. To James Bird, 9 April 1831, Moodie, *Letters of a Lifetime*, p. 60. Strickland continues: 'I refer you, my dear Bard, to the four several descriptions of the speed of our hero and heroine's horses. The Earl of Stadbrooke would give half his estate for such a brace of racers. Your thoughts my friend often outspeed the wind, the lightening, the shooting stars and meteors, but I don't see why your horses' legs should perform miracles to keep pace with the vivid imagination of their Master'.
20. In her preface to the *Narrative*, Strickland writes, 'While Mary's narrative shews the disgusting character of colonial slavery, this little tale explains with equal force the horrors in which it originates' (41).
21. S. Strickland, *Negro Slavery described by a Negro; being the Narrative of Ashton Warner, a Native of St Vincent's; with an Appendix containing the*

*Testimony of Four Christian Ministers Recently Returned from the Colonies on the System of Slavery as it now exists* (London: Samuel Maunder, 1831), p. 15. (Strickland 1831)
22. *Narrative of Ashton Warner*, p. 43, note.
23. *Narrative of Ashton Warner*, p. 17.
24. John Marrant, *A Narrative of the Life of John Marrant of New York in North America; Giving an Account of His Conversion When Only 14 Years of Age* (Halifax: J. Nicholson, 1813), p. v. (Marrant 1813)
25. James Ramsay, *An Essay on the Treatment and Conversion of African Slaves in the British Sugar Colonies* (London: James Phillips, 1784), p. 248. (Ramsay 1784)
26. Philip Gould, *Barbaric Traffic: Commerce and Antislavery in the Eighteenth-century Atlantic World* (Cambridge, MA: Harvard University Press, 2003), p. 68. (Gould 2003)
27. William Shenstone, 'Elegy XX', *Poetical Works of Will [sic] Shenstone, volume 1* (London: Joseph Wenman, 1780), p. 103. (Shenstone 1780)
28. William Wordsworth, Preface to *Lyrical Ballads* (1800), *Prose Works, volume 1*, eds. W.J.B. Owen and Jane Worthington Smyser (Oxford: Clarendon Press, 1974), pp. 118, 124. (Wordsworth 1974)
29. Olaudah Equiano, *The Interesting Narrative of the Life of Olaudah Equiano, or Gustavus Vassa, the African, Written by Himself* (London: Printed for the Author, [1789]), p. iii. (Equiano 1789)
30. Equiano, *Interesting Narrative*, p. iv.
31. *Monthly Review* (June 1789): 551.
32. Ottobah Cugoano, *Narrative of the Enslavement of Ottobah Cugoano, a Native of Africa; Published by Himself in the Year 1787, an Appendix to The Negro's Memorial, or, Abolitionist's Catechism* (London: Hatchard and Co., and J. and A. Arch, 1825), p. 120. (Cugoano 1825)
33. Sara Salih, '*The History of Mary Prince*, the Black Subject and the Black Canon', *Discourses of Slavery and Abolition*, p. 130.
34. *Narrative of Ashton Warner*, p. 44. The presence of the author in person was a form of surety for the authenticity of the works. Frank Shuffelton says of Phillis Wheatley: 'Because doubts had been raised about the authenticity of her writings, her presence was useful to her publisher, no doubt, to establish her credentials as well as to generate interest in the book that was in the press', 'On her Own Footing: Phillis Wheatley in Freedom', *Genius in Bondage: Literature of the Early Black Atlantic*, eds. Vincent Carretta and Philip Gould (Lexington: University Press of Kentucky, 2001), p. 175. (Shuffelton 2001)
35. Olaudah Equiano, *The Interesting Narrative of the Life of Olaudah Equiano*, ed. Angela Costanzo (Peterborough, CA: Broadview, 2004), Appendix A, p. 260; *The Monthly Review* (June 1789): 551. (Equiano 2004)
36. Shirley, Preface, *A Narrative*, p. iii.

37. Vincent Carretta, 'Olaudah Equiano: African British Abolitionist and Founder of the African American Slave Narrative', *The Cambridge Companion to the African American Slave Narrative*, ed. Audrey Fisch (Cambridge: Cambridge University Press, 2007), p. 54. (Carretta 2007)
38. Boyrereau was perhaps responsible for the material described in the sub-title as '*an Account of the Kingdom of Bow-Woo, in the Interior of Africa; with the Climate and Natural Productions, Laws, and Customs Peculiar to That Place; with an Account of His Captivity, Sufferings, Sales, Travels, Emancipation, Conversion to the Christian Religion, Knowledge of the Scripture*'; Prentiss for the '*Strictures on Slavery, Speculative Observations on the Qualities of Human Nature, with Quotation from Scripture*' (St. Albans, Vt.: Harry Whitney, 1810).
39. To James Bird, 9 April 1831, Moodie, *Letters of a Lifetime*, p. 60.
40. To James Bird, late January 1831, Moodie, *Letters of a Lifetime*, p. 57
41. John Jea, *The Life, History, and Unparalleled Sufferings of John Jea, the African Preacher; Compiled and Written by Himself* ('Printed by the author, n.d.), p. 95. (Jea n.d.)
42. To James Bird, late January 1831, Moodie, *Letters of a Lifetime*, p. 57. In keeping with the orientation of Canadian treatments of Strickland/Moodie, the editors give no footnote to indicate who the subject of the work might be.
43. On 21 February 1833, Pringle sued the editor of *Blackwood's Magazine* who had described him as 'taking that wretched tool, Mary Prince, from the washtub to the closet', *The Times*, 22 February 1833, p. 4. On 27 February 1833, Mr Wood sued him for the way the Woods were represented in the *History*. Pringle 'pleaded, besides the general issue, a justification to the greater part of the declaration', *The Times*, 1 March 1833, p. 6. In a 'Sketch' of Pringle's life Leitch Ritchie describes the *Blackwood's* attack as 'composed of the vulgar and silly blackguardism that usually distinguishes, in our civilised age, political partisanship, and confers upon the partisan the air of a common street ruffian', *The Poetical Works of Thomas Pringle, with a Sketch of his Life by Leitch Ritchie* (London: Edward Moxon, 1838), p. civ. (Pringle 1838). Pringle carefully exempts the Anti-Slavery Society from culpability for the contents of the *History* in his preface where he states they 'have no concern whatever with this publication, nor are they in any degree responsible for the statements it contains' (iv). See Sue Thomas, 'Pringle v. Cadell and Wood v. Pringle: the Libel Trials over *The History of Mary Prince*', *Journal of Commonwealth Literature*, 40: 1 (2005): 113–35. (Thomas 2005)
44. Moodie, *Voyages*, p. 227.
45. Misao Dean, 'Susanna Moodie', *Encyclopedia of Post-Colonial Literatures in English*, eds. E. Benson and L.W. Conolly (London: Routledge, 1994), p. 1037. (Dean 1994)

46. Ferguson says in a footnote that Pringle 'spent many years in South Africa... where he espoused traditional white supremacist attitudes towards Africans, evident in his published poetry', Moira Ferguson, *Subject to Others: British Women Writers and Colonial Slavery, 1670–1834* (London: Routledge, 1992), p. 376, footnote 25. (Ferguson 1992)
47. Ferguson, *Subject to Others*, pp. 281–98; p, 379, footnote 47. Strickland mentions her part in Prince's 'pathetic little history in a letter to James Bird (see pp. 16–17), describes herself as Prince's 'Biographer' in another letter (see p. 13), and describes admitting to being the author of 'that canting tract' in a sketch in 'Trifles from the Burthen of Life' (see p. 17). Prince's evidence in Wood *v.* Pringle, 27 February 1833, states 'The History of Her Life Was Written Down by Miss Strickland at Her (the Witness's) Request', *The Times*, 1 March 1833, p. 6.
48. Ferguson, *Subject to Others*, pp. 298, 284.
49. Susanna Moodie, *The Work of Words: the Writing of Susanna Strickland Moodie*, ed. John Thurston (Montreal and Kingston: McGill-Queen's University Press, 1996), p. 59. (Moodie 1996)
50. Gould, *Barbaric Traffic*, p. 145.
51. Salih, '*The History of Mary Prince*, the Black Subject and the Black Canon', *Discourses of Slavery and Abolition*, p. 134.
52. To James Bird, 9 April 1831, Moodie, *Letters of a Lifetime*, p. 60.
53. To James Bird, 11 November 1829, Moodie, *Letters of a Lifetime*, p. 44. The assertion by Ballstadt et al. (*Letters of a Lifetime*, p. 16) that this affiliation did not last, as demonstrated by her marriage in an Anglican church, St Pancras, in April 1831 is challenged by John Thurston: 'It would not be possible for her to get married in a Congregational chapel in 1831' as such places were not licenced for weddings until the civil register was established in 1836, *Voyages: Short Narratives of Susanna Moodie*, ed. John Thurston (Ottawa: University of Ottawa Press, 1991), p. 17. (Moodie 1991)
54. Thurston, *Work of Words*, p. 20.
55. To Mary Russell Mitford, 31 July 1829, *Letters of a Lifetime*, pp. 38–9.
56. Strickland, *Narrative of Ashton Warner*, pp. 6–7.
57. To John Fairburn, July 1834, Meiring, *Thomas Pringle*, p. 168.
58. *Narrative of Ashton Warner*, p. 139.
59. *The Times* (1 March 1833): 6.
60. The report describes 'lettered instruction the knowledge of reading' and explains 'They acquire it in Sunday Schools, which are chiefly attended by adult slaves, and *they* carry it home and spread it diligently'. *The Reporter* says that its source considers that '[w]ith respect to the provident or improvident use of money, he thought them pretty much like the peasantry of other countries, but considerably less given to intoxication than the

peasantry of Scotland, and infinitely less than the soldiery that go out to the colonies, the mortality among whom is attributed to their fondness for spirits,' *The Anti-slavery Reporter*, 5: 13 (31 December 1832): 321, 338.
61. Moodie, *Voyages*, pp. 227–8.
62. Mrs [Sarah] Trimmer, *The Charity School Spelling Book; Part One, Containing the Alphabet, Spelling Lessons, and Short Stories of Good and Bad Boys, in Words of One Syllable Only; and Short Stories of Good and Bad Girls, in Words of One Syllable Only*, new edition, (London: F.C. and J. Rivington, 1810) (Trimmer 1810). *Part Two* is subtitled *Containing Words Divided into Syllables; Lessons with Scriptural Names, etc.* and contains advanced lessons, with reading exercises of animal fables and Bible stories.
63. Thomas Laqueur, *Religion and Respectability: Sunday Schools and Working Class Culture, 1780–1850* (New Haven: Yale University Press, 1976), p. 191. (Laqueur 1976)
64. Trimmer, *Charity School Spelling Book; Part One*, p. 16.
65. Trimmer, *Charity School Spelling Book; Part One*, p. 17.
66. Trimmer, *Charity School Spelling Book; Part One*, pp. 34–5.
67. Trimmer, *Charity School Spelling Book; Part Two*, pp. 19–20.
68. Trimmer, *Charity School Spelling Book; Part One*, p. 34.
69. Trimmer, *Charity School Spelling Book; Part One*, p. 32.
70. Gould, 'The Rise, Development, and Circulation of the Slave Narrative', *Cambridge Companion to the Slave Narrative*, p. 13.
71. Moore, 'The Black Slave Trade', p. 381.
72. Dwight A. McBride, *Impossible Witnesses: Truth, Abolitionism, and Slave Testimony* (New York: New York UP, 2007), p. 94. (McBride 2007)
73. Markman Ellis, *The Politics of Sensibility: Race, Gender and Commerce in the Sentimental Novel* (Cambridge: Cambridge UP, 1996), p. 2. (Ellis 1996)
74. Ellis, *Politics of Sensibility*, p. 3.
75. Ellis, *Politics of Sensibility*, p. 49.
76. Trimmer, *Charity School Spelling Book; Part One*, pp. 21–2.
77. Susanna Strickland (now Mrs Moodie), 'An Appeal to the Free', *Enthusiasm; and Other Poems* (London: Smith, Elder, 1831), p. 78 (Strickland 1831). The volume is dedicated to James Montgomery, the poet and preacher. Cedrick May writes that 'throughout the eighteenth and nineteenth century, the word *enthusiasm* had pejorative connotations', *Evangelism and Resistance in the Black Atlantic, 1760–1835* (Athens, GA: University of Georgia Press, 2008), p. 18. (May 2008). The volume was reviewed by *La Belle Assemblée*, to which Strickland had been a regular contributor, who noted that 'with many of its brightest gems and sweetest flowers the pages of *La Belle Assemblée* have already been enriched' but felt that '[a] great portion of this volume, but, in our view, by far the least interesting, the least effective and meritorious in point

of talent, is of a religious cast', *La Belle Assemblée, or Court and Fashionable Magazine*, XIV (July–December 1831): 36.
78. *Narrative of the Enslavement of Ottobah Cugoano*, pp. 124–5.
79. Gillian Whitlock, 'Volatile Subjects: *The History of Mary Prince*', *Genius in Bondage: Literature of the Early Black Atlantic*, eds. Vincent Carretta and Philip Gould (Lexington: University Press of Kentucky, 2001), p. 76. (Whitlock 2001)
80. Salih, 'The History of Mary Prince, the Black Subject and the Black Canon', *Discourses of Slavery and Abolition*, p. 125.
81. *Narrative of Ashton Warner*, p. 15.
82. *Narrative of Ashton Warner*, p. 7.
83. *Northanger Abbey*, chapter 5.
84. Catherine Moreland is exercising her imagination 'over the pages of *Udolpho*, lost from all worldly concerns of dressing and dinner, incapable of soothing Mrs. Allen's fears on the delay of an expected dressmaker, and having only one minute in sixty to bestow even on the reflection of her own felicity, in being already engaged for the evening', *Northanger Abbey*, chapter 7.
85. Mary Shelley, *Frankenstein*, introduction.
86. Salih, '*The History of Mary Prince*, the Black Subject and the Black Canon', *Discourses of Slavery and Abolition*, p. 132.
87. Gillian Whitlock, *The Intimate Empire: Reading Women's Autobiography* (London: Cassell, 2000), p. 21. (Whitlock 2000)
88. Note to 'The Bechuana Boy', *Poetical Works of Thomas Pringle*, p. 72. A letter, recipient not given, quoted by Leitch Ritchie in the memoir contained in this volume, expresses the same feelings in slightly different language, p. cxliii–cxliv. The final stanza of 'The Bechuana Boy' is: 'We took him for "our own."'/ And One, with woman's gentle art,/ Unlocked the fountains of his heart;/ And love gushed forth – till he became/ Her Child in every thing but name', p. 8.
89. *Poetical Works of Thomas Pringle*, p. cxliv.
90. *Poetical Works of Thomas Pringle*, p. cxliii.
91. *Poetical Works of Thomas Pringle*, note, p. 72.
92. Pringle writes, 'The poor dear boy, whose history suggested those verses [i.e., 'The Bechuana Boy'], was received by me as a little servant for Mrs P., to whom he speedily became most affectionately attached; but as his intellect and disposition unfolded themselves, he exhibited so much amiable and excellent feeling, and good sense and delicacy, that he became to us rather a chid than a menial attendant', *Poetical Works*, p. cxliii.
93. *Poetical Works of Thomas Pringle*, p. cxliii–iv. Ritchie does not give the name of the recipient of the letter. Marossi was baptised in 1827 and died eighteen months later of 'a pulmonary complaint', *The Poetical Works of Thomas Pringle*, note, p. 72.

94. Pringle *v.* Cadell, Court of Common Pleas, 21 February 1833; *The Times*, 22 February 1833, p. 4.
95. *Morning Chronicle*, 22 February 1833, p. 4. The article continues: 'It was but a great criterion of the respectability of the female branches of Mr Pringle's family who consented to live in such a hotbed of immorality'.
96. Pringle, 'The Bechuana Boy', *African Sketches* (London: Edward Moxon, 1834), pp. 1–8. (Pringle 1834)
97. *African Sketches*, note, p. 501. In a letter of 29 August 1829 Pringle writes: 'I have not adhered strictly to his real story in every point, and have represented him as rather older than he was, and capable of more deep feeling and reflection than he appeared to possess when he *first* came under my charge, though not more than what he attained before he died. The destruction of his tribe and kindred, and his being sold to a boor, &c., are all as he related; but the springbok, and his mode of joining us, are poetical licenses', *Poetical Works*, p. cxliv. In the poem the child speaks 'in the language of his race'; in the notes describing the actual encounter, Pringle reports that Marossi said, 'Ik ben alleenig in de waereld' 'in his broken Dutch', *African Sketches*, note, p. 501. The child in the poem is older than Marossi was, 'though not more than what he had attained before he died', and what Pringle describes as 'his mode of joining us' was in actuality different, *Poetical Works*, p. cxliv.
98. *The Poetical Works of Thomas Pringle*, p. cxliii.
99. South African Library, Cape Town, MSB 393, 1 (8), 'Thomas Pringle'; see Peter Anderson, 'Home Truths: Samuel Taylor Coleridge Advises Thomas Pringle', *The Coleridge Bulletin*, new series, 28 (Winter 2006): 26 (Anderson 2006b). Coleridge suggested Pringle change the line, '"I have no kindred!" said the boy' to '"I have no Home" replied the boy'. Anderson (27) writes: 'Pringle went with his suggestion, though he dropped Coleridge's characteristic (and here significant) capital "H"'.

CHAPTER 5

# Culture's Artificial Note: E. Pauline Johnson, Tekahionwake, and her Audiences

On 10 October 1884, the *Washington Post* reported a curious ceremony which had taken place in the town of Buffalo on the previous day. 'The remains of the celebrated Iroquois Chief Red Jacket' and his fellow chiefs, identified by the *Post* as 'Destroy Town, Young King, Little Billy and Tall Peter', were re-interred in what the paper described as a 'beautiful lot donated for the purpose by the Forest Lawn Association'.[1] The *Post* carefully recorded the tribal affiliations of the pall-bearers – Onondaga, Cayuga, Oneida, Mohawk, Seneca and Tuscarora. Many were 'wearing their native costumes' and 'recit[ing] the usual Indian funeral dirge', although the cortege that escorted the cedar caskets was overwhelmingly composed of the local Historical Society, the 'lady members' laying flowers at the grave sites which were decorated with American flags. Although 'a short prayer in the Seneca tongue' began proceedings and the pall-bearers 'chanted a dirge which is introduced in burial ceremonies and where chiefs are elevated to places made vacant by death', the proceedings' dominant tone was ethnographic, and included 'an interesting and historical address' by Rev. William C. Bryant, who displayed a wampum belt 'which has been in the Iroquois tribe for 300 years'.

The reconciliatory tone of the occasion is utterly at odds with the history of Red Jacket's death and original burial in 1830. Then there had been conflict over his religious affiliations, accounts attributing to him, variously, a resolutely pagan end or Christian conversion. His biographer William L. Stone claimed that notwithstanding the brave resolutions in anticipation of the time of his departure, to die as he had lived and be buried as a pagan, there is reason to believe that he relented not a little in the bitterness of his hostility toward the missionary and the religion he taught.

But then Stone seemingly contradicted himself by saying that at the moment of death Red Jacket had deployed a vial of water 'all-sufficient to secure his spirit unobstructed flight to the fair hunting-grounds'. Stone quotes the *Missionary Herald* which claimed that 'very grievous misrepresentations' had been made by 'disappointed white pagans' whose accounts were 'like most other dramatic compositions... an entire fiction'. But he also cites Colonel McKenney who describes the Christian funeral, 'considering the opinions of the chief', as being 'as idle as it was indecorous... their lifeless chief in the sanctuary of that religion he had always opposed'. McKenney claimed that Red Jacket's kin had 'hastened from the scene which overwhelmed them with humiliation and sorrow'.[2]

Red Jacket's grave at the mission church at Buffalo Creek was originally unmarked until an admirer provided for a marble slab, which was then vandalised. As early as 1852, the Ojibwa missionary and writer George Copway gave two lectures in Buffalo pointing to the grave's neglect. The graveyard itself provides a small symbolic narrative of land alienation and bad faith. Although the 1842 Treaty with the Seneca seemed to imply that the church grounds were protected, they were sold to Ogden Land Company. Bryant, who was the secretary of the Buffalo Historical Society, wrote to Union Civil War general and Seneca chief Ely S. Parker in 1884 'the old Mission Cemetery, I grieve to say, has been invaded by white foreigners who are burying their dead there with a stolid indifference to every sentiment of justice or humanity'.[3] Copway, with a Buffalo business man named Hotchkiss and the local undertaker, exhumed the bones and placed them in Hotchkiss' cellar. Local Seneca confronted Hotchkiss, took the bones away and gave them to a stepdaughter of Red Jacket. She buried them secretly where they remained for some time. But as she got older she worried that knowledge of the grave might be lost, and consulted Rev. Asher Wright, 'a faithful missionary among the Senecas for nearly half a century',[4] who approached the Buffalo Historical Society.

This is a process common throughout the settler empire: Indigenous knowledge threatened as the owners of that knowledge become (or are believed to have become) extinct, and the transfer of that knowledge to the modern European systems of antiquarianism and ethnography. Red

Jacket's bones rested in a box in the storeroom of the Buffalo Historical Society, where the skull was measured and its remarkable likeness to 'that of a Caucasian rather than an Indian' was noted. The oral testimony of two old men who remembered Red Jacket was recorded: 'there is no doubt that he was a full-blooded Indian, though one says he had the eyes of a white man'.[5] Like the wampum belt, Red Jacket had, literally, become a collector's curio. The story provides an exhaustive list of Victorian attitudes to race: a dedication to Christian conversion versus admiration for the primitive pagan; land dispossession allied with a romanticised appropriation by the settler society of Indigenous cultural forms; the displacement of the figure of the native into archaic time and poetic space; the exact applications – computational and mathematical – of the emerging science of ethnography to codify racial distinctions. The Indian becomes a ghost in the settlers' self-narrative, his history re-enacted within settler history and his bones the raw data for ethnographic theorising. It is only – and this is quite a large proviso – the active presence of those Onondaga, Cayuga, Oneida, Mohawk, Seneca and Tuscarora pall-bearers at Red Jacket's interment, with their 'usual Indian funeral dirge[s]', who attest to an Indian presence.

Among those at the re-interment, the *Washington Post* recorded 'two young ladies in black, descendents of another noted Indian chief'.[6] Canadian Pauline Johnson and her sister Evelyn were the daughters of Mohawk George Johnson and English-born Emily Howells. The occasion's odd mixture of Indigenous ceremonial and antiquarian public lecture is not reflected in Pauline Johnson's poem 'The Re-interment of Red Jacket', which was published the next year in the *Transactions of the Buffalo Historical Society*.[7] The poem's tone is lyrical and elegiac, working as a mechanism for putting the memory of the Indigenous past somewhere safe – into officially sanctioned and sanitised history, and into literature, consigned to the poetic and the archaic, an even 'deeper quiet', as the poem puts it, than the quiet of the graveyard. Red Jacket is now part of the naturalised rather than acculturated order, and thus not part of modern discussions of community or nation:

> Sweet Indian Summer sleeps,
> Trusting a foreign and a paler race
> To give her gifted son an honoured place....[8]

The poem concedes Red Jacket's eloquence and his force, his 'higher flush of oratory' and his 'thought so vast, and liberal, and strong',[9] but that is cited as evidence of his membership of a dying race. Paradoxically, his very energy proves his people's exhaustion:

> The world has often seen
> A master mind pulse with the waning day
> That sends his waning nation to decay
> Where none can intervene.

The complex and conflicted narrative of Red Jacket's ante-mortem existence has no place in the poetic version of his reburial. The central voice in the poem is a personified 'Indian Summer', Indigenised Nature and sentimentalised Indigeneity, which welcomes the presence of the European, adopting their rhetoric of patriotism and settler justification:

> O, rising nation of the West,
> That occupies my land so richly blest;
> O, free, unfettered people that have come
> To make America your rightful home,
>
> Forgive the wrongs my children did to you,
> And we, the red skins, will forgive you too;
> To-day has seen your noblest action done,
> The honoured re-entombment of my son.

'[F]ew to-day remain' of Red Jacket's kin, the poem laments, but the poet herself can identify with remnants:

> ... copper-tinted face and smouldering fire
> Of wilder life, were left me by my sire
> To be my proudest claim.

Johnson's position as mixed-race, English mother and Mohawk father, is fashioned into a form of poetic authority as she speaks from one side of her heritage and to the other, implying that, as she in her person combines and embodies the two sides, there can be no conflict. But her poem, with its dying race frame and its conciliatory ventriloquism of Indigenous approval of the settler presence, is part of the Historical Society's civic celebration. It does not give a voice to the bones that are being interred or even reflect the evident, significant Indigenous presence at the re-interment.

The narrative her poem points to is not that of Red Jacket, or of his mourners, but of their necessary effacement by the modern settler nation.

When Pauline Johnson died in Vancouver on 7 March 1913 the Toronto *Globe* published an obituary on its front page.[10] Identifying her with 'that eminent group of writers who half a generation ago constituted the Augustan age in Canadian poetry', it described Johnson as a 'unique and individual singer, the lyricist of nature' noted for her 'epics of Canadian life and scenery in the broad outdoors of the north and west'. The writer notes the widening scope of her later work with its focus on the 'cosmopolitan' and her significance in expressing particularly Canadian aspirations of 'national development and civilization' as well as 'its individuality, its virility'. But it is, the paper decides, as 'the interpreter of the thoughts of a dying race' that she is most noteworthy, 'a spirit of rebellion breathing through those passionate verses, representing the red man's protest... its complete expression of love for the red men and their free life':

> [s]he became at once the voice of the hitherto inarticulate wards of the nation, and if she pictured a miserable present for the Indians, she was equally proud of a glorious past....

Johnson had made regular appearances in the *Globe* from the early 1890s until her move to Vancouver in 1909. As early as 1893, readers enjoyed a full page 'handsome photogravure' of 'this clever Canadian Indian... in a number of her platform representations'.[11] She featured in an 'Art Calendar' with poets of the 'confederation' school, Archibald Lampman, C.G.D. Roberts, Charles Heavysege, Bliss Carman and W.W. Campbell.[12] She was included in an article on 'what Canadian women had done and are doing in journalism'.[13] A piece on 'Canadian Literature' describes her as 'that interesting authoress... whose Indian songs are very vivid and full of spirit'.[14] 'Canadian Women Who Are Poets' in the 'Canadian Poets Series' notes that her 'Indian compositions [are] making her famous from the Atlantic to the Pacific', although the author here chooses to 'quote a stanza from her "Birds' Lullaby", which is an exquisite example of her work outside her Indian poetry'.[15] A review of *The Encylopaedia of Canada* notes her contributions on 'the organization and history of the Iroquois'.[16] And a review of Theodore Harding Rand's 1900 *Treasury of Canadian Verse* praises her poems, although in keeping with the collection's purpose (the *Globe's* reviewer states that it 'would do credit to any nation') her more inclusive pieces – the lyrical, the Christian and the patriotic – are preferred over her 'Indian compositions'.[17]

Performance was an essential component of Johnson's poetic practice; that her appearance was seen as an inextricable part of her poetic persona is suggested in a review that claimed that the reader 'has only to look upon the face of the portrait here reproduced to conclude that the poems of Indian life and love which make up this delightful edition are the work of a most accomplished writer'.[18] From the early 1890s the paper carried advertisements for and reviews of her public performances: taking part in a poets' evening with Miss Machar, Reade, Duncan Campbell Scott, Lampman and Campbell;[19] as member of the Gordon Shaw Opera Company (she played Nedda in *I Pagliacci* and Lola in *Cavalleria Rusticana*)[20]; and as a performer in her own right:

> One of the most popular forms of entertainment in Toronto is the dual recital, and certainly the most popular entertainment of this description is furnished by Miss Pauline Johnson, the Mohawk poetess, and Mr Owen Smily, the popular reader....[21]

The recital was a refined form of entertainment, on par with and often in the same bill as the public lecture or musical performance. Owen Smily, Johnson's professional partner from 1892 to 1897, had a reputation as a 'poet-elocutionist', often performing his own work, 'primarily in places like Massey Hall, a locale for serious theatre and symphonic concerts' for middle-class audiences. He was also the director of a school of elocution, and 'the preferred lecturer for unusual and high-profile events...his speciality was the patriotic'.[22] Reviewers praised his 'humorous and dialect work' and his Dickensian sketches. He might, one review conceded, 'almost be called the Canadian Grossmith'.[23] Walter McRaye, Johnson's partner from 1901 to 1909, was described, similarly, in terms of his refinement: 'Humour, rare goddess, is his and his also is romance. He is par excellence the best reader of dainty poems I have ever heard....'[24] McRaye specialised in dialect poetry, especially the 'habitant' poetry of William Henry Drummond[25] which mimicked the voice of the French-Canadian 'pauvre illettré':

> De place I get born, me, is up on de reever
> Near foot of de rapide dat's call Cheval Blanc

> Beeg mountain behin' it, so high you can't climb it
> An' whole place she's mebbe two honder arpent.
>
> De fader of me, he was habitant farmer,
> Ma gran' fader too, an' hees fader also,
> Dey don't mak' no monee, but dat isn't fonny
> For it's not easy get ev'ryt'ing, you mus' know –
>
> All de sam' dere is somet'ing dey got ev'ryboddy,
> Dat's plaintee good healt', wat de monee can't geev,
> So I'm workin' away dere, an' happy for stay dere
> On farm by de reever, so long I was leev.[26]

While Johnson's Indian poems are markedly different in tone and intent, being emphatically dignified and rhetorical, her Indians speaking in the cadences of Longfellow and Tennyson, it is worth thinking about the effect of their theatrical juxtaposition with McRaye's habitant items. Neither mode was intended to challenge or disturb the mainstream Canadian audience. 'One great merit of this style of poetry' said a reviewer of McRaye's habitant verse 'is that it is free from obscurity and can be easily followed and thoroughly comprehended by persons who are not acquainted, in the slightest, with the French language'.[27] Both enact a voice; in both cases that voice is other – demotic or marginalised. The performance not only invites sympathy but also allows amusement and condescension.

Johnson as 'lady-elocutionist' or 'lady-poetess' was praised for her 'unique and refined recitals'.[28] In their joint compositions she was 'Miss Poetry' to Smily's 'Mr Prose'.[29] In Toronto and Ottawa the socially select nature of their audience was stressed, the Lieutenant Governor and his wife being often in attendance. When she travelled with Smily and later with McRaye away from the main cities, their engagements were often held under the auspices of a local church, and often in aid of a worthy local cause. Thus Johnson's decision to dress in costume for the performance of her Indian poems needed to be carefully managed and calibrated. She needed to be dramatic but still lady-like. She needed to demonstrate the authority of her Indian blood without drawing attention to what was a less romantically conceived mixed-race status.[30] She needed to draw on the cultural capital of her poetry rather than call attention to the more unstable role of actress. And she certainly would not want to invite comparison with the 'Wild West' shows of Buffalo Bill Cody and the like.

Johnson developed her 'Indian princess' costume around 1892. The process was not straightforward. She wrote to W.D. Lighthall: 'For my Indian poems I am trying to get an Indian dress to recite in, and it is the most difficult thing in the world!'[31] There was, in fact, no 'Indian dress' for Six Nations women, who had habitually worn tunics, leggings and blankets like men. Moreover, Johnson and her sister had never worn anything other than decorous garb of the late nineteenth-century middle-class European woman. So the disposition of 'beads, quills, sashes, brooches, or indeed anything at all' that she sought had to be consciously invented, what she called 'getting up a costume'. She stressed that her dress should be 'one that is made up of *feminine* work'. 'Can you tell me', she wrote to Lighthall, 'if the "Indian Stores" in Montreal are *real* Indian stores, or is their stuff manufactured? I want a pair of moccasins, worked either in coloured moose hair, porcupine quills, or very heavily with *fine coloured beads*, have you ever seen any such there?' The final effect, purchased from the Hudson Bay Company in Winnipeg, demonstrated the eclectic nature of her affiliations, from the deeply authentic and personally sourced to the theatrical and manufactured: she decorated the department store tunic with animal pelts on which were pinned her grandmother's silver trade brooches. 'Several N.W. Reserves' were asked 'about getting some bead work done on my dress'. She wore her father's hunting knife; a Huron scalp which had belonged to her grandfather hung on her belt; and the scarlet blanket which had been used in 1869 when Prince Alfred, Queen Victoria's youngest son, had been made an honorary chief of the Six Nations was worn over her shoulders.[32] At Lighthall's suggestion, she asked Charles Mair, immigration agent and author of the verse drama *Tecumseh* (1886), for help with the more recondite items of decoration: eagles' feathers, bears' teeth and claws, arrows. At first, she wore a band embroidered with beads around her neck. Later Ernest Thompson Seton, founder of the boys' organisation Woodcraft Indians and first Chief Scout of the American branch of the Boy Scouts, gave her a necklace of bear's claws. Her influences thus demonstrate a circularity, Mair's poetry and Thompson Seton's Woodcraft Indians having themselves taken inspiration from the Indian material to which Johnson, by virtue of her family, had access.

Contemporary literary texts also offered inspiration, especially Longfellow's *Hiawatha* – Johnson' sister Evelyn said that she copied her dress from 'a picture we had of Minnehaha', perhaps one Frederic Remington's popular illustrations with their detailed concentration on clothes and accessories.[33]

The clothes worn by Longfellow's Indians are carefully described in his verse. At the wedding feast of Hiawatha and Minnehaha, for example, guests are 'clad in all their richest raiment,/ Robes of fur and belts of wampum,/ Splendid with their paint and plumage,/ Beautiful with beads and tassels'[34]. The warrior Pau-Puk-Keewis is:

> Dressed in shirt of doeskin,
> White and soft, and fringed with ermine,
> All inwrought with beads of wampum
> ...dressed in doeskin leggings,
> Fringed with hedgehog quills and ermine,
> And in moccasins of buck-skin,
> Thick with quills and beads embroidered.
> On his head were plumes of swan's down,
> On his heels were tails of foxes,
> In one hand a fan of feathers,
> And a pipe was in the other.[35]

Longfellow's poems were heavily influenced by the work of Henry Rowe Schoolcraft. In Schoolcraft's 1843 poem 'Alhalla, or the Lord of Talladega: a Tale of the Creek War', Clewalla wears 'the eagle plume' which

> Bespoke a warrior, not a groom
> Decked for the dance, with gay metasse,
> And figured band, and bell of brass.
> A collar of the sacred shell
> He wore, that graced his figure well.
> Loose was his robe of banded blue,
> And ample fold, and gather true.[36]

In her essay 'A Strong Race Opinion', written for the *Sunday Globe* at this time, Johnson attacks the bland and stereotyped Indian maiden of contemporary fiction, totally devoid of specific characteristics of tribe or even surname, though always the daughter of a chief, and always in the grips of a doomed love affair with the European hero.[37] This figure is the product, Johnson argues, of ignorance: 'half of our authors who write up Indian stuff have never been on an Indian reserve in their lives, have never met a "real live" Redman, have never even read Parkman, Schoolcraft or Catlin'.[38] But it is also, she claims, a function of the lazy invocation of established literary convention:

> The general author gives the reader the impression that he has concocted the plot, created his characters, arranged his action, and at the last moment has been seized with the idea that the regulation Indian maiden will make a very harmonious background whereon to paint his pen picture, that, he, never having met this interesting individual, stretches forth his hand to his library shelves, grasps the first Canadian novelist he sees, reads up his subject, and duplicates it in his own work.

Canadian authors, she writes, need to move beyond this shorthand and engage with the various aspects of the real thing, whether 'wild' or 'cultivated':

> [l]et the Indian girl of fiction develop from the 'doglike', 'fawnlike', 'deer-footed', 'fire-eyed', 'crouching', 'submissive' book heroine into something of the quiet, sweet womanly woman she is, if wild, or the everyday, natural, laughing girl she is, if cultivated and educated....

However, it is difficult to see how Johnson's carefully constructed stage persona differed from the clichés she so despises. The conflation of 'never been on an Indian reserve in their lives', 'never met a "real live" Redman' and 'never even read' the European ethnographers Parkman, Schoolcraft or Catlin is significant. Written sources are seen as equal to lived experience. Both aspects are presented as being essential and under Johnson's purlieu – as Cathy Rex puts it with regard to Copway, Johnson is 'placing [herself] on both sides of the ethnologist's office'.[39] In this, as in so much of Johnson's career, one senses the necessary negotiations and compromises she had to make with the middle-class Anglo-Canadian society she wished to inhabit, its expectations, not to mention the exigencies of financial survival, more and more precarious as she got older. The sharpness, the New Woman feminism, and the political engagement evident in her journalism are in marked contrast to the caution with which she conducted her career as a performer, and this caution is manifest in her poetry.

Johnson's appearance in her Indian garb was bracketed by the non-Indian portion of the evening's entertainment during which she wore an elegant evening dress. It has been suggested that her change from Indigenous to

European costume constituted a kind of dramatic vanishing.[40] In fact, reviews suggest that this was not necessarily the order of performance. *The Globe* in November 1893 described the sequence:

> The audience gave a fresh welcome when she appeared in her handsome striking Indian costume, in which she rendered a most powerful and graphic Indian poem, entitled 'The Cattle Thief'....[41]

In Nellie McClung's memoir *The Stream Runs Fast* she recalls a performance in the Methodist Church in Manitou, Manitoba in the early 1890s:

> Pauline's advertising had shown only the Indian girl in her beaded chamois costume and feather headdress, so when a beautiful young woman in white satin evening dress came out of the vestry door and walked to the platform, there was a gasp of surprise from the audience. Pauline smiled at us reassuringly, knowing what was in our minds.
> 'I am going to be a white woman first', she said in her deep voice, 'the Indian part will follow'.[42]

It was not, perhaps, the order in which the two costumes were worn that was the issue, but her facility to move from one to the other and back, the extreme formality of the evening dress being as important as the exoticism of the buckskin, especially in the more remote locations that she and McRaye toured in the early 1900s. McRaye describes Johnson in one small settlement being approached by a shabby Englishman who told her tearfully 'it was the first time in years he had seen a woman in evening dress' and that it reminded him of his mother.[43] As Mary Elizabeth Leighton suggests:

> [i]nstead of acknowledging the ways in which Johnson's performances hinted at the performability of identity, [her audience] interpreted her change of clothing as a barometer of her assimilation and the diminution of the threat that massed Native peoples, dissatisfied with such injustices, might have posed.[44]

In fact Johnson did not limit herself to the two alternative costumes of her stage performances. Of the cluster of seven photographs in *The Globe* of 23 September 1893 entitled 'Miss E. Pauline Johnson, the Indian Poet Reciter' only one is of her in her Indian costume; others show her in evening dress and in sporty outdoor wear, possibly the outfit of a skater or canoeist. These were pursuits which carried general nationalistic overtones. In an essay 'Outdoor Pastimes for Women' Johnson writes: '[o]n a midwinter's night one feels the pulse of a hot national blood awake in one's veins, that demands with every heart beat a special mention of Canada's national winter sports, in which both lads and lasses participate...And now abideth these three – skating, tobogganing and snowshoeing.' New Woman feminism, dress reform, and nationalism converge: the essay concludes with an image of 'little Lady Canada' making her way through a snowy landscape accompanied by a 'big jovial lad' whose help she declines, saying 'she can get along famously by herself, thank you'.[45]

The two Indian poems most commonly mentioned in accounts of Johnson's stage performances are 'A Cry from an Indian Wife', first published in *The Week* on 18 June 1885 and 'frequently reprinted in newspaper accounts of her performances from 1892 onward'[46] and 'The Cattle Thief', probably originally written for performance, which was first published in *The Week* on 7 December 1894.[47] Both poems function as performance texts, meaning that they were changed and adapted according to the demands of audience, programming and context, and the 'final' forms in which they appeared in Johnson's collections *The White Wampum* (1895), *Canadian Born* (1903) and the posthumous *Flint and Feather* (1912) do not necessarily convey the dynamics of this process.

'A Cry from an Indian Wife' was originally written at the time of the Northwest Rebellion, Louis Riel's loose alliance of Métis, Plains Indians, and white settlers. Linda M. Morra notes that the first performance of the poem 'attracted considerable notice, and is seen as launching Johnson on a touring career spanning fifteen years'.[48] The positive response, then and at later performances, Morra suggests, indicates 'that she was successful in her deployment of trauma and intimacy as the primary means to diminish the relational gap between her and her audience, to evoke sympathy, and to render a perspective that had been otherwise excluded'.[49] Yet, on the page, this is done very tentatively. The poem's position vacillates, moving from sympathy for the lamenting Indian wife to a patriotic affiliation to wider Canada. This ambiguity is encapsulated in the contradictory demands of the opening, as the wife commands her husband:

> Go; rise and strike, no matter what the cost.
> Yet stay, revolt not at the Union Jack....[50]

The invading militias are not only 'this stripling pack of white-faced warriors' but also 'young and beautiful and good'. The speaker urges savage retribution: 'Here is your knife... 'Twill drink the blood of a soldier host'. But at the same time she empathises with the mother and the sweetheart of the opposing militia who 'pleads her God to guard some sweet-faced child' and 'prays to shield her love from harm'. The despoliation of the plains, 'no roaming bison', its people 'starved, crushed, plundered', and the resultant 'wars and graves' are given a political reading:

> They but forget we Indians owned the land
> From ocean unto ocean; that they stand
> Upon a soil that centuries agone
> Was our sole kingdom and our right alone.

But it is framed with the conciliatory 'their [the colonists'] new rule and council is well-meant'. While Johnson uses the terms 'our little band' and 'our fallen tribe' to refer to the Plains Indians, she also calls them a 'kingdom' and a 'nation'. But their implied placement is in history rather than the present, a 'nation' in the past without a place in the nation of the modern. The speaker farewells her 'Forest Brave', her 'Red-skin love' as he leaves for war; that farewell encompasses both his inevitable death 'by a thousand rifle balls' and the extinction of his race. Despite the poem's forceful expression of the Indian cause, the assumption is that it is lost, especially in the conclusion to the 1912 *Flint and Feather* version:

> Go forth, nor bend to greed of white men's hands,
> By right, by birth we Indians own these lands,
> Though starved, crushed, plundered lies our nation low...
> Perhaps the white man's God has willed it so.[51]

What seems odd – this shifting, even contradictory stance of the speaker – may very well have been a function of its live performance, alert to the difficulty of critiquing the audience while keeping them on side. The Northwest Rebellion encapsulated so much of Canada's national narrative: the various peoples that comprised the nation, white, Indian, Métis and French; competition for land and anxiety over the formal ownership of that land; the relation between the settlers of the Northwest and the eastern establishment; anxieties over modernity clustered around the construction of the Canadian Pacific Railroad. Yet the poem's call to attend to the political concerns of the Indians, while present, is muted and deflected by the poem's seesawing, conciliatory sympathy and by its cloak of maternal sentimentality which makes the poem finally a cry against war in general rather than a cry against the particular wrongs of this particular war.

'The Cattle Thief' is a far more technically sophisticated, Kiplingesque piece, written in tetrameters, the favoured form of nineteenth-century recitation pieces, 'especially congenial to being set to the standard forms of Euro-Canadian music'.[52] The poem displays all the hallmarks of its oral performance – emphatic phrasing, rhetorical flourishes, a concentration of adjectives and expostulations:

> Mistake him? Never! Mistake him? the famous Eagle chief!
> That terror to all the settlers, that desperate cattle thief –
> That monstrous, fearless Indian, who lorded it over the plain,
> Who thieved and raided, and scouted, who rode like a hurricane![53]

This poem has none of the vacillations of sympathy of 'A Cry of an Indian Wife': the Indians' attackers are 'desperate English settlers...all their British blood aflame', 'a troop of demons', 'white-skins', 'that band of cursing settlers'. The old Indian, the eponymous cattle thief whom they have killed, is described as a 'lion', 'fearless', 'the famous Eagle Chief'. The bulk of the poem is spoken by a woman who protects the old man's dead body from desecration – 'If you mean to touch that body, you must cut your way through *me*'. Her stirring and dramatic demand of the 'white-skins', in performance, becomes a demand by Johnson of her audience:

> Give back our land and our country, give back our herds of game;
> Give back the furs and the forests that were ours before you came;
> Give back the peace and the plenty. Then come with your new belief,
> And blame, if you dare, the hunger that *drove* him to be a thief.

But the framing of these demands, spoken, the poem tells us, 'in the language of the Cree' by a character whom Johnson inhabits momentarily then steps back from, has a blunting effect. The woman voices a lament for the dead chief, rather than any programme of specific reform or restitution. Political complaint is contained by the literary convention used – the old man stands for his dying race, and the woman's oration is, finally, an example of the proleptic ode.

In the poetry, as opposed to her short stories and journalism, none of Johnson's Indian characters steps outside the narrowly defined set of characteristics she is so scornful of in 'A Strong Race Opinion'. None is portrayed as being part of the modern world, and none is portrayed with humour or satire – there is no Indian version of Drummond's 'habitant' in Johnson's verse. At the same time, there is a complete absence of specific ethnographic detail, even though such was commonplace in poetry of this kind – for example, in the works of Longfellow, Schoolcraft or Mair, all of whom carefully footnoted their sources and authorities. Johnson's Indians are, variously and without particular differentiation, identified as Mohawk, Huron, Plains, Cherokee, Sioux, Iroquois, Squamish, and, in 'The Cattle Thief', Cree. But they are characterised purely in terms of pre-existing literary stereotype. They are savage: 'Leans he low down above the snake-like flood/ To tell his world that law is blood for blood' ('The Death Cry'[54]). They are proud: 'Captive! But *never* conquered; Mohawk brave/ Stops not to be to any man a slave' ('As Red Men Die'[55]). They are the animating spiritual presence behind the landscape: 'a maiden misty as the autumn rains,/Guiding with her lamp of moonlight/ Hunters lost upon the plains' ('The Pilot of the Plains'[56]). They are at one with the natural world and its rhythms:

> So goes he forth beneath the planter's moon
> With sack of seed that pledges large increase,
> His simple pagan faith knows night and noon,
> Heat, cold, seedtime and harvest shall not cease.
> ('The Indian Corn Planter'[57])

And above all they are members – as ghosts, memories or remnants – of a dying race. The old woman in 'The Corn Husker', '[a]ge in her fingers, hunger in her face', thinks only

> ...of the days gone by,
> Ere might's injustice banished from their lands
> Her people, that today unheeded lie,
> Like the dead husks that rustle through her hands.[58]

Few of Johnson's contemporary reviews picked up any specific political message from the poems. They talked of the thrilling authenticity of voice but not of what that voice says. A reviewer in Brantford in 1894 wrote:

> Miss Pauline Johnson, in the course of an entertainment given in the city last night, took occasion to condemn the unnatural manner in which the Indian inhabitants of the Northwest are managed, in that the Indian children are separated from their parents. She did not think the churches would make any headway with the Indians by teaching children to despise their parents.[59]

But this is the exception. Most reviews concentrate on the theatrical aspects of the performance. Ann Arbour's newspaper *The Democrat* is typical. Under the headline 'Indian Trappings, Jewels, Scalps, Wampum, Fire Bags, Weird Symbols' is a list of breathless sub-headings: 'MOHAWK PRINCESS/ Of Royal Indian Blood and Native Indian Eloquence/ Beautiful and Young/ Recited Poems of Revenge, Hate and Deathless Love/ Entertainment Last Night in the Fountain Street Baptist Church'. The reviewer describes Johnson:

> Slender and graceful as a mountain gazelle, with her long, black, glossy hair hanging down her back and her buckskin dress covered with the mystic, symbolic jewels of the Mohawk tribe, she presented a picture seldom seen outside the imagination conjured in descriptive accounts of Indian princesses.[60]

\* \* \*

In *The Life, History, and Travels of Kah-Ge-Ga-Gah*-Bowh, George Copway describes his life before conversion to Christianity as being 'in *nature's wide domain*'. 'I am one of nature's children,' he declares, 'I have always admired her; she shall be my glory.'[61] Johnson echoes this: her poetry is presented as drawing force from her Indigenous identity but also from the natural world:

> My ears have heard some of nature's loveliest songs – the wild splash of the rapids in the great rivers as they leap over broken rocks and cascade in murmuring eddies away to the sea; the hushed melancholy of the winds in the forest pines away up in Northern Canada; the torturing loneliness that midnight airs breathe, when flapped through the pinions of migrating night birds, and one is conscious of the far-offness of any human habitation....[62]

Her audiences saw this as an appropriate conjunction. One reviewer expresses the sense that it is fitting that:

[a] singer who stands pre-eminent for expression of what is beautiful and ennobling in the scenes of our great continent should be an Indian; should come of that noble race which for centuries waxed strong and joyful in the primitive forest, but with all its primitive understanding and sympathy, with the great nature-spirit, has failed to survive contact with that paler race which loves better the world-spirit, and has for its heritage the instinct to trade and possess.[63]

Just as Copway sees his people's wigwams displaced by cities, their war-paths by railway lines, this association of Indigenous inhabitants and unspoilt nature was often linked with a sense of both being simultaneously under threat or vanishing. European settler society both celebrates the pristine beauty of the new place and sets about changing it in terms of the requirements of the modern nation. New Zealander William Pember Reeves expresses this disjunct at the conclusion of his 1898 poem 'The Passing of the Forest':

> Mighty are axe and fire, destroyers twain,
> Swift servants of the arch-destroyer, Man;
> And he is mighty as he hews amain,
> Bronzed pioneer of nations. Ay, but scan
> The ruined wonder never wrought again,
> The ravaged beauty God alone could plan!
> Bitter the thought: 'Is this the price we pay –
> The price of progress – beauty swept away?'[64]

Heroic and archaic Indigenous figures set in primeval landscape of sublimity can be accommodated, admired and celebrated in literature, and then set aside from consideration as having no place in the present. Heroic figures from the modern settler and pioneer experience may be problematic, both 'arch-destroyers' and 'bronzed pioneers of nations', but are figured as necessary. The landscape is both past and present – untouched in Indigenous memory and romanticised settler imagination; despoiled and remodelled in actuality.

In a fashion that is consonant with literature throughout the settler empire, Johnson's work offers various and sometimes mutually exclusive templates for the relationship between the Indigenous past, the settler present, and the landscape. Her setting is often not the absolute untouched wilderness but one which is more contrived, a formally sectioned-off, recreational portion of nature which preserves or at least mimics the pre-settler world. Within this reserved space, the appropriate activities of the recreational outdoors can be enacted and celebrated.

Two very similar poems, 'Bass Lake (Muskoka) ' and 'Star Lake (Muskoka) ', both written around 1890, address the delights of the recreational wild and compare them to the constraints of the city. In 'Bass Lake', the 'heron-haunted lake' is full of 'the sighs of gentle pine trees' that 'breathe the wind-taught song', acting like a sea shell which 'enthrals the voices of many deeps'.[65] This is a place where 'all the littleness of social living dies away forgot'. Significantly, only '[h]e, who so treasures wood and water lore', is entitled to experience the setting's 'silence, grandeur, soul and power'. In the second poem, 'Star Lake', the scenario is the same – this lake, too, is 'far from the work-encumbered world' and circled by 'storm-scorning cedar trees/ Whose aromatic branches sing whene'er/ A strolling zephyr threads the virgin air'.[66] However, here there are disturbing registrations of a human past, 'of the lonely years, when wildly rose/ The war cry of the Hurons' and their enemies the 'Bloody Iroquois':

> And Huron Brave to meet his doom went forth,
> Bathed with his blood the sands of Simcoe's shore,
> His war-song silenced now for evermore.

The voices of the natural world that are now heard at Star Lake are 'the voices that, succeeding, reign/ Usurpers of the Huron's old domain', that is, the birds – heron, owl and loon – who have replaced Indigenous human inhabitants. But they themselves have an uncertain place in the present. They are vulnerable to and will soon be replaced by 'pioneers of enterprise', 'the woodsman's axe' and 'the voice of the sportsman's rifle' – what the poem describes as the encroachment of 'culture's artificial note'.

The first poem sees an unpeopled landscape which can be possessed by those present-day Canadians with the knowledge and sensitivity to appreciate it. The second poem acknowledges an Indigenous past, though one fated to self-destruction and replaced by – and now only traceable through – an equally vulnerable natural world. This world is about to be annihilated, in its turn, by settler enterprise in all its various forms. The camper of Bass Lake 'sleep[ing] upon his bed of cedar boughs' is, at Star Lake, replaced by a rapacious but thoroughly modern 'sportsman'.

Johnson's most famous poem, the one that elderly Canadians of the twenty-first century can still recite by heart, is 'The Song My Paddle Sings', first published in 1892. The figure of Bass Lake's camper with his 'wood and water lore' is here given a more specific activity, one that links to and enacts a developing form of colonial nationalism, a particularised Canadian identity within empire. Canoeing is, as Daniel Francis puts it, one of the central myths of Canada, 'the mother image of our national dreamlife, a symbol of oneness with a rugged northern landscape, the vessel in which we are recreated as Canadians'.[67] It signifies an engagement with the healthy pursuits of the outdoors but, in contrast with Star Lake's sportsman, implies a benign relation with the natural world and an openness to the tutelage of its sublime. Canoeing is modern, with its associations with early twentieth-century health theorists, feminists and proto-eugenicists. In 'Outdoor Pastimes for Women', Johnson writes:

> Feminine beauty and feminine health are synonymous... strong life-giving airs and genial sunshine need not be filtered through glass and garniture of four square walls before it became refined sufficiently for female lungs to inhale and female faces to be bared to.[68]

But the image of the canoe and the canoeist is also open to archaising in a specifically Canadian way, as a mechanism of settler Indigenisation. The European canoeist mimics the activities and learns the skills of the displaced and disappeared Indian, and hence takes his or her place in the Indigenous landscape. Misao Dean warns:

> [t]he narrative that is elided in the dominance of the ideology of the canoe [is] the narrative of the way that First Nations were invaded, colonized, and subsumed by non-indigenous culture in Canada.[69]

Bruce Erikson argues that 'the sentimental place of canoe in Canada is the result of a set of narratives that attempt to legitimize a particular (and dominant) vision of the nation'.[70] Canoeing's cluster of associations works in a similar but far more effective manner than parallel mechanisms of appropriation in other settler societies, enfolding both the pre-contact natural world and its inhabitants, the canoe itself, as Dean puts it, 'metonymically part of the landscape'.[71] Mountaineering and 'tramping' (hiking) in New Zealand had something of the same nationalist connotations for the European population at the turn of the twentieth century, but without the Indigenous referents. Māori had not climbed mountains or hiked, although they might be imagined by settler mountaineers and hikers as ghostly figures in the landscape.[72] The Australian settler's relationship with the bush, a landscape which Marcus Clarke described as the 'strange scribblings of nature learning how to write',[73] was far more complex, without the automatic associations with the sublime found in both Canada and New Zealand, or any narrative of Indigenous presence which might be admired, mimicked or appropriated.

Johnson's use of the trope of the canoe is carefully calibrated, with no overt reference to her Indigenous persona or authority. 'The Song My Paddle Sings', with its reassuringly cultured Shelley-like overtones ('O! wind of the west, we wait for you/ Blow, blow!'), its inclusive sweep across the geographical nation ('blow from your prairie nest...from the mountains...from the west...down where the prairie grasses sweep'), its knowledgeable technical details (the 'white lateen', the stowed sail and unshipped mast, the 'trembling keel') and its absence of potentially alienating Indigenous detail, stands as a settler anthem.[74] The narrative – the wind picks up; the river current runs faster; the rapids approach, needing all the skill and courage the paddler can muster; safe passage is finally achieved – is eminently suited to metaphorical interpretation and nationalist application. In photographs of Johnson as a canoeist in the popular press at this time, she significantly not in her Indian costume but in modern European outdoor dress (blouse with crisscross lacing, striped tie, dark skirt, pompom hat), seated in her canoe 'Wild Cat' or posed leaning thoughtfully against her paddle: the knowledge of the Indian and in the setting of an Indian but with the reassuring appearance of the modern European.[75] As a reviewer writes: 'Her voice is far more than aboriginal – it is the voice which interprets not alone the hopes, joys, and sorrows of her race, but also the beauty and glory of the natural world around'.[76]

\*\*\*

Johnson's role as interpreter of the Indigenous past to modern settler society is a feature of *Legends of Vancouver*, a 1911 collection which had appeared as articles in the *Daily Province Magazine* and the *Mother's*

*Magazine* between 1908 and 1911[77] and was compiled by her friends who were concerned about her financial situation in her final years in Vancouver. Johnson explains the stories' genesis:

> These legends (with two or three exceptions) were told to me personally by my honoured friend, the late Chief Joe Capilano, of Vancouver... he frequently remarked that they had never been revealed to any other English-speaking person save myself.[78]

Initially, when the pieces were first published in the Vancouver newspaper, they were described as being narrated by Capilano and his wife Mary Agnes or Líxwelut. Described as 'a quaint old Indian mother', the latter was sole narrator of the original version of 'The Two Sisters' and a co-narrator of 'The Squamish Twins', which appeared in *Legends* as 'The Recluse'. In the collected *Legends* she transmogrifies into the non-specific 'klootchman' (Indian woman) who makes an occasional and unexplained appearance in several stories.

Although the general frame of the legends is that of private knowledge revealed with permission, Johnson's narration of first meeting with Capilano is very emphatically not in the context of shared Indigeneity, but that of empire and its networks. 'I had the privilege of first meeting [Capilano] in London in 1906', she writes, 'when he visited England and was received at Buckingham Palace by their Majesties King Edward VII and Queen Alexandra'.[79] Peripheral subjects meeting at the centre, Johnson and Capilano are linked by their inhabitation of both worlds, imperial metropole and Indigenous Canada. In 1906, Capilano and his fellow chiefs had travelled to London to make representations over land policies, but Johnson does not include this political and implicitly confrontational context in her literary frame; in her account, the circumstances of their first meeting are marked by shared sense of the two as imperial citizens, and by their ability to go between their places of origin and the imperial centre, figured here in the benevolently parental figures of the King and Queen.[80]

The first story in *Legends of Vancouver*, 'The Two Sisters: the Lions', develops this sense of the native subject as doubly fortunate, able to be part of the Indigenous and the natural local world as well as of the global empire. The story centres on the two peaks behind the city of Vancouver, and Johnson and Capilano discuss the similarity of the Vancouver formations to the Landseer Lions in Trafalgar Square. The story is framed by the memory of elsewhere: Capilano's 'fine face expressed the haunting memories of the far-off roar of Old London'.[81] But at the same time Capilano presents to Johnson an alternative, Indigenous reading of the landscape, using what Jay Arthur has described as 'lexical cartography', reshaping by renaming.[82] This reading is both private and, by virtue of its being offered to Johnson, and through her to the readers of the *Daily Province*, one which now moves into general currency. 'The Two Sisters', Johnson states, is 'a legend that I have reason to believe is absolutely unknown to the thousands of Palefaces who look on "The Lions" daily, without the love for them that is in the Indian heart'.[83] Her narration of his narration is designed to give the European reader a new context with which to read the local landscape – the rock formation the Two Sisters, and, in later stories, the Fraser River,[84] Coal Harbour[85] and the Grey Archway.[86] One of the central purposes of Johnson's retelling of Capilano's narratives is to overwrite the limited and imaginatively impoverished settler landscape. In the 1830s the newly arrived Catherine Parr Traill had written:

> As to ghosts or spirits they appear totally banished from Canada. This is too matter-of-fact country for such supernaturals to visit. Here there are no historical associations, no legendary tales of those that came before us. Fancy would starve for lack of marvellous food to keep her alive in the backwoods. We have neither fay nor fairy, ghost nor bogle, satyr nor wood-nymph; our very forests disdain to shelter dryad or hamadryad. No naiad haunts the rushy margin of our lakes, or hallows with her presence our forest-rills. No Druid claims our oaks; and instead of poring with mysterious awe among our curious limestone rocks, that are often singularly grouped together, we refer them to the geologist to exercise his skill in accounting for their appearance: instead of investing them with the solemn characters of ancient temples or heathen altars, we look upon them with the curious eye of natural philosophy alone.[87]

This is a common trope of settler poetics – the New Zealand poet Alexander Bathgate complains 'Why have we in these isles no faerie dell, / No haunted wood, nor wild enchanted mere?'[88] At times this anxiety is allayed by the tentative hope that a future poet may one day emerge to supply material for a local literature – one that will in turn inform the landscape with meaning. But another solution was to appropriate local Indigenous legends, traditions and literatures, since their owners were now figured as vanished.

Johnson is both complicit in this appropriation and a way of undermining it – ownership of the legendary material is passed from the Indigenous sphere to the general but it is passed by means of Johnson whose dual identity and interpretive authority can, it is implied, act as a safeguard. Moreover, her agency and her control of the text imply that the extinction of the Indian might be less than comprehensive. It is suggested that the material is not just preserved but is given a place in a more general global and modern system of signification. At the beginning of 'The Recluse' Johnson writes, 'the stream is haunted with tradition, teeming with scores of romances that vie with its grandeur and loveliness, and of which its waters are perpetually whispering'.[89] 'Haunted', 'tradition' and 'romances', 'grandeur and loveliness' are all terms taken from the conventions of European Romanticism – conveying, indeed, exactly what Traill and Bathgate saw as lacking in their respective settings – but are here used to refer to an appropriately Indigenous version of fairy, ghost, bogle, satyr, and wood-nymph.

In 'The Lure in Stanley Park', the double landscape – Europe and Vancouver – is again evoked:

> [I]n all the world there is no cathedral whose marble or onyx columns can vie with those straight, clean, brown tree boles that teem with the sap and blood of life. There is no fresco that can rival the delicacy of the lace-work they have festooned between you and the far skies. No tiles, no mosaic or inlaid marbles, are as fascinating as the bare russet fragrant floor outspreading about their feet.[90]

The local and the natural are favourably compared with the artificial beauty of European high culture, but at the same time Johnson is also demonstrating her knowledge of both worlds, local and international, and her ability to move between them. Johnson acts as the interpreter and mediator of the material she is given, and she takes on this role by virtue of her dual, mixed-race status.[91] As such she presents herself as a practised participant in two literary modes – the world of oral history, memory and tradition sanctioned by the links of blood, and the world of the professional writer, the newspaper article and the magazine short story. She makes it clear that she does not live in the world of Joe Capilano and the Squamish, and that she does not speak from it. Her position is removed, at times ethnographic in its objectivity. But the objectivity is tempered by sympathy, friendship and an appeal to blood. Much is made of her knowledge of Capliano's language, the basis of their first meeting in London – 'I was able to greet Chief Capilano in the Chinook tongue' she explains.[92] In 'The Grey Archway', she hopes that 'my Chinook salutation would be a drawbridge by which I might hope to cross the moat into his castle of silence',[93] and Capilano's willingness to talk to her comes after he gives 'a swift glance at my dark skin'. 'You are one of us,' he tells her, 'and you will understand, or I should not tell you. You will not smile at the story, for you are one of us.'[94] Markers of affiliation are here vague and generalised – 'blood', 'dark skin', 'one of us' – as Johnson homogenises tribal and regional difference. These credentials permit, she suggests, Capilano's confidences being passed on through her to the readers of the Vancouver *Daily Province* and *Mothers' Magazine*.

It is important for the authority of Capilano's stories that most of them are communicated to Johnson while they are in a natural setting which is often the key to unlocking the story's meaning. (One recitation takes place in her rooms, but it is on a rainy day, and nature is temporarily unavailable.) Each detail of Capilano's narrative has a correlative in the local landscape which validates its veracity.[95] In 'The Grey Archway', Johnson listens to him and then looks for some additional interpretive assistance from the world around her:

> As I brooded over this strange tale of a daughter's devotion I watched the sea and sky for something that would give me a clue to the inevitable sequel that the Tillicum, like all his race, was surely withholding until the opportune moment.[96]

Johnson signals her sensitivity as listener as she realises that the fish that she sees swimming by the boat are the characters from Capilano's story. The natural world – specifically that of the northwest coast – is a means of access to the past, though the depredations of settlement and industry are seen as destroying both. As Indian culture fades, so, Johnson suggests, the world itself – the physical landscape – is also fading. In 'The Lost Island' Capilano explains:

> [w]e Indians have lost many things. We have lost our lands, our forests, our game, our fish; we have lost our ancient religion, our ancient dress; some of our young people have even lost their fathers' language and the legends and traditions of their ancestors. We cannot call those things back to us; they will never come again. We may travel

many days up the mountains, and look in the silent places for them. They are not there. We may paddle many moons on the sea, but our canoes will never enter the channel that leads to the yesterdays of the Indian people. These things are lost, just like the Island of the North Arm. They may be somewhere nearby, but no one can ever find them.[97]

Two meanings of 'lost' are being conflated here – lands, forests, game, fish, religion, dress have all been destroyed by the processes of European settlement. But at the same time the story suggests they have been mislaid, are still physically somewhere, simply un-locatable by their previous owners. A political context for this loss is acknowledged, but then the reader's attention is diverted. Johnson conveys the particular injuries of a colonised Indigenous people, but then transfers that sense of loss and alienation to her wider readership. Capilano figures the pre-contact world as a mythical lost island, the Island of the North Arm: "'Why do you search for it" I lamented, thinking of the old dreams in my own life whose realization I have never attained....'[98] Her narration shifts the story from an implicitly political position to one that is more generalised, metaphorical and psychological, suggestive of European conventions of lost worlds of perfection or the depredations of modernity and thereby applicable to all readers.

Capilano is presented as being both in the world – in terms of his travels and the analogies he can thus make between London and Vancouver – and resonant with the pathos of a race consigned to the past. In 'The Recluse', he is described as having 'his heart... brimming with tales of the bygones, his eyes were dark with dreams and that strange mournfulness that always haunted them when he spoke of long-ago romance'.[99] Johnson combines the fact of his death – he died of tuberculosis in 1910 – with the wider rhetorical context of the dying race topos, where his individual mortality stands for that of his people.[100] The markers of mortality are registered on his body, and in the conventional use of the sea as a metaphor of eternity:

> He leaned a little backward against a giant boulder, clasping his thin, brown hands about his knees; his eyes roved up the galloping river, then swept down the singing waters to where they crowded past the sudden bend, and during the entire recital of the strange legend his eyes never left the spot where the stream disappeared in its hurrying journey to the sea.[101]

Paradoxically, Johnson links Capilano's imaginative power to his displacement or fading – he is archaic, rather than modern as Johnson is; his voice has 'a far-off cadence';[102] and when he concludes a tale 'the shadows of centuries gone crept into his eyes. Tales of the misty past always inspired him'.[103] The power of Indigenous narratives, it is suggested, lies in their location outside the present. In 'The Lost Salmon Run', the female storyteller is in a trance-like state specifically located in the past: 'I knew by the dusk in her eyes that she was back in her Land of Legends, and that soon I would be richer in my hoard of Indian lore'.[104] This story is linked to, almost synonymous with, the paddling of the speaker's canoe; when the journey is ended the story stops and the speaker returns to the present:

> The klootchman lifted her arms from the paddles as she concluded; her eyes left the irregular outline of the violet mountains. She had come back to this year of grace – her Legend Land had vanished.[105]

Despite her brisk marshalling of her material, and the sometimes prosaic way in which she sets out the pragmatics of each interview, Johnson implies that she is providing her readers with access to this vision of the spiritual, their own Legend Land.

More than a transcriber, Johnson conveys the performance values of Chief Capilano's renditions, as well as signalling that she has translated it from the restricted English of the speaker to the literary language of the published version. In 'The Two Sisters' she explains:

> The legend was intensely fascinating as it left his lips in the quaint broken English that is never so dulcet as when it slips from an Indian tongue. His inimitable gestures, strong, graceful, comprehensive were like a perfectly chosen frame embracing a delicate painting, and his brooding eyes were as the light in which the picture was hung. 'Many thousands of years ago,' he began....[106]

Rather than setting down the content of the story, Johnson is describing its performance, the stance and gestures of the teller.[107] In 'The Sea Serpent', she describes Capilano:

> During its recital he sat with folded arms, leaning on the table, his head and shoulders bending eagerly towards me as I sat on the opposite side. It was the only time he talked to me when he did not use emphasizing gesticulations, but his hands never once lifted: his wonderful eyes alone gave expression to what he called 'The Legend of the "Salt-Chuck Olak"' (sea-serpent).[108]

As both text and performance, she suggests, the stories are resistant to mediation or interpretation. Yet she does both. The performance of 'The Recluse', the story of the unpropitious consequences of the birth of twins, ends with the return of Capilano and Johnson from the wilderness, past the marks of the natural world's entanglement with commerce, to the city, moving from the archaic world of Capilano's recitation, to the settler past of landscape modification, to the city of the present and the modern:

> I nodded silently. The legend was too beautiful to mar with comments, and, as the twilight fell, we threaded our way through the underbrush, past the disused logger's camp, and into the trail that leads citywards.[109]

In fact, Johnson's position as an insider and sympathetic listener to Capilano's stories is balanced against her adoption of a more journalistic and ethnographic tone, as she explains and interprets his stories to his European audience in a way that at times separates her from the sympathetic positions she otherwise takes. In the story 'The Lost Salmon Run', she observes that

> those readers who are familiar with the ways and beliefs and faiths of the primitive races will agree that it is difficult to discover anywhere in the world a race that has not some story of the Deluge, which they have chronicled and localized to fit the understanding and the conditions of the nation that composes their own immediate world'.[110]

In 'The Sea Serpent', a story with the moral that 'avarice is unknown to the red man', she explains, 'All red races are born Socialists, and most tribes carry out their communistic ideas to the letter'.[111] In 'The Grey Archway' she explains that '[a]n Indian rarely uses the word "love"'.[112] In 'A Squamish Legend of Napoleon' Capilano himself, rather disconcertingly, is given this ethnographic tone of voice when he talks of 'the ever-romantic and vividly coloured imaginations of the Squamish people' and 'this beautifully childish, yet strangely historical, fairy-tale'.[113]

Johnson frames the Squamish material so that the reader can both accept and condescend to its magical and non-rational world. In 'The Grey Archway' she describes the landscape 'loom[ing] almost above us, the mysticism crowded close, it enveloped me, caressed me, appealed to me'.[114] In 'The Sea Serpent' Capilano worries that Johnson's lack of belief in sea-serpents means that she will not 'believe' his story. She answers:

> I shall believe whatever you tell me, Chief... I am only too ready to believe. You know I come of a superstitious race, and all my association with the Paleface has never yet robbed me of my birthright to believe strange traditions.[115]

It is, she assures him, not her rational Western self that she employs in listening to his tales: 'It is my heart that understands'. But this understanding by the heart is not, it is made clear to the reader if not to Capilano, the same as literal belief. Johnson acts as a filter between Capilano's beliefs and what the reader is asked to accept. In 'The Sea Serpent', Capilano and Johnson discuss the appropriate category in which the tale might be placed. Capilano suggests it is a legend. Johnson says that 'the white people would call it an allegory',[116] a term which she then must explain to Capilano – 'with his customary alertness he immediately understood'. But this shift in category, away from the 'legends' of the collection's title, is a signal from Johnson to her European readers that they should view Capilano's story not as the actual truth of reportage, or even the mythic truth of legends, but as having only an artificial relationship with the real. Johnson's own acceptance – 'It is my heart that understands' – differs from the way she expects her readers to see the story. 'Primitive' insight and wisdom are being sympathetically presented but their limits are also being clearly marked – the story is allegory rather than truth. As allegory, it needs its interpreter, and as allegory its meaning is external to its narrative, and arbitrary. Because of her intermediary status, Johnson represents herself as not primitive but as having access to the primitive. As George W. Lyon puts it in his discussion of her poetry, 'she assert[s] that her genetic history [gives] her the privilege of addressing certain subjects'.[117] Capilano is her specimen primitive, but even he does not any longer have complete access. In 'The Sea Serpent', Johnson asks the chief if he has ever seen the creature he describes: '"No", he answered simply. But I have never heard such poignant regret as his wonderful voice crowded into that single word'.[118]

It has been pointed out that the stories Johnson records in *Legends of Vancouver* do not conform to standard accounts of Salish mythology.[119] All but one appeared after Capilano's death in 1910. *Legends* is, at least in part, the product of Johnson's parents' library of 'Milton, Scott, Longfellow, Browning, Tennyson, Keats and Byron' and her own early fondness for 'stories about the nobility of Indians...John Richardson's *Wacousta* (1832) and *The Legends of Hiawatha*'.[120] It is indebted to the ethnographers she recommends in 'A Strong Race Opinion', Francis Parkman, Henry Rowe Schoolcraft and George Catlin. She may also have been responding, as the professional journalist she was, to the expectations of the *Mother's Magazine* whose stated aim was to 'better the conditions of the mothers and children and strengthen the home as the mainstay of the nation'.[121] Johnson sees the source material in *Legends* as entirely consonant with the values of the *Mothers' Magazine*: 'there is rarely a tradition among the British Columbian Indians that does not have at its base womanhood – wifehood, and above all, motherhood'.[122] 'Almost without exception' she states, 'their legends deal with rewards for tenderness and self-abnegation, and personal and mental cleanliness',[123] that is, they have a moral shape in keeping with turn of the century Canadian European society. But in this process Johnson necessarily depoliticises her material. It may be given to her under privileged conditions, but its import is shaped for a wider audience:

> Call them fairy-tales if you wish to, they all have a reasonableness that must have originated in some almighty mind, and, better than that, they all tell of the Indian's faith in the survival of the best impulses of the human heart, and the ultimate extinction of the worst.[124]

'Fairytales', 'reasonableness', 'some almighty mind', 'the best impulses of the human heart' – all these phrases generalise, remove the particularity that might be attached to the material, suggest that whatever the ethnographic truths of the material Johnson reports, it has no confrontational edge that might disturb the European reader.

\*\*\*

Because of the undeniably attractive and (literally) theatrical nature of her personality, it is tempting to see Johnson's work in terms of biography, and this is especially the case in *Legends of Vancouver*, with its accompanying narrative of the dying chief, the landscape of sea, river and forest, the sense of the reader's access to material otherwise unobtainable deriving from Johnson herself. But if we see *Legends* in literary rather than in personal terms it can be read as a text which solves a number of conventional problems of colonial writing.[125] Johnson is remembered by a friend as having said 'one of the secrets of good writing of any kind is the power of being someone else.... How can one be consistent until the world ceases to change with the changing days?'[126] In *Legends*, as in her other writing and in her theatrical career, her narrative persona is a carefully managed one. Inevitably, as an educated member of the literary as well as the social and political empire, she inhabits the formal literary structures of empire. *Legends* addresses one of the central issue of colonial writing, authenticity. It allows its reader to enjoy a privileged sense of access to 'primitive' material, while being reassured of the correct moral placement of that material. *Legends* imaginatively recreates a landscape before European settlement, one given meaning by a spiritual system organically connected to that landscape and to those who inhabit it. As such it re-inscribed the Romantic vision of a world before modernity and fracture.[127] The validity of this material is continually affirmed by Johnson's reportage of the chief's acceptance of her as a proper intermediary – a translator, just as her father was. But her reportage is continually framed in language that de-particularises and universalises her material, expressing it in terms that would be entirely familiar to the European reader. And at the foundation of *Legends* is the Victorian dying race topos: the stories are told by a dying man from a dying race and describe a landscape that is, like Capilano's lost island, becoming more and more difficult to gain access to.

Johnson is reported as having said, 'Writing was never the Indian's mode of expression. It was the speech, the oration of which was his greatest achievement. And that, like all the old customs, is dying out'.[128] Finding ways of conveying that orality, while preserving the material it expressed, was a common enterprise of colonial writers. Persuading readers of the authenticity of the resulting literary voice was an additional requirement to be built into the way a text was constructed. Johnson's membership of the literary community of empire, alongside her carefully and somewhat selectively maintained Indigeneity, put her in a particularly strong position in both regards. Franz Fanon wrote, 'A colonized people is not alone. In spite of all that colonialism can do, its frontiers remain open to new ideas and echoes from the world outside'.[129] But Johnson's *Legends* suggest that those new ideas and echoes from outside her particular world that she was able to access were still those of empire and its dialects.

## NOTES

1. *Washington Post*, 10 October 1884, p. 1.
2. William L. Stone, *The Life and Times of Red Jacket, or Sa-Go-Ye-Wat-Ha; being a Sequel to the History of the Six Nations* (New York and London: Wiley and Putnam, 1841), pp. 391–4 (Stone 1841). The colonel is referred to variously as 'McKenney' or 'McKinney'. See introduction, p. 4.
3. Correspondence between Parker and Bryant appeared in the *Buffalo Commercial Advertiser* and was reprinted in the *New York Times*, 1 July 1884, p. 2.
4. Ibid.
5. *New York Times*, 23 March 1884, p. 7.
6. *Washington Post*, 10 October 1884, p. 1.
7. *Transactions of the Buffalo Historical Society*, vol III, Appendix no. 20 (1885).
8. E. Pauline Johnson, Tekahionwake, *Collected Poems and Selected Prose*, eds. Carole Gerson and Veronica Strong-Boag (Toronto: Toronto University Press, 2002), p. 11. (Johnson 2002)
9. Red Jacket's single recorded characteristic was his eloquence – he had an ambiguous record as soldier, but was successful as a negotiator on behalf of the Seneca people in a delegation in Philadelphia in 1792, and was given a medal by George Washington.
10. *The Globe*, 8 March 1913, p. 1.
11. *The Globe*, 25 September 1893.
12. *The Globe*, 22 November 1894.
13. *The Globe*, 3 June 1893.
14. This article groups her with other women writers: 'Miss Machar (Fidelis), Mrs Harrison (Seranus), Mrs Curzon', *The Globe*, 6 November 1897, p. 4.
15. She is associated here with other poets: Ethel Wetherald, Jean Blewett, Helen Merrill, Mrs Machar, Miss Elizabeth Roberts McDonald and Evelyn Durand, *The Globe*, 10 December 1904, p. 9.
16. *The Globe*, 3 March 1898, p. 6.
17. *The Globe*, 10 December 1904. Johnson appears alongside Lampman, Carman, Roberts, Jean Blewett, Edward Dewart, William Drummond and Arthur Stringer.
18. Advertisement for *Flint and Feather* in *The Bookman*, January 1913, reproduced in Linda Quirk, 'Skyward Floating Feather: A Publishing History of E Pauline Johnson's *Flint and Feather*', *Papers of the Bibliographical Society of Canada* 44: 1 (2006):75.(Quirk 2006)
19. *The Globe*, 18 October 1893, p. 8.
20. *The Globe*, 15 April 1903, p. 14.
21. *The Globe*, 18 October 1893, p. 8.

22. Marta Braun and Charlie Keil, 'Sounding Canadian: Early Sound Practices and Nationalism in Toronto-based Exhibition', *The Sounds of Early Cinema*, eds. Richard Abel and Rick Altman (Bloomington and Indianapolis: Indiana University Press, 2001), pp. 201–3. (Braun and Keil 2001)
23. *The Globe*, 22 September 1893, p. 8.
24. *The Mail and Empire*, 30 May 1902.
25. Audiences praised 'the illusion he gives of an easy amiable interchange between the two cultures, French- and English-speaking', Roy Daniels, 'Minor Poets 1880–1920', *Literary History of Canada: Canadian Literature in English*, second edition, vol 1, ed. Cark F Klinck (Toronto: University of Toronto Press, 1977), p. 438. (Daniels 1977)
26. William Henry Drummond, 'De Habitant', *The Habitant and Other French-Canadian Poems* (New York: G P Putnam's Sons, 1897), p. 6. (Drummond 1897)
27. *Daily Examiner*, 20 May 1903, n.p., E Pauline Johnson Fonds, Box 4, File 8, William Ready Division of Archives and Research Collections, McMaster University Library.
28. Flyer from Johnson's 1900-1 tour of the Maritimes, reproduced in Sheila M.F. Johnson, *Buckskin and Broadcloth: A Celebration of E. Pauline Johnson-Tekahionwake 1861–1913* (Toronto: Natural Heritage Books, 1997), p. 157. (Johnson 1997)
29. *Collected Poems and Selected Prose*, p. 306.
30. Walter McRaye is at pains to distinguish between the status of 'half-breed', that is, having an Indian mother, and Johnson who with an Indian father 'was Indian by race and by law', *Pauline Johnson and Her Friends* (Toronto: Ryerson Press, 1947), p. x. (McRaye 1947)
31. Charlotte Gray, *Flint and Feather: The Life and Times of E. Pauline Johnson, Tekahionwake* (Toronto: Harper Collins, 2002), pp. 156 ff. (Gray 2002)
32. See Jane Stafford and Mark Williams, 'Indian Mysteries and Comic Stunts: The Royal Tour and the Theatre of Empire', *Journal of Commonwealth Literature*, 44: 2 (June 2009): 87–105, for a discussion of this visit. (Stafford and Williams 2009)
33. Carole Gerson and Veronica Strong-Boag, *Paddling Her Own Canoe: the Times and Texts of E. Pauline Johnson, Tekahionwake* (Toronto: Toronto University Press, 2000), p. 110 (Gerson and Strong-Boag 2000); Archives of Ontario, E. Johnson, 'Chiefswood'.
34. Longfellow, *The Song of Hiawatha*, XI, 'The Wedding Feast' (London: Harrap, 1911), p. 108. (Longfellow 1911)
35. Ibid., p. 110.

36. Henry Rowe Schoolcraft, 'Alhalla, or the Lord of Talladega: A Tale of the Creek War', *Alhalla, or the Lord of Talladega* (New York: Wiley & Putnam, 1843), p. 81, lines 133–140. (Schoolcraft 1843)
37. 'A Strong Race Opinion: on the Indian Girl in Modern Fiction', *Sunday Globe*, 22 May, 1892, p. 1.
38. Henry Rowe Schoolcraft (1793–1864), ethnographer and poet; Francis Parkman (1823–93), historian and travel writer; George Catlin (1796–1872), painter and travel writer.
39. Cathy Rex, 'Survivance and Fluidity: George Copway's *The Life, History, and Travels of Kah-Ge-ga-gah-bowh*', *Studies in American Indian Literatures*, 18: 2 (2006): 21. See introduction, p. 5. (Rex 2006)
40. See Mary Elizabeth Leighton, 'Performing Pauline Johnson: Representations of "the Indian Poetess" in the Periodical Press, 1892–95', *Essays on Canadian Writing* 65 (Fall 1998): 149. (Leighton 1998)
41. *The Globe*, 1 November 1893, p. 3.
42. Nellie L. McClung, *The Stream Runs Fast: My Own Story* (Toronto: Thomas Allen, 1945), p. 35. (McClung 1945)
43. Walter McRaye, *Town Hall Tonight*, intro. Lorne Pierce (Toronto: Ryerson Press, 1929?), p. 44. (McRaye 1929?)
44. Leighton, 'Performing Pauline Johnson': 159.
45. 'Outdoor Pastimes for Women', *Collected Poems and Selected Prose*, pp. 176–7.
46. *Collected Poems and Selected Prose*, note, p. 292.
47. *Collected Poems and Selected Prose*, note, p. 306.
48. Linda M. Marra, *Unarrested Archives: Case Studies in Twentieth-Century Canadian Women's Authorship* (Toronto: University of Toronto Press, 2014), p. 33. (Marra 2014)
49. Marra, *Unarrested Archives*, p. 34.
50. 'A Cry from an Indian Wife', Johnson, *Collected Poems and Selected Prose*, p. 14–15; first published in *The Week*, 18 June 1885; *White Wampum* version revised.
51. Earlier versions were more stirring, and more accusatory of the Canadian public, possibly reflecting their performance while the Rebellion was still in progress:

> O! coward self – I hesitate no more.
> Go forth – and win the glories of the war.
> O! heart o'erfraught – O! nation lying low –
> God, and fair Canada have willed it so.
> Johnson, *Collected Poems and Selected Prose*, p. 292.

52. Gerson and Strong-Boag, *Paddling Her Own Canoe*, p. 137.
53. 'The Cattle Thief', *Collected Poems and Selected Prose*, pp. 97–9; first published in *The Week*, 7 December 1894, p. 34.
54. 'The Death Cry', *Collected Poems and Selected Prose*, p. 32.
55. 'As Red Men Die', *Collected Poems and Selected Prose*, p. 68.
56. 'The Pilot of the Plains', *Collected Poems and Selected Prose*, p. 80.
57. 'The Indian Corn Planter', *Collected Poems and Selected Prose*, pp. 124–5.
58. 'The Corn Husker', *Collected Poems and Selected Prose*, p. 121.
59. 'Brantford Briefs', *The Globe*, 7 December 1894, p. 8.
60. *The Democrat*, Grand Rapids Michigan, 10 November 1896.
61. George Copway, *The Life, History, and Travels of Kah-Ge-Ga-Gah-Bowh (George Copway) a Young Indian Chief of the Ojebwa Nation, a Convert to the Christian Faith and a Missionary to his People for Twelve Years; with a Sketch of the Present State of the Ojebwa Nation in Regard to Christianity and Their Future Prospects; also an Appeal; with all the Names of the Chiefs now Living who have been Christianized, and the Missionaries Now Laboring Among Them; Written by Himself* (Albany: Weed and Parsons, 1847), p. 16. (Copway 1847)
62. 'Royal Iroquois Chief', Clipping from Johnson's collection, n.p., n.d., [Toronto newspaper?], E Pauline Johnson Fonds, Box 4, File 15, William Ready Division of Archives and Research Collections, McMaster University Library.
63. Clipping from Johnson's collection, n.p., n.d., E. Pauline Johnson Fonds, Box 4, File 19, William Ready Division of Archives and Research Collections, McMaster University Library.
64. William Pember Reeves, 'The Passing of the Forest', *New Zealand, and Other Poems* (London: Grant Richards, 1898), pp. 7–8. (Reeves 1898)
65. 'Bass Lake (Muskoka)', *Collected Poems and Selected Prose*, pp. 46–7; first published in *Saturday Night*, 2 August 1889, p. 6.
66. 'Star Lake (Muskoka)', *Collected Poems and Selected Prose*, pp. 73–4. Gerson and Strong-Boag use a version from *The Young Canadian*, 22 April 1891, p. 198 as their copy text. It is not clear whether this was where the poem was first published.
67. Daniel Francis, *National Dreams: Myth, Memory, and Canadian History* (Vancouver: Arsenal Pulp Press, 2010), p. 129. (Francis 2010)
68. 'Outdoor Pastimes for Women', *Collected Poems and Selected Prose*, p. 175.
69. Misao Dean, *Inheriting a Canoe Paddle: The Canoe in Discourses of English-Canadian Nationalism* (Toronto: University of Toronto Press, 2013), p. 39. (Dean 2013)
70. Bruce Erikson, *Canoe Nation: Nature, Race, and the Making of a Canadian Icon* (Vancouver: U.B.C. Press, 2013), p. xiii. (Erikson 2013)
71. Dean, *Inheriting a Canoe Paddle*, p. 49.

72. For the experience of other settler cultures in this regard, see Kirstie Ross, *Going Bush: New Zealanders and Nature in the Twentieth Century* (Auckland: Auckland University Press, 2008) (Ross 2008) and Libby Robin, *How a Continent Created a Nation* (Sydney: University of New South Wales Press, 2007). (Robin 2007)
73. Marcus Clarke, Preface, Adam Lindsay Gordon, *Sea Spray and Smoke Drift* (Melbourne: Clarson, Massina and Co, 1876), p. vi. (Clarke 1876)
74. 'The Song My Paddle Sings', *Collected Poems and Selected Prose*, p. 81; first published in *Saturday Night*, 27 February 1892, p. 7.
75. Brant Historical Society no. 563, Brant County Museum and Archives.
76. Thomas O'Hagan, 'Some Canadian Women Writers', *The Week*, 5 September 1896, p. 1053.
77. Several of the stories were published in both journals, and republished after the appearance of *The Legends of Vancouver*. See Gerson and Strong-Boag, *Paddling Her Own Canoe*, pp. 230–32 for a list of publication details.
78. E. Pauline Johnson, *Legends of Vancouver* (1911) (Vancouver: Douglas and McIntyre, 1997), p. vii. (Johnson 1997)
79. *Ibid*.
80. Their shared identity is to a great extent manufactured by Johnson. She and Capilano were in fact from different groupings, and she employs here the imperial practice of conflating and eliding difference between colonised groups. Elleke Boehmer, in *Empire, the National, and the Postcolonial 1890–1920* (Oxford, 2002), p. 6, talks of the way in which at this time 'the entire imperial framework becomes... at once decentred and multiply-centred, a network, one might say, of interrelating margins' but this must be set against the way in which the dominant discourse of empire was, inevitably, adopted by colonised writers. (Boehmer 2002)
81. Johnson, 'The Two Sisters', *Legends of Vancouver*, p. 2.
82. Jay Arthur, 'Natural Beauty, Man-Made', *Words for Country: Landscape and Language in Australia*, eds. Tim Bonyhady and Tom Griffiths, Sydney: University of NSW Press, 2002, pp. 190–205. (Arthur 2002)
83. Johnson, 'The Two Sisters', *Legends of Vancouver*, p. 2.
84. Johnson, 'Deer Lake', *Legends of Vancouver*, p. 122.
85. Johnson, 'Deadman's Island', *Legends of Vancouver*, p. 96. Johnson renames Coal Harbour called so because of its proximity to a railway coal-yard, the Lost Lagoon: 'I always resented that jarring, unattractive name... This was just to please my own fancy', Gray, *Flint and Feather*, p. 353.
86. Johnson, 'The Grey Archway', *Legends of Vancouver*, p. 83.
87. Catherine Parr Traill, *The Backwoods of Canada* (1836) (Toronto: McClelland and Stewart, 1989), p. 128. (Traill 1989). Daniel Coleman points out that the young George Copway who was at that time at school

nearby could have supplied Traill with an abundance of 'historical associations' and 'legendary tales'. See 'Grappling with Respect: Copway and Traill in a Conversation that Never Took Place', *English Studies in Canada* 39: 2–3 (June–September 2013): 63–88.
88. Alexander Bathgate, 'Faerie', *Far South Fancies* (London: Griffith, Farran, Okenden, and Welsh, 1890), p. 99. (Bathgate 1890)
89. Johnson, 'The Recluse', *Legends of Vancouver*, p. 17.
90. Johnson, 'The Lure in Stanley Park', *Legends of Vancouver*, p.113.
91. See Margo Lukens, '"A Being of a New World": the Ambiguity of Mixed Blood in Pauline Johnson's "My Mother"', *MELUS* 27: 3 (Fall 2002): 43–58 for a discussion of Johnson's own writings on her mixed race background. (Lukens 2002)
92. Johnson, 'The Two Sisters', *Legends of Vancouver*, p. 2.
93. Johnson, 'The Grey Archway', *Legends of Vancouver*, p. 84.
94. Johnson, 'The Grey Archway', *Legends of Vancouver*, p. 84. In fact, Johnson knew very little of the Chinook – or her own language, Mohawk.
95. In 'The Legend of the "Salt-Chuck Oluk"', for example, he assures Johnson 'If you care to go there one day I will show you the hollow in one great stone where that head lay', Johnson, 'The Legend of the "Salt-Chuck Oluk"', *Legends of Vancouver*, p. 53.
96. Johnson, 'The Grey Archway', *Legends of Vancouver*, p. 91.
97. Johnson, 'The Lost Island', *Legends of Vancouver*, p. 59.
98. Johnson, 'The Lost Island', *Legends of Vancouver*, p. 60
99. Johnson, 'The Recluse', *Legends of Vancouver*, p. 18.
100. Lee Schweninger discusses the use of the term 'terminal creeds' in the writing of Gerald Vizenor to describe the deployment of this motif in contemporary Native American literature, 'Radicalism and Liberation in Native American Literature', *Post-Colonial Literatures: Expanding the Canon*, ed. Deborah L Madsen (London: Pluto, 1999), pp. 206–7. (Vizenor 1999)
101. Johnson, 'The Recluse', *Legends of Vancouver*, pp. 19–20.
102. Johnson, 'The Deep Waters', *Legends of Vancouver*, p. 47.
103. Johnson, 'The Deep Waters', *Legends of Vancouver,* p. 43.
104. Johnson, 'The Lost Salmon Run', *Legends of Vancouver*, p. 32. Johnson addresses the narrator as 'Dear old klootchman!'
105. Johnson, 'The Lost Salmon Run', *Legends of Vancouver*, p. 36.
106. Johnson, 'The Two Sisters', *Legends of Vancouver*, p. 2. For a discussion of the poetic expression of oral Indigenous literature see Jane Stafford, 'Immeasurable Abysses and Living Books: Oral Literature and Victorian Poetics in Alfred Domett's *Ranolf and Amohia*', *Bulletin of the Bibliographical Society of Australia and New Zealand*, Special Issue 28: 1,2 (2004), pp. 161–71. (Stafford 2004) Okereke discusses the ways in which performance values might be recorded in an oral text, Augustine Okereke, 'The Performance and

the Text: Parameters for Understanding Oral Literary Performance', *Across the Lines: Intertexuality and Transcultural Communication in the New Literatures in English*, ed. Wolfgang Kloss, Amsterdam: Rodopi, 1998, pp. 39–50. (Okereke 1998)
107. In the introduction to *Performance and Cultural Politics Context* (London: Routledge, 1996), pp. 1–2, Elin Diamond discusses the relation between the immediate context and the historic and on-going cultural contribution that such performances consist of. He quotes James Clifford (*Writing Culture: the Poetics and Politics of Ethnography* [Berkeley: University of California Press, 1986], p. 19): 'Twentieth-century identities no longer presuppose continuous cultures or traditions. Everywhere individuals and groups improvise local performances from (re)collected pasts, drawing on foreign media, symbols, languages... culture is contested, temporal, and emergent'. (Clifford 1986)
108. Johnson, 'The Sea Serpent', *Legends of Vancouver*, pp. 51–2.
109. Johnson, 'The Recluse', *Legends of Vancouver*, p. 27.
110. Johnson, 'The Lost Salmon Run', *Legends of Vancouver*, p. 39.
111. Johnson, 'The Sea Serpent', *Legends of Vancouver*, p. 49.
112. Johnson, 'The Grey Archway', *Legends of Vancouver*, p. 86.
113. Johnson, 'A Squamish Legend of Napoleon', *Legends of Vancouver*, p. 110.
114. Johnson, 'The Grey Archway', *Legends of Vancouver*, p. 86.
115. Johnson, 'The Sea Serpent', *Legends of Vancouver*, p. 51.
116. Johnson, 'The Sea Serpent', *Legends of Vancouver*, p. 56.
117. George W. Lyon, 'Pauline Johnson: A Reconsideration', *Studies in Canadian Literature* 15, no. 2 (1990), p. 136. (Lyon 1990)
118. Johnson, 'The Sea Serpent', *Legends of Vancouver*, p 57.
119. See a discussion of early reservations by Johnson's contemporaries, Gerson and Strong-Boag, *Paddling Her Own Canoe*, p. 176.
120. Gray, *Flint and Feather*, p. 53.
121. 'Current News of Interest to Mothers', *Mothers' Magazine*, December 1906, p. 51. See Gerson and Strong-Boag, *Paddling Her Own Canoe*, p. 170.
122. 'The Great Deep Water: a Legend of "The Flood"', a *Mothers' Magazine* early version of 'The Deep Waters'. See Gerson and Strong-Boag, *Paddling Her Own Canoe*, p. 173 and note 85.
123. Johnson, 'The Lure in Stanley Park', *Legends of Vancouver*, p 119.
124. Johnson, 'The Lure in Stanley Park', *Legends of Vancouver*, p 119.
125. Deena Rymhs describes Johnson's writing as 'deal[ing] with Native cultures and issues, curiously yoked with western, European literary forms', 'But the Shadow of her Story: Narrative Unsettlement, Self-inscription and Translation in Pauline Johnson's *Legends of Vancouver*', *Studies in American Indian Literatures* 13.4 (Winter 2001), p. 52 (Rymhs 2001). But there is nothing curious about the incorporation of ethnological material into Victorian

colonial literature. Anne Collett, discussing the poetry, usefully points to Johnson's use of the literary ballad, a form which traditionally transgresses boundaries, 'Pauline Tekahionwake Johnson: Her Choice of Form', *Kunapipi* 19:1 (1997), p. 63. (Collett 1997)

126. Isabel Ecclestone Mackay, 'Pauline Johnson: A Reminiscence', *Canadian Magazine* 41 (1913), p. 274. (Mackay 1913)
127. See Diana Brydon's critique of critics such as Frederic Jameson who assume 'a first world criticism respectful of a third world authenticity that it is believed his own world has lost', 'The White Inuit Speaks', *Past the Last Post: Theorizing Post-Colonialism and Post-Modernism*, eds. Ian Adam and Helen Tiffin (Hemel Hempstead: Harvester, 1991), p. 195 (Brydon 1991). Katja Sarkowsky warns of a tendency in postcolonial criticism of 'a dangerous reduction to a dualistic or monolithic understanding as divided exclusively along ethno-cultural and political lines', 'Writing (and) Art – Native American/First Nations' Art and Literature: Beyond Resistance and Reconciliation', *Resistance and Reconciliation: Writing in the Commonwealth*, eds. Bruce Bennett, Susan Cowan, Jacqueline Lo, Satendra Nandan and Jen Webb (Canberra: ACLALS, 2003), p. 91. (Sarkowsky 2003)
128. Mackay, 'Pauline Johnson: A Reminiscence', pp. 273–4.
129. Franz Fanon, 'Concerning Violence', *The Wretched of the Earth*, trans. Constance Farrington (Harmondsworth: Penguin, 1961), pp. 54–5. (Franz 1961)

# CHAPTER 6

# 'Pressed Down by the Great Words of Others': Wiremu Maihi Te Rangikaheke and Apirana Ngata

In the New Zealand colony's foundational poem, *Ranolf and Amohia* (1872), the British hero sets out to explain to his beloved, the Māori princess Amohia, what he describes as 'the stately Ship of Western Thought'.[1] In keeping with his literary model and personal friend Robert Browning, the poem's author Alfred Domett relaxes into the task – *Ranolf and Amohia* is 500 pages of close print, longer than *Paradise Lost*. Even Tennyson, not noted for his brevity, remarked on the poem's 'want of limitation'.[2] But in return for Ranolf's exposition of 'the Soul and God',[3] and in keeping with the poem's generic mode of fictive ethnography, Amohia is also allowed her say, meeting Ranolf's philosophising with her own systematic exposition of Indigenous lore and custom.

*Ranolf and Amohia* is that very Victorian beast, a poem with footnotes. Amohia may inhabit the airy realms of Maoriland, the romantic, archaised version of the past that was the construct of settler New Zealand. But her sources are all impeccably scholarly and their citations given in full. Her voice, the narrative trick whereby she speaks in Māori but is transliterated on the page in high Victorian verse, is explained in an appendix in terms of contemporary translation theories of Matthew Arnold and Friedrich Wolf. And the synchronicity of her world view with that of Ranolf demonstrates a key concept in nineteenth-century intellectual and imperial thought, the ultimately unitary nature of all systems of knowledge.

© The Author(s) 2016
J. Stafford, *Colonial Literature and the Native Author*,
DOI 10.1007/978-3-319-38767-3_6

Behind much colonial literary production lies issues of transmission, translation and transliteration. Domett's chief source for his poem was the work of his friend and political ally George Grey, governor of New Zealand from 1845 to 1853 and 1861 to 1868, the only person to read *Ranolf and Amohia* before Domett carried it back to London in 1872 as colonial booty, its mixture of erudition and sensation – cannibal feasts, volcanic eruptions, and beastly superstitions – intended to win Domett a place in the English literary establishment. It was Grey's collections of Māori material, published in 1853[4] and translated as *Polynesian Mythology* in 1855[5] which gave the poem its snap of the authentic.[6]

George Grey was a Victorian type, the scholar colonialist. As a young army officer he had undertaken exploration in Western and South Australia and accompanied his exploits with the composition of a grammar of Aboriginal languages, an account of their customs and a survey of local botany. Appointed governor of New Zealand in 1845 when he was thirty-three, he found an edgy and unsettled colony, racked with enmity between settler and native, settler and governor, and governor and missionary. In 1847 Grey wrote:

> I have neither read in history nor met in real life with such a case as the present in which a few individuals... have acquired such large tracts of land from ignorant savages over which they have acquired a religious influence, and who being themselves missionaries have then assailed with such violence and obloquy a person [i.e. himself] who has endeavoured to protect the rights of the suffering and complaining natives.[7]

In 1848 one of his settler adversaries wrote, 'He never offends one's self love, he listens as well as he talks and he leaves you with a notion that you have made some impression on him when in fact you have made none.'[8]

Given this context, the preface to Grey's 1855 *Polynesian Mythology* is a statement of political pragmatism as much as it is a scholarly exposition. Grey begins with an acknowledgement of the hostility and discontent his governorship encountered:

> I soon perceived that I could neither successfully govern, nor hope to conciliate, a numerous and turbulent people, with whose language, manners, customs, religion, and modes of thought I was quite unacquainted. In order to redress their grievances, and apply remedies, which would neither

wound their feelings, nor militate against their prejudices, it was necessary that I should be able thoroughly to understand their complaints....[9]

Aware of the debates surrounding translation that Domett would later reference, Grey describes his initial intention to learn the Māori language giving way to an awareness that simply finding the exact equivalence between English and Māori words would be to ignore more complex undercurrents which were cultural rather than linguistic:

> To my surprise... I found that these chiefs, either in their speeches to me, or in their letters, frequently quoted, in explanation of their views and intentions, fragments of ancient poems or proverbs, or made allusions which rested on an ancient system of mythology... it was clear that the most important parts of their communications were embodied in these figurative forms....[10]

Māori fondness for figurative speech quickly became a colonial truism. C.O.B. Davis, a government translator, wrote in 1855 of 'the metaphorical mode of expression in use among these singularly interesting tribes',[11] and in 1865 the *New Zealand Herald* expressed the view that Māori had a 'natural turn for word painting' and would 'search for a second meaning in every sentence'.[12] Grey's task, faced with such literary allusiveness, was not merely to attain knowledge of the language – an issue of grammar and vocabulary – but to enter into a system of rhetorical translation and transposition which recognised that seemingly extraneous, ornamental and literary features of expression convey actual, pragmatic meaning. What was needed, Grey realised, was the necessary interpretive trick. As with his research in Australia, he needed to construct a grammar, but a grammar of the metaphorical rather than the physical world, deploying the tools of interpretive criticism. As in biblical exegesis, the outcome of the enquiry will be not merely aesthetic enjoyment, but access to fundamental information. His purpose is not aesthetic but empathetic. At the conclusion of his endeavours, he says, he is confident that

> [f]or the first time... a European reader will find it in his power to place himself in the position of one who listens to a heathen and savage high-priest explaining to him, in his own words, and in his own energetic manner, the traditions in which he earnestly believes, and unfolding the religious opinions upon which the faith and hopes of his race rest.[13]

This is a key moment in imperial systematics. The cultural relativism of the early empire is shifting to a more rigid, evangelically driven position. Grey stands on the cusp. He recognises the intellectual pleasure in inhabiting the world of a 'heathen and savage high-priest', and at the same time deplores what he describes as the 'awful superstitions' and 'cruel and barbarous rites' of their 'puerile' traditions.[14] He follows Victorian ethnographic and philological scholars in seeing an identity between Māori mythology and that of Saxon, Celtic and Scandinavian societies, but he primly considers that ignorance of *all* systems has 'too generally led to their being considered far grander and more reasonable than they really were'.[15]

With his intellectual sympathies finely balanced by his Christian fastidiousness, Grey soon finds that his project's difficulties are not conceptual or intellectual, but practical – negotiations with the powerful and quixotic sources, uncomfortable travel to obscure parts of the country, the organisation of material collected, the collating of different traditions from different sources and the chance of random mishap, such as the fire at Government House in Auckland in June 1848 where as he put it bleakly 'all the Maori notes' were lost. As he observes, 'A man employed in the service of a great and extensive Empire can...never perfectly adjust or arrange his entire life'.[16]

In *Ranolf and Amohia*, Ranolf is told his Māori lore in post-coital conversation. Grey's account of his sources is far from lubricious, but no less romanticised, as he claims privileged access to a generation unsullied by colonial contact:

> [p]robably to no other person but myself would many of their ancient rhythmical prayers and traditions have been imparted by their priests; and it is less likely that any one could now acquire them, as I regret to say that most of their old chiefs, and even some of the middle-aged ones who aided me in my researches, have already passed to the tomb.[17]

Grey is being deliberately vague. His purpose is to establish an unimpeachable authenticity for his material. But in fact, logically, much of his information came not from the high romance of old chiefs, but from a class of Christian converts, Church Missionary Society-educated young men with links to chiefly families but not necessarily chiefly themselves – literate but, in the manner of this particular generation, literate in Māori rather than English.[18] Just as Grey suppresses the references to sexual activity and bodily excretions in the myths he transcribes, so he suppresses the in-between status of his informants, the Christian framework with which they viewed their material, and the contemporary, tribal and partisan nature of each man's stance, highly political, though not necessarily in a sense that Grey would understand the term.

These men – Grey's secretary and interpreter Pirikawau of the Ngatitoa and Te Atiawa tribes, who was educated by the missionary Octavius Hadfield at Otaki and travelled with him to England and South Africa; Te Riwau Ropiha; Te Rangi Matanuku; and Wirimu Maihi Te Rangikaheke – are that significant but overlooked element in the cultural conversations of settler nations. They were difficult to fit into colonial binary structures of thought and were figured variously as loyal servant or Christian convert. They present similar difficulties today, too often seen by postcolonial critics as dupes, collaborators and embarrassments, or anachronistically enrolled into the ranks of postcolonial resistance: Māori critic Linda Tuhiwai Smith, in her 1999 work *Decolonizing Methodologies*, describes these figures as 'problematic', 'closely allied to the colonizers in terms of their class interests, their values and their ways of thinking'.[19] They hint at separate agendas, hidden or lost to the official record, alien world views difficult to contain within Victorian ideological formations or modern theoretical ones. Viewed by their colonial employers as a means to the authenticated past of pre-modernity, they were in fact significant actors in and products of the colonial present.

Tony Ballantyne describes the effect on Indigenous societies of projects such as Grey's:

> The processes by which [these collections] were created profoundly altered the knowledge they recorded, disembodying these traditions, wrenching them free of the traditional social contexts of knowledge transmission to revalue them as an aid to the operation of imperial authority.[20]

But Ballantyne stresses that the two-way process such information gathering entailed was also enabling. Grey's collaborators were not without agency and influence, and not without understanding of the implications of what they were involved in. As Ballantyne writes:

> [i]n many instances, colonized peoples embraced the printed word's ability to preserve 'tradition' through the recording of genealogies, the documentation

of oral traditions, and the production of tribal and caste histories. These texts allowed colonized groups to record their understandings of the past and to articulate their vision of the future. In many cases, we should see this response to colonization not as conservative or reactive but rather a creative and powerful response that turned the colonial state's fetishization of documents and history against itself.[21]

In the New Zealand context, Jane McRae points to 'the interactions between print and orality and the transformative effects of these changes'.[22] Literacy, she argues, was seen by Māori as a 'key to European religious and technical knowledge'.[23] Lindsay Head writes: 'Maori adopted literacy for the same reasons as Pakeha [Europeans]: as an information technology – not a trivial or imitative skill, but a useful one.'[24] The Māori newspaper *Te Wananga* produced in the 1870s saw the danger in being excluded from this new order: 'How the Pakeha is saved is that they write down everything they say. How we Maori are lost is that we don't record what we say.'[25]

Grey's chief source from 1846 to 1853 was Te Rangikaheke of Ngati Rangiwehiwehi of Te Arawa, also known by his baptismal name William Marsh and its Māori transliteration Wiremu Maihi. There are two photographic images of Te Rangikaheke.[26] In one he is pictured in the role of traditional warrior; the other he presents very differently, in conventional Victorian suit and tie, indicating the performative nature of both personae and his pivoting position between two cultures. Such dual representations were not uncommon.[27] Michael Jackson talks about the intersection of oral and written culture as bringing 'challenges to traditional chiefs from the literate who acquired prestige that had no precedent in custom'.[28] Opposing and strongly voiced opinions as to Te Rangikaheke's character reflect this. Lady Martin, wife of the chief justice, described him as 'very quaint and clever in his talk with us'[29] but said that on his first visit to Auckland he was denied entrance to her house because he wore 'a dirty blanket', that is, the normal clothing of the postcontact Māori. When he returned 'dressed in such a good suit of clothes' – that is, European dress – she recounted that he 'quoted the bible against her inhospitality'.[30] In his 1967 history of the Arawa people, Don Stafford describes Te Rangikaheke as 'one of [its] more turbulent characters' and 'the son of a celebrated priest', though he was 'claimed by some to be a chief of the highest rank and by others a person of much less dignity'. He is reported to have been 'a wild looking handsome fellow',[31] possessed of 'an oily tongue', 'a dangerous character, and cordially hated by a portion of Te Arawa'.[32] Stafford positions Rangikaheke in the changing context of mid-century New Zealand:

> [a] highly intelligent and gifted man, at a time when Maori thought was being greatly influenced by new knowledge, and by the pressure of a rapidly increasing Pakeha population.... Much of his work has a literary sophistication not to be found in the writings of the more strictly traditional recorders of Maori material. He was very talented writer who achieved in his work a unique blend of old and new....[33]

McRae describes his work as 'fluent and sophisticated... some of the finest Maori literature'.[34]

Te Rangikaheke was around 30 years old when he first met Grey. He had been educated in and had access to Māori traditional knowledge, and his European education was gained from Church Missionary Society lay missionaries, Thomas and Ann Chapman. Te Rangikaheke saw his role, he later wrote, to serve 'the Governor's desire to learn the Maori language, in fact all Maori custom'.[35] As he wrote to Queen Victoria in 1850, 'the governor has a double task of looking after Maori and Pakeha; matters within Maoridom are neglected because of the governor's ignorance of language and custom... Te Rangikaheke was living with the governor to teach him'.[36] Grey paid him 2/6 a day, or £36 a year, housed him, providing a 'whare tuhituhi' or writing place, and supplied flour, sugar, tobacco, and other goods. Te Rangikaheke later wrote:

> I... lived with [the governor] and his wife in their house. We ate together every day of the week; we talked together, played together, were happy together. His kindness to me was like his kindness to his own child, his younger brother or relation.[37]

It is difficult to know how to define such relationships, let alone to know how the participants defined them. Te Rangikaheke's biographer Jenifer Curnow writes that the three draft letters to Queen Victoria which he wrote between 1845 and 1850 'indicate the political purpose he intended with his association with Grey'.[38] Grey and Te Rangikaheke were master and servant, governor and governed, coloniser and colonised, Pākehā and Māori. But they were both Christian, and both, in some sort of sense, scholars. Were they friends? How applicable are Victorian notions of male friendship in such circumstances? Were there equivalent Māori concepts? How much did Christian ideals of fellowship and joint evangelical endeavour apply? Alex Frame, recounting the trip Grey and Iwikau Te Heu Heu took in 1849–1850 through the central North Island of New Zealand, describes that relationship as 'in essence a combination of elementary good manners and respectful curiosity and scholarship in a spirit of co-operation in the full sense of that deceptively simple activity'.[39] Could this be applied to Grey and Te Rangikaheke? Iwikau was the Upoko Ariki, or paramount chief, of Tuwharetoa, a very powerful figure, and perhaps would have enjoyed a more equal relationship with the governor than Te Rangikaheke was able to.

What is not disputed is Te Rangikaheke's authority when it came to his writing. He was considered by contemporaries as 'a person of some repute in [knowledge of legendary material]'.[40] Stafford considers that 'at least a considerable part of *Polynesian Mythology*, published under the name of Sir George Grey in 1855, was in actual fact compiled and written by Wiremu Marsh',[41] although, as Stafford demonstrates, his sources and authority were the subject of debate within Māoridom. Some of the Arawa people

> [c]laimed that much of the material Maihi gave Sir George was false; but there would be without a doubt a certain amount of jealousy in this, making it an unrealistic appraisal of Maihi's worth. Certainly the large amount of evidence that Maihi gave in later times during Land Court hearings, and which was very largely undisputed by some of his former critics, is evidence of his genuine or at least superior knowledge of things Maori.[42]

Te Rangikaheke is the sole author of twenty-one extant manuscripts, a collaborator in seventeen, some 800 pages, although there is no evidence that he knew or ever wrote in English.[43] Some of the manuscripts display evidence of close collaborative composition with Grey, with interlinear notes, commentaries and records of discussions written in both men's hands. Others were written with different purposes and for different audiences. They range in subject matter. Donald Jackson Kerr describes them as 'encompass[ing] most aspects of Maori culture: language usage, genealogies, legends, contemporary history, political commentary, customs, annotation of moteatea (chants) and autobiographical material, waiata (songs) and proverbs'.[44]

One of Te Rangikaheke's manuscripts, dated October 1853, is entitled 'Ancient Poems, Legends, Ceremonies and Services appropriate to nearly all circumstances of New Zealanders [i.e., Māori]'. In this document, Te Rangikaheke sets out what Curnow describes as an 'exposition of

Maori knowledge and its skilful retention by the Maori people from the time the world was covered in darkness' to the present. The manuscript moves from the strictly practical – matters such as the weather, the fertility of the land and people, the theory and practice of dogs, canoe building – to the esoteric, 'sacred matters, ceremonies and incantations'. But there is a purpose to this compendium: 'although some knowledge was lost, the Maori people were more skilled at retaining knowledge from one generation to another than were other peoples... the ancestors left nothing to chance'.[45] In Te Rangikahke's manuscripts, the skilfully retained knowledge of Māori tradition is being shifted from the rhetorical structures of oral transmission into the methodically organised and systematically classified archive of the governor. Two manuscripts translated by Margaret Orbell illustrate his consciousness of this relationship and his role within it. Both are transcriptions of dreams, but they are cast in a conventional form, that of the matakite or visionary song. Orbell writes, 'The language of these... was usually metaphorical and often cryptic'.[46] Te Rangakaheke's first dream is as follows:

> I saw some men walking along with a dog. I could not clearly distinguish whether these people were Pakeha or Maori. They said to me, 'Let us fight!' I said, 'No, those evil customs of former days are ended. Let us instead carefully discuss the mater [sic]. We can fight later.'
> They said, 'Let a document be written: afterwards we will fight.'
> And so it was written, and was finished. Then we fought.[47]

The setting of the dream is one of contention and possible warfare, and the necessity of 'those evil customs of former days' to be rejected. Whether this refers to inter-tribal conflict of the first decades of the century or the conflict with European settlement is not clear, perhaps intentionally: the speaker quite carefully notes that the figures in his dream could be either Pākehā or Māori. What is interesting about the dream is the central role of writing, of documentation, even though in the conclusion – 'And so it was written, and was finished. Then we fought' – there is a sense of the inevitability of conflict.

The second dream has the same structure as the first – a setting, actors, the immanence of conflict:

> After this we came together at the edge of the ocean; some were on a bridge, and some were below it. I saw tables standing there with paper and pens and

inkwells. One of them said, 'My friend Maihi, go to that table and write your views on the battle that is about to begin.'[48]

Again, there is Te Rangikaheke the clerk at his desk recording it. In both cases the written record – his written record – is a central part of the vision.

\*\*\*

Between 1855 when Grey wrote his first preface to *Polynesian Mythologies* and 1885 when he revised it for the second edition, New Zealand transformed itself into, if not quite a nation, then certainly a recognisable society within the ambit of empire – bustling, modern and enterprising. In 1855, the small settler community had been an irritant – Domett had written to Robert Browning of its dreary provincialism, a 'damned dull collection of log huts'[49] – and the chief business of the governor had been relations with the far more numerous Māori. By 1885 the European population was vastly larger in number, increasingly urbanised and busily constructing its own mythologies. The military engagements of the 1860s and 1870s and the widespread land dispossession that followed fuelled the expectation of Māori's immanent extinction. The role of settler society was, as one commentator put it, to 'smooth the pillow of the dying race'.[50]

Thus in 1885 Grey's purpose in writing a second preface to a new edition of *Polynesian Mythology* differed from the carefully focused pragmatism of his 1855 version. The collection of myths is no longer a tool to deal with an unruly people with a bent for metaphor, but a way of defining an imaginative space now emptied of its original owners. The aim of the editor is now not political but scholarly. He is no longer an actor, and the material has been separated from its original owners and exists as a scholarly text rather than as reported speech. In the *Transactions and Proceedings of the Royal Society* 1892, R. Harding Coupland reflects this shift when he writes:

> It is easy to disparage the quality of native lore on the ground that it is elliptical, obscure, and at times when literally translated wholly unintelligible. The difficulty which meets the translator or collector on the very threshold of his work is the allusiveness characteristic of all the songs and sayings. The most brief and pointed proverb may embody some reference to an old hero, a national custom, the habit of some obscure plant or animal, or to some well-known fable or story. Before it can be understood, a great mass of native lore must be mastered, and if literally rendered it is meaningless without annotation.[51]

## 6 'PRESSED DOWN BY THE GREAT WORDS OF OTHERS': WIREMU MAIHI...

The differences between Coupland writing in 1892 and Grey's initial 1855 Preface to *Polynesian Mythology* are instructive. The allusiveness of Māori rhetoric is now not a barrier to governing and conciliating a 'numerous and turbulent people'. It is an academic challenge to textual interpretation and annotation. Its place in national and political life now marginal, Māori culture is viewed as a collectable, with no direct line of ownership, much like the collection of artefacts that surrounded Grey in his retirement on Kawau Island.

Because of this removal, Grey's 1885 introduction can spell out the mechanics of the work's production. This is, after all, now a scholarly rather than administrative exercise, and Grey is anxious to convey the sense of the New Zealand material as constituting a growing and reputable scholarly domain, equal to and connected with imperial intellectual networks. His activities are part of local institutions such as the Polynesian Society, the New Zealand Institute, provincial mechanics' institutes and libraries, and the newly formed university colleges with their public lecture programmes, dialectic debating societies and English language and literature departments.[52] Grey's debt is now not to his original sources, the vaguely described great chiefs now gone, but to the work of other scholars, some overseas – 'my friend Dr Bleek...the greatest of living philologists' – but others who are local: John White, Octavius Hadfield, William Martin, Robert Maunsell, J.F.H. Wholers.

In the same vein, he acknowledges the work of his Māori collaborators, computing the number of manuscripts 'written by natives from the dictation of the most celebrated old chiefs' and 'all gone over and corrected by natives who could read and write'. 'In many cases' Grey writes, 'I told them exactly what I wanted, supplied them with the requisite writing materials, and some months afterwards received a valuable manuscript which had been dictated to an educated native.'[53]

But unlike the confidence and sense of community with which Grey can enumerate his fellow European scholars, his Māori collaborators, 'fellow-labourers and assistants', have an ambiguous place in the 1885 preface, reflecting their uneasy place in the modern settler nation. Some, he writes, have assimilated British values and are remembered in monuments raised by 'European hands and European regard' testifying to 'British admiration for nobility of character and purpose, wherever these qualities may be found'. But others have broken out of their 'whare tuhituhi', and, 'led astray by designing men', have fought against the government in the military engagements of the 1860s and 1870s, withdrawing 'in a state of obstinate and resolute isolation from the Europeans, under a native king, in the mountainous fastnesses of the interior of the North Island'.

What Grey cannot acknowledge is the attraction of those 'fastnesses' – geographical and intellectual – for his former collaborators, given the unaccommodating nature of the developing settler nation, where Māori are allowed to exist only in scholarly catalogues, or in the sentimental imagination of the European in an artfully conceived and winsomely archaised past. Such imaginative formations leave no space for the realities of Māori existence in the late colonial period – realities suggested by Te Rangikaheke's career after 1855. He fought on the side of the government in the wars in 1860s, and his son was killed fighting against the rebel prophet Te Kooti Arikirangi Te Turuki. He was in government employment for eighteen years; he worked as a land purchase agent and was an assessor for the Native Land Court. He was a vocal critic of the separatist Kingitanga or Māori King movement, the 'mountainous fastnesses' which Grey refers to. He was an active letter writer and translations of his letters concerning local political affairs were published in the local press. But when he stood for parliament in a European electorate in 1875 he gained only ten votes out of 616.

What happens to settler societies when the bush is cleared, the cities built and the natives relegated to a twilight world, delineated not by the careful, traditionally formed cosmologies of Te Rangikaheke and his fellows, or by their canny negotiations with modernity, but by the European poets of Maoriland? In the work of these writers the texts of Te Rangikaheke become the source material for poetic whimsy – albeit whimsy with footnotes and an ethnographical twang of authenticity. This material is not a transcription of Te Rangikaheke's skilfully retained knowledge, but a local version of Victorian medievalism, highly wrought, consciously inauthentic, with the same collaborative relation to the nationalist project that medievalism had for late Victorian England. It may be sourced from Māori material, through the channels of Te Rangikaheke and his fellows, Grey, and the scholars and popularisers of late colonial culture. But the material is divorced from its originators and bent towards a nationalist purpose, although not entirely without a sense of what it is excluding. A 1899 poem by Arthur Adams, 'The Brave Days to Be', begins with an optimistic vision of a future New Zealand:

> My Maoriland! she sat a new-crowned queen,
> Hilarious and radiant with youth,

> Superbly throned above world of peace
> By the mere power of loveliness.[54]

But the poem ends with a description of an absence:

> But alas!
> Over the isles a whispered story went–
> A memory of vague laughter and of life
> Irrevocably mute, for ever mourned.
> From his high place the Maori, the erect
> Brown, sturdy efflorescence of the isles
> Had fallen. Nevermore the warriors
> Superb in pride of kingly thews, with spear
> And murdering mere [club] through the shrinking land
> Imperiously strode....[55]

The language here is Victorian-archaic, Tennysonian cadences and Ossianic sentiments. And in a poem about the future – 'The Brave Days to Be' – the present and the past are carefully segmented and each given its own rhetorical register. Māori in the present are 'whispered', a 'memory', 'vague', 'mute', 'mourned', 'fallen'. What is so forcefully – so floridly – described, 'the erect/Brown, sturdy efflorescence [with] kingly thews [striding] imperiously' with 'spear and murdering mere', is what no longer exists. But it is also what never existed, any more than Tennyson's knights or Mathew Arnold's Vikings ever existed.

Te Rangikaheke died in 1896, two years before Grey. In 1903 there was a short piece written by S. Percy Smith entitled 'Wairemu [sic] Maihi Te Rangikaheke, of Rotorua' in the Dunedin newspaper the *Otago Witness* in which Te Rangikaheke is praised as 'a great friend of Sir George Grey's', a significant contributor to *Polynesian Mythology*, 'full of story, songs, traditions, etc.'.[56] But he is also pictured as a comical rogue, 'a very amusing old fellow, very fond of jokes...a good deal given to the wine bottle, and to the charms of female society...a great beggar'. Percy Smith's piece serves as a caption to a large illustration based on the photographs taken of Te Rangikaheke in the 1860s. The artist is James McDonald who at this time was employed by the Department of Tourist and Health Resorts, mainly as a photographer. He later worked for the Dominion Museum and, with the encouragement of Apirana Ngata and Peter Buck (Te Rangi Hiroa), made a series of films of Māori life – the first, in 1918, is named by Jonathan Dennis as 'the earliest known ethnographical film to be made in New Zealand'.[57]

The rest of the newspaper page is taken up with photographs – the *Otago Witness* was a weekly supplement to the *Otago Daily Times* and its selling point was its illustrations. There are photos of the Hanover Street Baptist Church Mission picnic ('Tug of war, won by the Chinese'), the Merton Creamery Milk Supplies First Annual Picnic, and the launch of the Westport Coal Company's new steamer – all the activities of a modern thriving colony. It seems to be a significant moment in the life of the settler nation: the picnicking Baptists and Creamery employees; the heroic stance of Te Rangikaheke's picture and the disparaging tone of the caption; and the career of the illustrator McDonald – a recorder of the past with the technologies of the future, though not an unsympathetic one. Where in all of this is the voice of Te Rangikaheke? In December 1867 he had written a letter to Prince Alfred, son of Queen Victoria, who had just completed a tour of the colony. The letter was translated and published in the *Daily Southern Cross*. It finishes with a 'Song' which concludes:

> This was the ancient saying:–
> After our death, O son, suffer not thyself to be pressed down
> By the great words of others;
> Lift up thy voice, speak on war; and speak on peace;
> So that you may be lifted up by thousands lying here.[58]

It seems reasonable to suppose that, despite the poem's advice to 'lift up thy voice', Te Rangikaheke had been 'pressed down by the great words of others'.

\*\*\*

Three years before Te Rangikaheke's death, the first Māori graduate of a New Zealand university published an essay 'The Past and Future of the Maori' in the Christchurch *Press*. Apirana Ngata was educated at Te Aute College, a school for Māori students initially founded in 1854 by the Anglican Church but later, after a number of years of decline, taken into the Native Schools system.[59] John Thornton, headmaster from 1878 to 1912, was a product of the Church Missionary Society and the Indian colonial education system and Te Aute's atmosphere was bracingly Christian in the manner of *Tom Brown's Schooldays*. An old boy remembered Thornton telling his boys of '[l]ife as a game of football in which our chief opponent was Satan, and on no account were we to let Satan hook the ball from us'.[60] At a time when secondary schooling for Māori (or indeed for the majority of European) children was rare, and the few dedicated schools limited in their curriculum, Thornton decided to prepare his more able students for the university matriculation exam by offering them a syllabus comparable to that of an English grammar school. It was a defiantly literary programme, redolent of David Lester Richardson's development of English studies in the Indian education system, with which Thornton was familiar. The prescription for Te Aute's second highest class in 1898, for instance, specified:

> English literature: Byron's 'Prisoner of Chillon' and Macaulay's 'Armada' to be learnt by heart; extracts from Scott, for reading only; Macaulay's 'Hampden', 11 pages, the text to be learnt by heart; English Grammar: Smith's 'Manual of English Grammar', all the syntax noun, adjective, pronoun, verb and adverb; Latin: English into Latin, Wilkin's Prose Exercises, the 'Eclogue' to the end of 'Hannibal'.[61]

The success of Te Aute graduates at university, in the professions, and in politics endorsed Thornton's belief that Māori students were educable to the same degree as the sons of settlers, and that, to survive, Māori society needed Māori doctors, lawyers, and teachers as well as farmers. The Young Maori Party, which developed out of the Te Aute College Students' Association and was initially called 'The Association for the Amelioration of the Condition of the Maori Race', was a significant political and social force in the early decades of the twentieth century, and its annual conferences, with Thornton as secretary, 'presented in miniature', according to its 1898 report, 'the spectacle of a noble race in immediate danger of sinking but still struggling to keep its head above water'.[62]

Thornton's philosophy was not universally appreciated, and was, by the turn of the century, increasingly at odds with the carefully demarcated fashion in which 'native' education was officially conceived. His concentration on what the Education Department Report of 1902 described as 'the more bookish forms of instruction which tend to unfit Maori boys and girls for the simple life at the pa [Māori settlement]'[63] contravened the belief that such systems should not encourage social mobility. And in the aftermath of the land alienation of the second half of the nineteenth century, and in the throes of the economic depression at the end of the century, even former students such as the Young Maori Party's Maui Pomare complained: 'You have taught us how to read and write, you have taught us Greek and Latin, you have taught our girls how to couch endearing terms to their lovers, teach us also to cultivate our lands.'[64] While some Māori parents appreciated the intellectual sweep of Te Aute, some, such as Ngata's father Paratene, felt that Māori students would be better at an 'industrial school' teaching 'agriculture, poultry-farming, dairy-farming, pig-raising, horticulture and all classes of farm work' along the lines of American Indian schools such as the Federal Sherman Institute in California, which was viewed with admiration by the New Zealand education establishment.[65]

Ngata's essay 'The Past and Future of the Maori' was probably written for Canterbury College's debating society[66] and reflects this intellectual background. It expresses theories of native educability, and the settler agendas and Darwinian stringencies implicit within them, as well as reflecting the way that ethnography had become a popular amateur pastime for educated gentlemen. The professor of English at Canterbury College was John Macmillan Brown, a Scots polymath, amateur ethnographer and utopian novelist, author of the profoundly didactic and almost unreadable fictional duet *Riallaro: the Archipelago of Exiles* (1901) and *Limanora: the Island of Progress* (1903).[67] Macmillan Brown's educational philosophy was a combination of Arnoldian high-mindedness and canny pragmatism. During his job interview in London, Lord Lyttleton, the university's agent, accused him of not being able to write Greek verse, to which Macmillan Brown replied, 'God help me, what would be the good of Greek verse for pioneers in a new colony?'[68] He felt that there was a danger in 'the production of a bookish community unable to bring what they read in relation to what they have to be and to do'. But he also believed in the power of literature 'to bring the highest faculties of the student into play, appeal to his finest emotions and knowledge of life, stimulate and practice his powers of thought and expression'.[69] He defined the new subject

> [a]s a humanity and as the practical art of expression... as a revelation of life and character by its greatest authors... and as a training in the ready and correct manipulation of ideas and phraseology, in oral or in written form. No professional man, no specialist, no citizen of the world, but has need of these.[70]

Ngata's essay begins by emphasising the importance of the past in understanding the present condition of Māori society: 'the feelings and motives that influence [Māori] today are the same that influenced him ages ago'.[71]

Civilisation is a mere veneer, and while Christianity might have been formally accepted, the superstitions of the tohunga (Māori priest) are still secretly adhered to: 'Your Maori today is but the savage of yesterday, polished and draped in European finery...his hands are bound with the manacles of civilisation and humanity, but they are restless to grasp once more the spear, the taiaha (javelin), and mere (club).'[72] The Māori past and Māori culture, Ngata suggests, may be 'a large area for speculation and fruitful pastures for the imagination', but so little is known of the origins and history that

> [w]e are stranded on a strange shore with waves of civilization rolling in dull monotony behind us, and the towering unscaleable precipice of the Maori past locking us in before and on either side. And a dark cloud rests on the edge of the precipice above, and we long for some breath of wind to waft it away that we might catch a glimpse of the confines of that strange land.'[73]

'We' here denotes not Māori – Ngata's identification of himself as Māori is wholly absent throughout the essay – but educated men, enquiring ethnographers, common (European) readers. But the spatial imagery in the passage is configured in accordance with the Māori conception of the past as being ahead. The term for the past in Māori is 'i nga wa o mua', meaning 'from the times in front'. For Ngata, as for Māori in general, the future, civilisation, is 'behind us'. A 'dark cloud' – the present uncertain state of Māoridom, perhaps – is above. The nature of the 'strange land' – the future of modern New Zealand, perhaps – is presented as an intellectual problem which the community the educated Ngata is now part of must decipher.

In contrast with his later incarnations, the Ngata of this period is no culturalist. He is scathing of 'the few customs that still remain among the Maoris, as an inheritance from their ancestors' and dismisses accounts of the Māori legendary past as 'crude and almost childish', marked by 'savage hue and immoral colouring'.[74] In this he takes a harsher stand than his teacher John Macmillan Brown who described Māori as a 'highly intelligent...primitive race'.[75] But Ngata concedes that, depleted by land alienation, depopulated by disease and demoralised by the consequences of war, Māori face an uncertain future deprived of what might sustain them: 'the legendary lore, the metaphysic traditions of his ancestors...the record of the race of heroes and demigods that inhabited these islands'. Indeed, cultural memory has been so affected that 'long genealogies, once his delight to commit to memory, flit in confused array across his diseased and troubled mind'.[76] Living in a present in which he has no place, and deprived of the cultural mechanisms that might connect him to the past,

> [y]et he hears around him echoes from the days gone by; strange antique figures hover round him and will not let him rest, but ape his newfangled manners, mock him for his downfall and jeer at him for his degeneracy. He wanders in fancy back to the days before ever the European set foot on his Arcadia and imported such woe. Where are the mana and prestige of the ancient chiefs, the tapu, the chants and incantations of the priests? Surrendered to the white man, disdained by him and laughed to scorn, nay, abused by those of his own race. Where are those lands over which his ancestors held such absolute sway? Gone, stolen, robbed, the chief source of perplexity to his day, the bane of his race. And the hosts of warriors that traversed forest and plain on the warpath? They, too, are gone, they, too, have disappeared before the advancing tide of immigration. Then he recoils startled and trembling, for the gain of civilisation falls far short of the loss he has suffered.[77]

The rhetorical frame Ngata is using here is the 'ubi sunt' motif, a convention of medieval literature. In Old English poems such as *The Wanderer*, *The Ruin* and *The Seafarer*, an individual bereft of his community and isolated in a bleak and ruined physical landscape reflects on the transience of human life, and nostalgically remembers former glories in a series of rhetorical questions. In *The Wanderer* the narrator laments:

> The Maker of men hath so marred this dwelling
> that human laughter is not heard about it
> and idle stand these old giant-works.
> A man who on these walls wisely looked
> who sounded deeply in this dark life
> would think back to the blood spilt here,
> weigh it in his wit. His word would be this:
> 'Where is that horse now? Where are those men? Where is the hoard-sharer?
> Where is the house of the feast? Where is the hall's uproar?
>
> Alas, bright cup! Alas, burnished fighter!
> Alas, proud prince! How that time has passed,
> dark under night's helm, as though it had never been!'[78]

In the nineteenth century, lines 2247 to 2266 from *Beowulf* were routinely excerpted and titled 'The Lay of the Last Survivor':

'No trembling harp,
no tuned timber, no tumbling hawk
swerving through the hall, no swift horse
pawing the courtyard. Pillage and slaughter
have emptied the earth of entire peoples.'
And so he mourned as he moved around the world,
deserted and alone, lamenting his unhappiness
day and night, until death's flood
brimmed up in his heart.[79]

Old English or, as it was termed in the nineteenth century, Anglo-Saxon poetry and its allied discipline of philology, disseminated by publications such as Henry Sweet's *Anglo-Saxon Reader in Prose and Verse* (1876) and *Anglo-Saxon Primer* (1882) or Morris and Sceat's *Specimens of Early English* (1887), was at the core of the newly conceived university subject, English literature.[80] Though unsympathetic to the philological bias of some universities' brand of English studies, 'a subject', he snorted, 'no more worthy of being the basis of culture than Sanskrit',[81] Macmillan Brown nonetheless introduced Anglo-Saxon literature into the Canterbury College English degree in the early 1890s. He writes:

I could not bear to do this in a superficial or cramming way. I traced the Anglo-Saxon word down to its ultimate English form and also into its relations in other Indo-European languages. I aimed to give each student as large a vocabulary and such ease in translation that he could find pleasure in tackling any piece of Anglo-Saxon at sight.[82]

Macmillan Brown's Scottish education had given him a grounding in the rhetorical, 'belle lettres' mode of teaching university English. Erica Schouten notes his propensity for 'using the literary text as simply a model form of writing rather than as a sanctified form of expression which cannot be emulated'.[83] As early as 1880 when he began as professor of English literature at Canterbury College he had, he wrote later, 'resolved that I should make my chief aim the teaching of the art of writing English'. To this end, he developed an exercise in which students were given a piece of foolscap paper, half a dozen subjects and a choice of literary forms – sonnet, epigram, lyric, story, dramatic scene. The results were then read aloud and the students voted for the best. 'In this way' Macmillan Brown wrote, 'there developed in the class a number of genuine poets and original writers'.[84]

This mode of teaching, allied with the vogue for Anglo-Saxon literature, encouraged the kind of writing that Ngata deploys. The elegiac poems of the newly evolving Anglo-Saxon canon had obvious parallels with the 'dying race' complaint. In both forms, the individual contemplates the remnants of a society and a culture that have been destroyed. In both, the speaker is alone, bereft of his comrades and the community within which he had status and function. In both, he inhabits a blighted, hostile and unsustaining physical landscape. In both, memory is the only way that he can return to the golden age of the past. In both the reader is invited to sympathise with the bereft speaker. Critics have noted the tension in the medieval poems between the Christian framework, with its confidence in the eternal, and the overriding tone of melancholy and transience. As Rosemary Woolf says, the 'ubi sunt' may have been a popular sermon convention, but these poems, 'far from suggesting that their subjects are worthless... confer a deep nostalgic value on them, and the very fleetingness which the questions call to mind enhances rather than diminishes their preciousness'.[85] In much the same way, the nineteenth-century dying race poems tend to eschew the more moralistic contemporary explanations for extinction – 'savage practices', inter-tribal warfare, a lower evolutionary status – and concentrate on the pathos of the individual. Following this pattern, Ngata's version of the 'ubi sunt' asks and answers a series of rhetorical questions: Where are the mana and prestige of the ancient chiefs? Surrendered to the white man. Where are those lands over which his ancestors held such absolute sway? Gone. Where are the hosts of warriors? They, too, are gone.

Ngata's poem 'A Scene from the Past' was written at the same time as the essay 'The Past and Future of the Maori'.[86] Although the same 'dying race' assumptions and 'ubi sunt' plangency underlie the poem, its emphasis is less pessimistic than the essay, more in tune with Woolf's idea of 'nostalgic value', as it locates itself in a past which can be celebrated rather than in a present which must be endured. The narrator begins with an expression of dislocation:

> We reck not that the day has past;
> That Death and Time, the cruel Fates,

Have torn us from the scenes we loved,
And brought us to this unknown world.[87]

Māori are, the poem suggests, 'a race that's speeding/ Sadly onwards to oblivion'. Māori society is a boat – a 'humble reed' – which cannot compete with the 'iron-clad' of colonial modernity. Traditional culture is now accessed only in memory, 'all too hazy,/ Blurred, uncertain', and when that memory is translated and fixed into a literary form the process is necessarily compromising:

> Language doth but
> Clothe in artifice our passion,
> Doth but to the world proclaim
> We are traitors to the past.[88]

So 'language', the framework of the literary empire that the educated Ngata now has at his disposal, is a dangerous tool. The act of recording, of aestheticising the past and adopting the models of Macmillan Brown's composition classes necessarily involves a move from the authentic to the inauthentic.

The poem's answer to this charge is to insist on the validating force of memory. While 'The Past and Future of the Maori' asserts that the memory of traditional forms has been lost to Māori society, in the contemporaneous 'A Scene from the Past', memory is the only resource remaining, a means of connecting to the past, and to demonstrate this, much of the poem is a re-enactment or performance of that past: '[f]or mem'ry, like that herb, embalms/ Preserves, endears our recollections'. While conceding that the Māori population will soon die out, the poem presents not an elegy but a vigorous recreation of what has been lost: a Māori powhiri (ceremony of greeting) at a marae (meeting ground), with challenge, haka (war dance), and waiata (songs). In this re-enactment, the various streams of Ngata's education are apparent. Language pivots between the Indigenous and the classical. Traditional Māori protocol is carefully replicated. The 'maidens lovely' are 'dressed in mats of finest fibre'/ Cheeks with *takou* (red ochre) gaily hued,/ Plumed with quills of rarest *huia* (a native bird prized for its white feathers)'. But they are also favourably compared to classical nymphs and naiads. The warriors chant '*Au, au, au e ha!*', the stage direction given in Māori: '*Ko te iwi Maori e ngunguru nei!*' ('Here the Māori tribe chants'). But they are also described as a fit sight for Mars and Apollo. The ceremony is '[s]taged in meads that heard no bleating,/ Save of savage babes at play', both evoking and rejecting the idea of the English pastoral. And as a balance to the bland conventionality of the poetic language, there is a sharp specificity with a roll call of chiefs and tribes: Rewi, Taonui, Kahungunu, Te Rarawa, Tainui me Te Whakatohea, Whakaata, Taupare, Tuwhakatohea, historical groupings and actual individuals rather than the mythic stereotypes of colonial literature.

In keeping with his experience as the first Māori to study at university, Ngata uses his knowledge of traditional Māori literature, but frames and orientates it in terms of the European literary world he encountered at Te Aute and at Canterbury College. But there is an intermediate stage in this process, the move within the Māori language community from oral literature to written. Written Māori had been developed by missionaries in the early 1800s, and until 1847 the Māori language was their usual teaching medium. It was only subsequent to the second Native Schools Act of 1867 that instruction was solely in English – Te Rangikaheke, born around 1815, wrote only in Māori. Although figures are complex and arguable, Shef Rogers suggests that, at least in the first part of the century, 'the literacy rate in Maori among Maori was higher than the literacy rate in English among the colonists'.[89] Moreover, the ability to read was matched by an enthusiasm by Māori for what the new skill could provide: fixity of expression, the provision of an authoritative record, communication beyond the immediate oral encounter and a way of entering into the world of the Pākehā on a more equal footing. Māori newspapers were widely read, and there was a proliferation of letter writing – personal, official and in the correspondence columns of those newspapers – by those literate in Māori. And, significantly for Ngata's poem, despite their missionary education, writers were not cowed by the stylistic forms of the schoolroom essay or exercise, and adapted the written medium to the conventions of oral performance with which they were more familiar. Timoti Karetu writes:

> In their correspondence with each other and to the newspapers – whether about land, politics, daily events or personal matters – Maori developed a protocol, a convention based largely on the etiquette and protocol of the *marae* or tribal meeting-ground, and particularly on that of the *whaikorero*, the formal speech-making.[90]

As Lyndsay Head puts it, 'Most Maori do not distance themselves from their words, but write as if they were standing to speak'.[91] And that speech is organised in terms of the rules of Māori public oratory.

While Jane McCrae suggests that '[a] perceptible shift to a literate style and mentality by the end of the century might be proposed',[92] Ngata's poem demonstrates that the situation may be more complex. 'A Scene from the Past' uses the English language, Victorian poetic rhetoric, and a colonial narrative of racial effacement. But it is structured as a traditional Māori welcome, a powhiri. The poem thus links the literary rhetoric of Thornton and Macmillan Brown's English classes with the oral world of the poet's upbringing. Ngata is not an innovator here – he utilises the adaptations that Māori language users had made during the first half of the nineteenth century, as they formed a hybridised mode of public address. As Karetu suggests, writers in the Māori press transferred Māori oral forms over into the medium of the printed page. Ngata, writing in English, follows the pattern these writers had established: the literary gestures to its origins in the oral. His unique position – a child of the tribal groupings of Ngati Porou, Te Whanau-a-Te Ao, Ngati Rangi, Te Whanau-a-Karuai and Ngati Rakairoa but also a B.A. (Cantab) – means that, unlike earlier writers, he can move between not two but three worlds: that of traditional Māori public protocol, that of his European education, and the adaptive innovations of the first generation of literate Māori.

Ngata's education at Canterbury taught him the systematic categorisation of knowledge which was central to both the imperial project and the professionalisation of university study. From Macmillan Brown he learnt not just literary style but the scholarly framework within which information should be presented, and the sense that the poetic voice and the ethnological record could exist side by side, each giving authority to the other. Domett's epic poem *Ranolf and Amohia* was the canonical New Zealand example of this, with its romance narrative and its encyclopaedic detail – historical, mythological, geographical, botanical and cultural – coexisting within its massive 500-page text. Domett's poem has footnotes and appendices; Ngata's more modest effort has, in the version that appeared in the *Auckland Star*, a number of glosses which point to its academic pedigree. The glosses have various functions. Māori words are defined and given a place within the European systems of scientific categorisation, for example:

Tukutuku – A kind of mosaic work in kiekie. (Bot. Treycinetia banksii.) The kiekie is dyed. The back ground consists of narrow slits of wood laid transversely in parallel lines across reeds of kakaho (Bot. arundo conspicua) weaved together. Each tukutuku is placed between the side posts of a whare.[93]

Significantly here the word 'whare', house, is not translated. Ngata assumes some Māori knowledge on the part of his largely European newspaper readership.

But generally, Māori phrases are translated and their place within the description of the ceremonial explicated: 'Word of command – tender ye your welcome... Word of command – Clap your hands (on your knees)'. Individual and tribal names are identified. There is a sense here that Ngata, like Te Rangikaheke fifty years earlier, is between two systems of knowledge, the interpreter of one side to the other, and, given what seems to be his acceptance of the 'dying race' axiom, the scholarly recorder of what might otherwise be lost. Ngata's command of English and his success in the colonial education system gives him an authority – a voice, even – that Te Rangikaheke lacked. But there is still a suggestion that the movement between these two systems – Māori knowledge and European structures of categorisation – is not entirely seamless. In his note to 'our war dance' in the poem's eighth stanza, Ngata glosses:

> The dance – This cannot be rendered literally into English. It dates back to about 1865, and was the substance of a dream by a Maori priest just before the capture of Ngatapa. A later generation has transferred the prophecy to New Zealand: – 'Oh, let me by this side creep in: mayhap then we will meet a pupukarikawa or a pupuharerorero. She is tottering, she is falling; New Zealand is tottering to her fall.' Pupukarikawa – A kind of periwinkle, seen at low tide. Pupuharerorero – another kind. Here the fish lolls out of its shell like a tongue. The two terms are applied to an old man who was speared and clubbed on the incline leading up to Ngatapa. His tongue lolled out when dying, and his death was forecast in the dream and it was considered a good omen.[94]

There is a sense in this gnomic passage of what cannot be contained in any of the rhetorical systems Ngata has mastered in his time at Canterbury. That the dance 'cannot be rendered literally in English' points to the limits of Ngata's interpretive role, even if he can translate pupukarikawa and pupuharerorero. The mix of information that the note contains – unofficial history, dream lore, Indigenous zoological systems, prophecy – is resistant to European explication or rational organisation. It depends on a cultural system in which dreams and prophecies have equal status with facts, a world which Judith Binney describes as existing in 'the shadow of prediction',[95] an orientation towards the future which sits oddly within the dying race frame of the poem which defines Māori society as inhabiting the archaic past. Ngata's fussy academic annotation paradoxically refers to a system of orally maintained knowledge without the fixed textual authority of the written record. As Binney writes,

> [t]he oral narratives of the elders and the kupu whakaari (words of foresight and promise), allow for independent understandings, and these different understandings co-exist. Meanings are ascribed according to the place, the context, the narrator. This is the strength and scope of orality, which the printed page sometimes circumscribes and inhibits.[96]

There are more personal, more contentious undercurrents in Ngata's gloss which are not spelt out for the uninformed reader. Ngatapa was a fortified settlement occupied by the rebel leader Te Kooti in December 1868, and its fall in January1869 was effected in part by Ngata's paternal great-uncle Rapata (or Ropata) Wahawaha who was part of a loose alliance of Māori who supported the crown and colonial forces. Ngata's father Paratene was also present at this engagement. One hundred and twenty male prisoners were summarily executed after the battle.[97] As Binney writes, 'within this war... there were many wars; and not the least was the retaliation of the Ngati Porou against East Coast and Urewera tribal enemies'.[98] The old man whose grotesque death on the slopes of the hill the poem considers to be an omen of good luck is presumably one of Te Kooti's supporters, an opponent of Ngata's tribe. Te Kooti's death the year before Ngata's poem was published may have supplied an added unspoken context for some readers. But what is the import of the suggestion that the fall of Ngatapa be reinterpreted as the fall of New Zealand: 'a later generation has transferred the prophecy to New Zealand'? Is this an attempt to incorporate the European dying race trope, 'New Zealand' referring to the Māori population? Or is it an attempt to signal information, custom and usage that falls outside the explanatory systems of Ngata's European education and thus outside the scope of the poem? There is an argumentative tension in 'A Scene from the Past' in its pivoting position between past and present, between Indigenous detail and classical referent, between its late-Victorian literary structure and the sharpness of its ethnological detail, between its public rhetoric and its private knowledge which reflect contemporary Māori political contentions. Ngata was a reformer and a moderniser at a time when some sectors of Māori society were looking to separatist agendas.

Ngata resists the suggestion that he is a traitor to his past by demonstrating within his poem the force and vitality of Māori cultural forms. But he does so by appealing to the authority of memory. Traditional Māori society exists as performance within a literary frame which concedes its transient status and within a scholarly apparatus which allows that even the most central aspects of cultural practice now need footnotes.

## NOTES

1. Alfred Domett, *Ranolf and Amohia: A South-Sea Day-Dream* (London: Smith, Elder, 1872), p. 44. (Domett 1872)
2. Alfred Domett, *The Diary of Alfred Domett 1872–1885*, ed. E.A. Horsman (London: Oxford University Press, 1953), p. 69. (Domett 1953)
3. Domett's friend James Fitzgerald, pointing to the 'Browningite' aspects of *Ranolf and Amohia*, Alfred Domett papers, MS-Papers-1632-2, Alexander Turnbull Library, National Library of New Zealand.
4. George Grey, *Ko Nga Moteatea, Me Nga Hakirara o Nga Maori or Poems, Traditions and Chaunts of the Maories* (Wellington: Robert Stokes, 1853). (Grey 1853)
5. George Grey, *Polynesian Mythology and Ancient Traditional History of the New Zealand Race, as furnished by their Priests and Chiefs* (London: John Murray, 1855). (Grey 1855)
6. As early as 1852, there was a plan to collaborate with the illustrator Richard Oliver in a volume which would combine Grey's legends and Domett's poems. It did not progress. The publisher William Boone, who had published Grey's Australian works, said 'New Zealand is overdone', Leonard Bell, *Colonial Constructs: European Images of Maori 1840–1914* (Auckland: Auckland University Press, 1992), p. 33. (Bell 1922)
7. Edmund Bohan, *To Be a Hero: Sir George Grey* (Auckland: Harper Collins, 1998), p. 100. (Bohan 1998)
8. Bohan, *To Be a Hero*, p. 101.
9. Grey, *Polynesian Mythology*, pp. iii–iv.
10. Grey, *Polynesian Mythology*, p. vii.
11. C.O.B. Davis, *Maori Mementos: Being a Series of Addresses, Presented by the Native People to His Excellency Sir George Grey, KCB, FRS, Governor and High Commissioner of the Cape of Good Hope, and the Late Governor of New Zealand; with Introductory Remarks and Explanatory Notes, to Which is Added a Small Collection of Laments, etc.* (Auckland: Williamson and Wilson, 1855), p. ii. (Davis 1855)

12. Lachy Paterson, *Colonial Discourses: Nuipepa Māori, 1855–1863* (Dunedin: Otago University Press, 2006), p. 42. (Paterson 2006)
13. Grey, *Polynesian Mythology*, p. xi.
14. Grey, *Polynesian Mythology*, pp. xii–xiii.
15. Grey, *Polynesian Mythology*, p. xii.
16. Grey, *Polynesian Mythology*, p. xix.
17. Grey, *Polynesian Mythology*, p. x.
18. Paterson writes of the mid-century, 'it is reasonably clear that *Māori* literacy rates were probably higher than for some segments of the English population at the time and that, while some areas may have had higher concentrations of literate people, there were individuals able to read and write in most Māori communities', *Colonial Discourses*, p. 38.
19. Linda Tuhiwai Smith, *Decolonizing Methodologies: Research and Indigenous Peoples* (Dunedin: Otago University Press, 1999), pp. 69–72. (Smith 1999)
20. Tony Ballantyne, 'What Difference Does Colonialism Make? Reassessing Print and Social Change in an Age of Global Imperialism', *Agents of Change? Print and Culture Studies after Elizabeth L. Eisenstein*, eds. Sabrina Alcorn Baron, Eric N Lindquist and Eleanor F Shevlin (Amherst and Boston: University of Massachusetts Press, 2007), p. 345. (Ballantyne 2007)
21. Ballantyne, 'What Difference Does Colonialism Make?', p. 350.
22. Jane McRae, '"Ki nga pito e wha o te ao nei [To the Four Corners of This World]": Maori Publishing and Writing for Nineteenth-century Maori-language Newspapers', *Agents of Change*, p. 287.
23. Jane McRae, 'Maori Literature: A Survey', *The Oxford History of New Zealand Literature*, rev. ed., ed. Terry Sturm (Auckland: Oxford University Press, 1998), p. 4. (McRae 1998)
24. Lyndsay Head, '*Kupu Pai, Kupu Kino*: Good and Bad Words in Maori Political Writing', *Rere Atu, Taku Manu! Discovering History, Language and Politics in the Maori-Language Newspapers*, eds. Jenifer Curnow, Ngapare Hopa and Jane McCrae (Auckland University Press, 2002), p. 136. (Head 2002)
25. Quoted in Head, '*Kupu Pai, Kupu Kino*', p. 134.
26. One of these photographs is in the National Library collection, one in the Auckland Public Library collection. Both seem to have been taken at the same sitting, though Te Rangikaheke strikes slightly different poses in each. The second photograph is reproduced in Jenifer Curnow, 'Wiremu Maihi Te Rangikaheke: His Life and Work', MA Thesis, University of Auckland, 1983, p. 38. Its location is not given. (Curnow 1983)
27. See for example George Angas's two portraits of one of Grey's sources, Tamihana Te Rauparaha, one entitled 'Civilised and Christianised New Zealand Chief', the other 'Te Rauparaha and Ko Katu'. Bell, *Colonial Constructs*, p. 25, and figures 9 and 10. Tamihana wrote 'The History of

Te Rauparaha' c.1845 (GNZ MMSS 27). By the 1920s the value placed on the contrasting representations had changed. The magazine *South Africa* contained two photographs of King Sobhuza of Swaziland, 'one – in which he was in traditional dress – given the caption "natural"; the other, next to it, in which he was dressed in conventional western attire, had the epithet "unnatural"', Brian Willan, *Sol Plaatje: South African Nationalist, 1876–1932* (Berkeley: University of California Press, 1984), p. 289. (Willan 1984)

28. Michael Jackson, 'Literacy, Communication and Social Change', *Conflict and Compromise*, ed. I. H. Kawharu (Wellington: A. H. and A. W. Reed, 1975), pp. 35–44. (Jackson 1975)
29. D. M. Stafford, *Te Arawa: A History of the Arawa People* (1967) (Auckland: Reed, 2005), p. 362. (Stafford 2005)
30. Curnow, 'Wiremu Maihi Te Rangikaheke', p. 15.
31. Stafford, *Te Arawa*, p. 8. The speaker was Lady Martin.
32. Stafford, *Te Arawa*, p. 3364, quoting Grey's secretary, George Sisson Clarke.
33. Stafford, *Te Arawa*, p. 9.
34. McRae, 'Maori Literature: A Survey', p. 8.
35. Curnow, 'Wiremu Maihi Te Rangikaheke', p. 16.
36. The letters are in GNZMA 723,724 and 323.
37. Curnow, 'Wiremu Maihi Te Rangikaheke', p. 17.
38. Curnow, 'Wiremu Maihi Te Rangikaheke', p. 19.
39. Alex Frame, *Grey and Iwikau: A Journey into Custom [Kerei Raua Ko Iwikau Te Haerenga me Nga Tikanga]* (Wellington: Victoria University Press, 2002), p. 13. (Frame 2002)
40. G.C. Cooper, *Journal of an Expedition Overland from Auckland to Taranaki by Way of Rotorua, Taupo, and the West Coast Undertaken in the Summer of 1849–50 by His Excellency the Governor-in-Chief of New Zealand* (Auckland: Williamson and Wilson, 1851), p. 128. (Cooper 1851)
41. Stafford, *Te Arawa*, p. 362.
42. Stafford, *Te Arawa*, p. 363.
43. Curnow, 'Wiremu Maihi Te Rangikaheke', p. 15.
44. Donald Jackson Kerr, *Amassing Treasure for All Times: Sir George Grey, Colonial Bookman and Collector* (Delaware: Oak Knoll Press/Dunedin: Otago University Press, 2006), p. 79. (Kerr 2006)
45. Summarised by Curnow, Wiremu Maihi Te Rangikaheke, p.118, Grey Collection, APL, pp. 84–138.
46. Margaret Orbell, 'Two Manuscripts of Te Rangikaheke', *Te Ao Hou*, 62 (March 1968): 9. (Orbell 1968)
47. Orbell, 'Two Manuscripts of Te Rangikaheke': 9–10.
48. Orbell, 'Two Manuscripts of Te Rangikaheke': 8–12. The dream is described in GNZMMSS 93, the letter in GNZMMSS 45.

49. *Robert Browning and Alfred Domett*, ed. Frederick Kenyon (London: Smith, Elder, 1906), p. 81.
50. Attributed to Dr Isaac Featherstone by Walter Buller, 1905. See Stafford and Williams, *Maoriland: New Zealand Literature, 1872–1914*, p. 289, note 47, for a discussion of this often cited phrase.
51. R. Coupland Harding, 'Unwritten Literature', *Transactions and Proceedings of the Royal Society of New Zealand*, 25 (1892): 443. (Harding 1892)
52. Mark Williams, 'Literary Scholarship, Criticism, and Theory', *The Oxford History of New Zealand Literature*, p. 697; see also Bettina Kaiser, 'Collegiate Debating Societies in New Zealand: The Role of Discourse in an Inter-Colonial Setting, 1878–1902', PhD Thesis, Canterbury University, 2008. (Kaiser 2008)
53. George Grey, Preface, *Polynesian Mythology and Ancient Traditional History of the New Zealand Race* (Auckland: H. Brett, 1885), p. xvi. (Grey 1855)
54. Arthur Adams, 'The Brave Days To Be', *Maoriland and Other Verses* (Sydney: The Bulletin, 1899), p. 24. (Adams 1899)
55. Adams, 'The Brave Days To Be', p. 26.
56. *Otago Witness*, 13 May 1903, p. 41.
57. *Ibid*. McDonald retired from the museum in 1926 and lived the rest of his life in Tokaanu where he helped found Te Tuwharetoa School of Maori Arts and Culture. When he died in 1935, Dennis writes, 'a tribute appeared in *Te Waka Karaitiana*, honouring his decision to live and work with the Maori people of Tokaanu, and his desire to continue learning from them was noted with approval', Jonathan Dennis, 'McDonald, James Ingram 1865–1935', *Dictionary of New Zealand Biography*, http://www.dnzb.govt.nz
58. *Daily Southern Cross*, 24 December 1867, p. 3.
59. With an endowment from the local Chief Te Hapuku and grant of land under the control of the Crown at the time.
60. 'Reminiscences' by George Bertrand, in R.R. Alexander, *The Story of Te Aute College* (Wellington: A.H. & A.W. Reed, 1951), p. 103. (Alexander 1951)
61. Quoted in John Barrington, *Separate but Equal? Maori Schools and the Crown 1867–1969* (Wellington: Victoria University Press, 2008), p. 146. (Barrington 2008)
62. *Report of the Third Conference of the Te Aute College Students' Association* (Gisborne: The Poverty Bay Herald, 1898), p. 6.
63. Barrington, *Separate but Equal?*, p. 151.
64. Barrington, *Separate but Equal?*, p. 152.
65. Barrington, *Separate but Equal?*, p. 159.
66. It seems likely that it is the prize-winning essay referred to in Ngata's entry in *A Short History of Canterbury College (University of New Zealand) with a Register and Graduates and Associates of the College* by James Hight and Alice M.F. Candy (Christchurch: Whitcombe and Tombs, 1927), p. 204. (Hight and Candy 1927)

67. See Erica Schouten, '"The Encyclopaedic God-Professor": John Macmillan Brown and the Discipline of English in Colonial New Zealand', *Journal of New Zealand Literature*, 23:1 (2005): 109–23. (Schouten 2005)
68. John Macmillan Brown, *Memoirs* (Christchurch: Canterbury University Press, 1974), p. 75. (Brown 1974)
69. John Macmillan Brown, *Modern Education: Its Defects and their Remedies* (Christchurch: *The Lyttleton Times*, 1908), p. 39 (Brown 1908).
70. Macmillan Brown, *Modern Education*, p. 42.
71. The essay appeared serialised the newspaper on 3, 12 and 19 December 1892, and was reprinted as a pamphlet: Apirama [sic] Turupu Ngata, *The Past of Future of the Maori* (Christchurch: 'The Press' Office, 1893), p. 1. (Ngata 1893)
72. Ngata, *The Past of Future of the Maori*, p. 1.
73. Ngata, *The Past of Future of the Maori*, p. 1.
74. Ngata, *The Past of Future of the Maori*, p. 2.
75. Macmillan Brown, *Memoirs*, p. 97.
76. Ngata, *The Past of Future of the Maori*, p. 6.
77. Ngata, *The Past of Future of the Maori*, p. 6.
78. 'The Wanderer', lines 85–96, trans. Michael Alexander, *Earliest English Poems* (Harmondsworth: Penguin, 1966), pp. 72–3. (Alexander 1966)
79. *Beowulf*, lines 2262–70, trans. Seamus Heaney (London: Faber, 1999), p. 72.
80. The Rawlinson chair of Anglo-Saxon literature was established at Oxford in 1803, but Oxford and Cambridge were slower than the Scottish universities and London University to take up English literature as a part of the curriculum.
81. Macmillan Brown, *Modern Education*, p. 42.
82. Macmillan Brown, *Memoirs*, p. 129.
83. Schouten, 'The Encyclopaedic God-Professor', p. 115. For a discussion of this process, see Thomas P. Miller, *The Formation of College English: Rhetoric and Belles Lettres in the British Cultural Provinces* (Pittsburgh: University of Pittsburgh Press, 1997), pp. 265–76. (Miller 1997)
84. Macmillan Brown, *Memoirs*, p. 92.
85. Rosemary Woolf, '*The Wanderer, The Seafarer*, and the Genre of Planctus', *Art and Doctrine: Essays on Medieval Literature*, ed. Heather O'Donoghue (London: Hambleton, 1986), p. 166. (Woolf 1986)
86. The poem won the Canterbury College Dialectic Society prize in 1892. For a discussion of the Dialectic Society, see Jane Stafford and Mark Williams, *Maoriland: New Zealand Literature, 1872–1914* (Wellington: Victoria University Press, 2006), p. 258. (Stafford and Williams 2006)
87. Hone Heke and A.T. Ngata, *Souvenir of the Maori Congress, July 1908: Scenes from the Past with Maori Versions of Popular English Songs*

(Wellington: Whitcombe and Tombs, 1908), p. 5 (Heke and Ngata 1908). The poem was also printed in the *Auckland Star*, 25th October 1894 and in R. A. Loughnan, *Royalty in New Zealand: The Visit of their Royal Highnesses the Duke and Duchess of Cornwell and York to New Zealand, 10th–27th June 1901: A Descriptive Narrative* (Wellington: Government Printing Office, 1902), pp. 102–4. (Loughnan 1902)
88. Ngata, 'A Scene from the Past', *Souvenir of the Maori Congress*, p. 5.
89. Shef Rogers, 'Crusoe among the Maori: Translation and Colonial Acculturation in Victorian New Zealand', *Book History* 1, 1(1998): 183. (Rogers 1998)
90. Timoti Karetu, 'Maori Print Culture: The Newspapers', *Rere Atu, Taku Manu! Discovering History, Language and Politics in the Maori-Language Newspapers*, eds. Jenifer Curnow, Ngapare Hopa and Jane McCrae (Auckland: Auckland University Press, 2002), p. 1. (Karetu 2002)
91. Lyndsay Head, '*Kupu Pai, Kupu Kino*: Good and Bad Words in Maori Political Writing', *Rere Atu, Taku Manu!*, p. 135.
92. Jane McRae, '"Ki nga pito e wha o te ao nei" (To the four corners of this world)': Maori publishing and writing for nineteenth-century Maori-language newspapers', *Agents of Change? Print and Culture Studies after Elizabeth L. Eisenstein*, eds. Sabrina Alcorn Baron, Eric N Lindquist and Eleanor F Shevlin (Amherst and Boston: University of Massachusetts Press, 2007), p. 297. (McRae 2007)
93. Apirana T. Ngata, 'A Scene from the Past', *Auckland Star*, 25 October 1894, p. 2. (Ngata 1984)
94. *Ibid*.
95. Judith Binney, *Redemption Songs: A Life of Te Kooti Arikirangi Te Turuki* (Auckland: Auckland University Press, 1995), p. 11 (Binney 1995). Binney is specifically referring to Te Kooti, but Ngata was associated with similar auguries. See Ranginui Walker, *He Tipua: The Life and Times of Sir Apirana Ngata* (Auckland: Penguin, 2001), pp. 54–5. (Walker 2001)
96. Binney, *Redemption Songs*, p. 25.
97. See James Belich, *The Victorian Interpretation of Racial Conflict: The Maori, the British, and the New Zealand Wars* (Montreal: McGill-Queen's University Press, 1989), pp. 260–7 (Belich 1989), and Steven Oliver, 'Wahawaha, Rapata, ?-1897', *Dictionary of New Zealand Biography*, http://www.dnzb.govt.nz/ Belich writes 'The killings were primarily carried out by Ngati Porou, but the colonists must bear a large share of responsibility. Ropata [sic] was praised for the killings and, though this was generally glossed over, the Arawa – colonial regulars – also took part in them', p. 266.
98. Binney, *Redemption Songs*, p. 146.

CHAPTER 7

# Conclusion: Secret Fountains and Authentic Utterance

In a 1933 review of Sol Plaatje's *Mhudi* in the *Times Literary Supplement*, the anonymous reviewer expresses not only approval – 'it is believed to be the only novel written by a South African native'; it is 'written in English, which the author used with exceptional facility and understanding' – but also disappointment:

> Plaatje's whole endeavour and mental direction were towards Europeanism and away from Africanism. 'Mhudi', accordingly, might almost be the first novel of a new European writer of promise. That in itself is no small achievement. But one wonders what secret fountain of African art might not have been unsealed if, in interpreting his people, a writer of Plaatje's insight had thought and written 'like a Native'. That might well have been the first authentic utterance out of the aeons of African silence.[1]

This uneasiness – that in using the English language and the literary forms of the English canon the native author was in some way invalidating the very qualities of authenticity that were his or her claim to attention – was common during the period covered by this book. Laurence Binyon was disconcerted by the poetic style of his friend Manmohan Ghose, a fellow student at Oxford in the 1890s: 'I had imagined', he confesses, 'that an Oriental's taste must of necessity be for the luxuriant and ornate, and was surprised that he should feel such as strong attraction to the limpid and severe'.[2] Edmund Gosse scrutinised Toru Dutt's work for signs of the 'littleness and frivolity' which he felt 'seems, if we may judge by a slight experience, to be the bane of modern India'.³ James Cousins, writing in 1918, warns young Indian writers not to use Tennyson or Swinburne as models:

> You will never sing your own song if you are content to echo another's: four lines struck from the vina of your own heart experience or mental illumination will be worth infinitely more to you than reams of mimicry.⁴

What he describes as 'Anglo-English poetry', presumably David Richardson's 'British-Indian Poetry', is, he warns, an especial danger for Indian poets:

> They may try their sitar with English poetry – and fail, and in the failing may learn a valuable lesson; but they may try it with Anglo-English poetry – and succeed, and in the succeeding, achieve a useless mediocrity.⁵

To use the English language but to avoid 'its point of view, its temperament, its mannerisms' is the preferred aim. Cousins acknowledges that, as an Irishman, he is hardly in a position to talk about linguistic purity, '[having] had several generations of English-speaking ancestors, and [having] had English as our own, so to speak, mother-in-law-tongue, as the result of what our education bureaucracy ironically called National Education'. 'And yet' he continues, referring to his participation in the Celtic Revival, 'we have created a new English': W.B. Yeats' Anglo-Irish variety, J.M. Synge's more realistic approximation of peasant diction, both 'as far as possible from the "eftsoons" and "methinks" style of English poetry, and as near as possible to their own spiritual and emotional centre, which was also Ireland's'. This is what Indian writers should emulate:

> Let their ideal be the expression of themselves, but they must be quite sure that it *is* their *self*, not merely faint echoes and shadows from others or from the transient phases of desire.

However, while the native author could be critiqued for not writing sufficiently 'like a native', he or she could also attract opprobrium by engaging too strongly or unconvincingly in the performance of authenticity. In a review of Pauline Johnson's 1895 collection of poetry, *The White Wampum*, the London *Saturday Review* expressed disapproval of her poetic voice, seeing it as an unfortunate artistic choice rather than an intrinsic expression of identity:

> Miss Johnson is undoubtedly something of a poet, but we do not think the idea of posing as an Indian bard can be counted among her happiest inspirations. It is true she has so successfully caught the Mohawk frenzy as to break quite naturally into the cry of 'Wah' and to warn her enemies, in a rather doubtful rhyme, of the day when –
> Reeking, red, and raw
> Their scalps will deck the belts of the Iroquois.
> But on the whole, though we like to hear of the Indians virtues, and fully believe at least in their wrongs, the fiery strains of 'Tekahionwake' leave us unmoved; and we much prefer the poems in which Miss Johnson, who is, it appears, a Canadian, condescends to touch the humbler lyre of the paleface.[6]

*The Guardian* agreed, finding '[a]n ancient dying race, strange customs and costumes, fierce passions, barbaric heroisms, long unpronounceable names such as "Yakonwita" and "Ojistoh", tomahawks, happy hunting grounds, canoes, "red men", cattle thieves, melodrama and rhetoric' all too much. '[H]er poems seem contrived and self-consciously fashioned' the reviewer complained, 'They have too much the appearance of being made, as the degenerate Red-skin has learned to make his moccasins and snowshoes, and even his gods, for the European bric-a-brac market.'[7] What was offered as a thrilling experience of the authentic was received as manufactured and commodified.

It is perhaps significant that these two reviews are from London publications. Canadian audiences tended to be more enthusiastic, their enthusiasm having decidedly nationalistic overtones. In settler societies whose identities within empire were often partly constructed from the appropriated material of their Indigenous populations, work such as Johnson's was uncritically celebrated, seen as attesting to a co-opted romanticised past which countered the brief historical span and unromantic realities of settlement – 'roughing it in the bush' as Susanna Moodie, neé Strickland, termed it in her 1852 memoir of the same name. Writing 'like a native' was less important in this context than sentimental archaising, at what David Attwell identifies as 'the point of rupture between tradition and modern neo-traditionalism, the point at which a historically retroactive, fiction-making consciousness is called into play for the building of a national culture'.[8]

The creator of such 'historically retroactive' and 'fiction-making' texts was as likely to be a settler mimic as a native author, albeit one whose work might depend on ethnographic collections of traditional material. The distinction between the two was seen as moot. If the native author could learn to write in the tones of the English literary canon, could not the European author mimic the native voice, especially if that voice was configured as coming from a dying race? W.A. Cawthorne concludes *The Legend of Kuperree; or, the Red Kangaroo* with the declaration:

> Ah, native man! thy race is run;
> Jacob supplants the first-born son.
> 'To adorn a tale,' thine immortality;
> 'To point a moral,' thy only history.[9]

Cawthorne's subtitle, *An Aboriginal Tradition of the Port Lincoln Tribe; A Metrical Version by the Author of 'The Islanders'*, etc., is intended to signal his work's ethnographic veracity and minimise the degree of his own creative intervention. His name does not appear anywhere in the text, there are scholarly footnotes and the inference is that the work is in some sense a translation, albeit in metre. The distinction between translation and original composition was at times deliberately blurred, given the desire to reproduce indigenous literary forms and diction. This could verge on the duplicitous. Adela Nicholson, under the pseudonym Laurence Hope, initially offered her 1901 collection *The Garden of Kama* as a translation of original Indian material 'arranged in verse' by herself – a phrase as ambiguous as Cawthorne's 'metrical version'.[10] Sarojini Naidu's marginalia in her copy reflects a varying degree of approval – 'pretty', 'beauty with a touch of vulgarity', 'how vulgar' and 'this poem would strike wondrous music on the chord of an artistically-moulded heart'[11] – but suggest that an actual native author could be influenced by the artificial and constructed variety.

Conventional expectations of what writing 'like a native' would look like were well established by the mid-nineteenth century and paradoxically set the standard by which native authors were judged. Binyon laments that English readers would probably feel 'much readier sympathy' for 'the Orientalism of a Flecker or a Lafcadio Hearn' – that is, the florid and uncompromisingly Romantic and orientalist works of European authors – than for Ghose's verse. Rabindranath Tagore, in his foreword to the 1918 *Bengali Book of English Verse*, expresses a preference for the India as expressed in the work of Ralph Waldo Emerson, Alfred Lyall or Edwin Arnold to the early generation of Bengali authors writing in English: 'The reason may be that these early writers in an alien tongue were anxious to anglicise not only their vocabulary but their ideas.'[12] One of Johnson's reviewers sees little difference between her work and the 'pseudo-Indian ballads after the manner of Mr Bret Harte or Mr G. R. Sims'.[13] Even Johnson herself concedes the possibility of authorship based purely on the inventive and the imaginative:

> Perhaps, sometimes an Indian romance may be written by someone who will be clever enough to portray national character without ever having come into contact with it. Such things have been done before, for are we not told that Tom Moore had never set foot in Persia before he wrote *Lalla Rookh*?[14]

Her disapproval of those who write on Indian subjects and who 'have never even read Parkman, Schoolcraft or Catlin'[15] suggests that research could take the place of 'authentic utterance'.

What does the stipulation 'to write like a native' mean in terms of the individual author and text? Who defines what 'native writing' looks like? How far is the author's voice bound by his or her traditional culture, identity and practices? And how far is writing, of any kind, a direct unmediated expression of the author? Might the 'contrived and self-consciously fashioned' nature of the work of the native author be inevitable, and not necessarily disadvantageous, working as they are both with the English language and English literary conventions and with traditional material and forms? Plaatje was quite conscious of his use of the imperial adventure story genre, interwoven though it might be with content and forms of Tswana oral traditions, 'the aeons of African silence' that the *TLS* reviewer so patronisingly refers to (silent to the European ear, presumably, not the African). As a late nineteenth-, early twentieth-century member of the Anglophone world and its literary empire he found it perfectly natural to make use of the forms and genres that were current among his potential readership without invalidating the status of his novel as 'authentic utterance'. The tone of *Mhudi* is both modern and eclectic. In his poem 'A Scene from the Past', Apirana Ngata anticipates such criticism – that his work might be 'clothed in artifice' – by inserting into the high Victorian form of the proleptic elegy the untranslated voices of a Māori powhiri or welcome. The poem is thus both modern and a container for the archaic, written for a university competition, published in a colonial newspaper, but gesturing to pre-contact oral literary modes. Sarojini Naidu and Toru Dutt were conscripted into versions of their native identities as constructed as Johnson's stage costume, 'Vedic solemnity and simplicity of temper', as Edmund Gosse noted approvingly of Dutt.[16] But at the same time both women eagerly embrace the literary modes of the mid-nineteenth century and *fin de siècle* circles which they inhabited, actually in the case of Naidu, intellectually in the case of Dutt. Naidu takes on the tones and attitudes of Arthur Symons and his fellow decadents; Dutt integrates the world of Christian didacticism with that of Hindu mythology, infused and given resonance by personal memory. Neither is at a disadvantage. Indeed, Edward Marx suggests, 'Coming to *fin-de-siècle* English poetry as an outsider, Naidu seems to have found it easier to blend styles that a British poet might have found incongruous.'[17]

For some, writing 'like a native' was not a possibility. Neither Chief Joe Capilano nor Wiremu Te Rangikaheke could do so directly or indeed exercised control over the textualisation of their material. Cathy Rex describes George Copway as 'placing himself on both sides of the ethnologist's office'.[18] In a similar fashion, in *The Legends of Vancouver*, Johnson performs the role of licensed intermediary between indigenous and European Canada, a conduit between a now vanished past and the settler present. In a more effaced way, George Grey's collections and Alfred Domett's verse preserve but also reorient Te Rangikaheke's indigenous knowledge in keeping with the agendas of settler New Zealand. Mary Prince is not required to 'write like a native'. To be acceptable and effective her *History* must use the offices of Susanna Strickland to deal with her repetitions, prolixities and 'gross grammatical errors' – that is, modify any sense of a direct voice – just as Johnson adjusts Capilano's 'quaint broken English' in her transmission of his legends.[19] Prince's *History* is presented as the 'voice of truth and nature'[20] rather than 'authentic utterance', the anti-slavery campaign being more interested in the claims of and to humanity in general than in a particular ethnographic examination of the rare and the strange. It is the work's claim to *emotional* truth that gives it its force.

Readers of this material looked for a voice, the sense of an immediate presence within the writing, as figured by Johnson's literal performance, replete with animal pelts, trade brooches, eagle feathers and bear claws. 'One cannot comprehend the moving strength of such a composition until an Indian woman, who lives its words while she speaks, recites them', wrote a reviewer in the Toronto *Globe* of her performances.[21] But Meenakshi Mukherjee warns against attempting to locate 'authentic utterance' in such texts:

> ...words like 'voice', or 'authenticity' are not innocent signifiers, imbricated as they are with possibilities of insidious complicity with, or co-option by, the prevailing literary culture. In both cases the dominant and the resistant impulses tend to operate simultaneously in constructing the subject, rendering inconclusive any attempt at locating an unsullied or pristine 'voice'.[22]

The binaries Mukherjee suggests – 'insidious complicity with, or co-option by'; 'the dominant and the resistant impulses' – seem, for the works this study examines, too extreme. Rather, the forces 'constructing the subject' in these texts are demonstrably more variable, ambiguous and open to modification. But she is right to aver that the search for a voice, the voice, which engenders and authorises these texts, will be futile. Instead of conveying 'secret fountains' of arcane knowledge or being the 'authentic utterance' of one pristine and unsullied speaker, the work of the native author acts against the univocal. If there is one thing that sounds in all these works, it is a productive inability to cohere. This writing, overtly artificial, self-consciously constructed, demonstrates flexibility and eclecticism, an openness to the multiplicity of influences which the literary empire – and the social and political empire – brings to bear on its production and articulation. Its influences range from traditional indigenous forms with their traces of oral performance to Victorian canonical and popular responses to the nineteenth- and early twentieth-century modernity. This fluidity, instability and porousness looks forward to modernist and postcolonial texts of the twentieth and twenty-first centuries which are relaxed about competing voices and incongruous sources, which acknowledge what cannot be understood, translated or contained within the English language or English literary conventions.

## Notes

1. 'Review', *Times Literary Supplement*, 31 August 1933, p. 574.
2. Laurence Binyon, Introduction, Manmohan Ghose, *Songs of Love and Death* (Oxford: Basil Blackwell, 1926), p. 22. (Binyon 1926)
3. Edmund W. Gosse, Introductory Memoir, Toru Dutt, *Ancient Ballads and Legends of Hindustan* (London: Kegan Paul, 1882), p. xxii. (Gosse 1882)
4. James H. Cousins, *The Renaissance in India* (Madras: Ganesh and Co, 1918), p. 156. (Cousins 1918)
5. Cousins, *Renaissance in India*, pp. 176–7.

6. *Saturday Review*, 4 September 1895, n.p.; E. Pauline Johnson Fonds, Box 4, File 14, William Ready Division of Archives and Research Collections, McMaster University Library.
7. *The Guardian*, 5 July 1895, n.p.; E. Pauline Johnson Fonds, Box 4, File 14, William Ready Division of Archives and Research Collections, McMaster University Library.
8. David Attwell, 'Reprisals of Modernity in Black South African "Mission" Writing', *Journal of Southern African Studies*, 25:2 (1999): 281. (Attwell 1999)
9. William Anderson Cawthrone, *The Legend of Kuperree; or, the Red Kangaroo; An Aboriginal Tradition of the Port Lincoln Tribe* (Adelaide: Alfred N. Cawthrone, n.d. [1858]), [p. 36]. (Cawthorne 1858)
10. Laurence Hope (Adela Nicolson), *The Garden of Kama and other Love Lyrics from India* (London: William Heinemann, 1901). (Hope 1901)
11. Edward Marx, 'Decadent Exoticism and the Woman Poet', *Women and British Aestheticism*, eds. Talia Schaffer and Kathy Alexis Psomiades (Charlottesville: University Press of Virginia, 1999), pp. 152–4. (Marx 1999)
12. Rabindranath Tagore, Foreword, *The Bengali Book of English Verse*, selected and arranged by Theodore Douglas Dunn (Bombay: Longmans, Green and Co, 1918), p. xxi. (Tagore 1918)
13. *The Guardian*, n.p., 5 July 1895. George R. Sims, *The Dagonet Ballads* (London: E.J. Francis, 1879) was a popular collection of humorous and pathetic verse, including one piece which opens with the immortal line, 'It is Christmas Day in the workhouse'. None have colonial subject matter though many are concerned with social injustice. Many reproduce demotic and dialect speech in the manner of the 'habitant' poetry of William Henry Drummond. (Sims 1879)
14. Pauline Johnson, 'A Strong Race Opinion: on the Indian Girl in Modern Fiction', *Sunday Globe*, 22 May, 1892, p. 1.
15. *Ibid.*
16. Edmund W. Gosse, 'Introductory memoir' to Toru Dutt, *Ancient Ballads and Legends of Hindustan*, (London: Kegan Paul, 1882), p. xxii.
17. Marx, 'Decadent Exoticism', p. 143.
18. Cathy Rex, 'Survivance and Fluidity: George Copway's *The Life, History, and Travels of Kah-Ge-ga-gah-bowh*', *Studies in American Indian Literatures*, 18: 2 (2006): 21. (Rex 2006)
19. T.P [Thomas Pringle], Preface, *The History of Mary Prince, A West Indian Slave, Related by Herself* [1831], ed. Sarah Salih (London: Penguin, 2000), p. 3; E. Pauline Johnson, 'The Two Sisters', *Legends of Vancouver* [1911] (Vancouver: Douglas and McIntyre, 1997), p. 2. (Johnson 1997)

20. S. Strickland, *Negro Slavery described by a Negro; Being the Narrative of Ashton Warner, a Native of St Vincents* (London: Samuel Maunder, 1831), pp. 6–7. (Strickland 1831)
21. 'Music and Drama', *Globe*, 1 November 1898, p. 3.
22. Meenakshi Mukherjee, 'Hearing Her Own Voice: Defective Acoustics in Colonial India', *The Perishable Empire: Essays on Indian Writing in English* (New Delhi: Oxford University Press, 2000), p. 89. (Mukherjee 2000)

# Bibliography

Adams, Arthur. 1899. *Maoriland and Other Verses*. Sydney: The Bulletin.
Alexander, Michael. 1966. *Earliest English Poems*. Harmonsworth: Penguin.
Alexander, R.R. 1951. *The Story of Te Aute College*. Wellington: A.H. and A.W. Reed.
Allen, Chadwick. 2002. *Blood Narrative: Indigenous Identity in American Indian and Maori Literary and Activist* Texts. Durham: Duke University Press.
———. 2014. Decolonizing Comparison: Toward a Trans-Indigenous Literary Studies. In *The Oxford Handbook of Indigenous American Literature*, edited by James Cox and Daniel Heath Justice. Oxford: Oxford University Press.
———. 2012. *Trans-Indigenous: Methodologies for Global Native Literary Studies*. Minnesota: University of Minneapolis Press.
Anderson, Benedict. 2006a. *Imagined Communities: Reflections on the Origins and Spread of Nationalism*. Rev. edition. London: Verso.
Anderson, Peter. 2006b. Home Truths: Samuel Taylor Coleridge Advises Thomas Pringle. *The Coleridge Bulletin*. New series, 28: 21–28.
Anon. 1933. Review of Sol Plaatje, *Mhudi*. Times Literary Supplement, August 31: 574.
Aptheker, Herbert. 1989. *The Literary Legacy of W.E.B. Du Bois*. New York: Kraus.
Armstrong, Isobel. 1999. Msrepresentations: Codes of Affect and Politics in Nineteenth-Century Women's Poetry. In *Women's Poetry, Late Romanticism to Late Victorian: Gender and Genre, 1830–1900*, edited by Isobel Armstrong and Virginia Blain. London: Macmillan.
Arnold, Edwin. 1888. *The Light of Asia: The Great Renunciation*. London: Trübner and Co.

Arthur, Jay. 2002. Natural Beauty, Man-Made. In *Words for Country: Landscape and Language in Australia*, eds. Tim Bonyhady and Tom Griffiths, 190–205. Sydney: University of New South Wales Press.

Attwell, David. 1999. Reprisals of Modernity in Black South African 'Mission' Writing. *Journal of Southern African Studies* 25(2): 267–285.

Bader, Clarisse. 2005. Introduction to the Original French Edition, Toru Dutt, *The Diary of Mademoiselle D'Arvers*. Trans. N. Kamala, 5–20. New Dehli: Penguin India.

Ballantyne, Tony. 2002. *Orientalism and Race: Aryanism in the British Empire*. Basingstoke: Palgrave.

———. 2012. *Webs of Empire: Locating New Zealand's Colonial Past*. Wellington: Bridget Williams Books.

———. 2007. What Difference Does Colonialism Make? Reassessing Print and Social Change in an Age of Global Imperialism. In *Agents of Change? Print and Culture Studies after Elizabeth L. Eisenstein*, eds. Sabrina Alcorn Baron, Eric N. Lindquist and Eleanor F. Shevlin, 342–350. Amhert and Boston: University of Massachusetts Press, 2007.

———, and Antoinette Burton 2014. *Empires and the Reach of the Global, 1870–1945*. Cambridge, MA: Harvard University Press.

Banerjee, Sudeshna. 1997–8. Spirituality and Nationalist Domesticity: Rereading the Relationship. *Calcutta Historical Journal*, 19–20:173–204.

Barrington, John. 2008. *Separate but Equal? Maori Schools and the Crown, 1867–1969*. Wellington: Victoria University Press.

Bathgate, Alexander. 1890. *Far South Fancies*. London: Griffith, Farran, Okenden, and Welsh.

Beckson, Karl. 1987. *Arthur Symons: A Life*. Oxford: Clarendon.

Beecher, Henry Ward. 1858. *Life Thoughts*. Boston: Phillips, Sampson.

Belich, James. 1989. *The Victorian Interpretation of Racial Conflict: The Maori, the British, and the New Zealand Wars*. Montreal: McGill-Queen's University Press.

Bell, Leonard. 1992. *Colonial Constructs: European Images of Maori, 1840–1914*. Auckland: Auckland University Press.

*Beowulf*. 1999. Trans. Seamus Heaney. London: Faber.

*The Bengali Book of English Verse*. 1918. Edited by Theodore Douglas Dunn. Bombay: Longmans, Green and Co.

Beveridge, William. 1947. *India Called Them*. London: Allen and Unwin.

Binney, Judith. 1995. *Redemption Songs: A Life of Te Kooti Arikirangi Te Turuki*. Auckland: Auckland University Press.

Binyon, Laurence. 1926. Introduction. In *Songs of Love and Death*, edited by Manmohan Ghose, 7–23. Oxford: Basil Blackwell.

Boehmer, Elleke. 2002. *Empire, the National, and the Postcolonial, 1890–1920*. Oxford: Oxford University Press.

Bohan, Edmund. 1998. *To Be a Hero: Sir George Grey*. Auckland: Harper Collins.
Bohn, Henry George. 1902. *Dictionary of Quotations from the English Poets*. London: George Bell and Sons.
*A Book of Homage to Shakespeare; To Commemorate the Three Hundredth Anniversary of Shakespeare's Death*. Edited by Israel Gollancz. Oxford: Humphrey Milford; Oxford University Press, 1916.
Borthwick, Meredith. 1984. *The Changing Role of Women in Bengal, 1849–1905*. Princeton: Princeton University Press.
Boswell, James. 1934. *The Life of Samuel Johnson*, vol. IV. Edited by George Birbeck Hill. Rev. edition L.F. Powell. Oxford: Clarendon.
Braun, Marta, and Charlie Keil. Sounding Canadian: Early Sound Practices and Nationalism in Toronto-Based Exhibition. In *The Sounds of Early Cinema*, edited by Richard Abel and Rick Altman, 198–203. Bloomington and Indianapolis: Indiana University Press, 2001.
Brinch, Boyrereau. 1810. *The Blind African Slave; or, Memoirs of Boyrereau Brinch, Nick-named Jeffrey Brace*. St. Albans, VT: Harry Whitney.
Brydon, Diana. 1991. The White Inuit Speaks. In *Past the Last Post: Theorizing Post-Colonialism and Post-Modernism*, edited by Ian Adam and Helen Tiffin, 136–142. Hemel Hempstead: Harvester, 1991.
Burns, Robert. 1950. *Poetical Works*, edited by J. Logie Robertson. London: Geoffrey Cumberlege, Oxford University Press.
Burton, Antoinette. 1998. *At the Heart of the Empire: Indians and the Colonial Encounter in Late-Victorian Britain*. New Delhi: Munshiram Manoharlal.
Byrd, Jodi A. 2011. *Transit of Empire: Indigenous Critiques of Colonisation*. Minnesota: University of Minneapolis Press.
*The Cambridge History of English Literature*, vol. XIII. Cambridge: Cambridge University Press, 1916.
Cariou, Warren. 2010. Going to Canada. In *Across Cultures, Across Borders: Canadian Aboriginal and Native American Literatures*, edited by Paul DePasquale, Renate Eigenbrod, and Emma LaRocque, 17–23. Peterborough: Broadview Press.
Carretta, Vincent. 2007. Olaudah Equiano: African British Abolitionist and Founder of the African American Slave Narrative. In *The Cambridge Companion to the African American Slave Narrative*, edited by Audrey Fisch, 44–60. Cambridge: Cambridge University Press.
Castillo, Susan. 2006. *Colonial Encounters in New World Writing, 1500–1786*. London: Routledge.
Cawthorne, W. A. n.d. [1858]. *The Legend of Kuperree; Or, the Red Kangaroo; An Aboriginal Tradition of the Port Lincoln Tribe*. Second edition. Adelaide: Alfred N. Cawthorne, stationer; Scrymgeour and Sons, Printers.
Chaudhuri, Rosinka. 2002. *Gentlemen Poets in Colonial Bengal: Emergent Nationalism and the Orientalist Project*. Calcutta: Seagull.

Clarke, Marcus. 1876. Preface. Adam Lindsay Gordon, *Sea Spray and Smoke Drift*, p. vi. Melbourne: Clarson, Massina and Co.

Clifford, James. 1988. *The Predicament of Culture: Twentieth-Century Ethnology, Literature and Art*. Cambridge, MA: Harvard University Press.

———. 1986. *Writing Culture: The Poetics and Politics of Ethnography*. Berkeley: University of California Press.

Coleman, Daniel. 2013. Grappling with Respect: Copway and Traill in a Conversation that Never Took Place. *English Studies in Canada* 39: 2–3 (June–September): 63–88.

Collett, Anne. 1997. Pauline Tekahionwake Johnson: Her Choice of Form. *Kunapipi* 19(1): 59–66.

Collis-Buthelezi, Victoria J. 2009. 'A Native Venture': Sol (Solomon Tshekisho) Plaatje Defining South African Literature. *Xcp: Cross-Cultural Poetics, Special Issue: South Africa: Literature and Social Movements*, 21–22: 118–136.

Conder, Joseph. 1835. Biographical Sketch of the Author. Thomas Pringle, *Narrative of a Residence in South Africa*. New edition. London: Edward Moxon, pp. v–xxxiv.

Cooper, G.C. 1851. *Journal of an Expedition Overland from Auckland to Taranaki by Way of Rotorua, Taupo, and the West Coast Undertaken in the Summer of 1849–50 by his Excellency the Governor-in-Chief of New Zealand*. Auckland: Williamson and Wilson.

Copway, George, Kah-Ge-Ga-Gah-Bowh. 1847. *The Life, History, and Travels of Kah-Ge-Ga-Gah-Bowh (George Copway), a Young Indian Chief of the Ojebwa Nation, a Convert to the Christian Faith and a Missionary to his People for Twelve Years; with a Sketch of the Present State of the Ojebwa Nation in Regard to Christianity and Their Future Prospects; also an Appeal; with all the Names of the Chiefs now Living who have been Christianized, and the Missionaries now Laboring among them*. Albany: Weed and Parsons.

———. 1850a. *The Life, Letters and Speeches of Kah-Ge-ga-gah-bowh, Or, G. Copway*. New York: Benedict.

———. 1850b. *Recollections of Forest Life; or, the Life and Travels of Kah-Ge-ga-gah-bowh, Or George* Copway. London: Gilpin.

Coupland Harding, R. 1892. On Unwritten Literature. *Transactions and Proceedings of the Royal Society of New Zealand* 25: 439–448.

Cousins, James H. 1918. *The Renaissance in India*. Madras: Ganesh and Co.

Couzens, Tim. 1978. Introduction. In *Mhudi*, edited by Stephen Gray, 1–20. Oxford: Heinemann.

Couzens, Tim, and Stephen Gray. 1978. Printers and other Devils: the Texts of Sol Plaatje's *Mhudi*. *Research in African Literatures*, 9(2): 98–215.

Cowper, William. 1967. *Poetical Works*. Edited by H.S. Milford. Fourth edition. London: Oxford University Press.

Chrisman, Laura. 2000. *Rereading the Imperial Romance: British Imperialism and South African Resistance in Haggard, Schreiner and Plaatje*. Oxford: Clarendon.
Cugoano, Ottobah. 1825. *Narrative of the Enslavement of Ottobah Cugoano, a Native of Africa; Published by Himself in the Year 1787, an Appendix to The Negro's Memorial; or, Abolitionist's Catechism*. London: Hatchard and Co., and J. and A. Arch.
Curnow, Allen. 1960. Introduction. In *The Penguin Book of New Zealand Verse*, edited by Allen Curnow, 17–67. Harmondsworth: Penguin.
Curnow, Jenifer. 1983. Wiremu Maihi Te Rangikaheke: His Life and Work. MA Thesis, University of Auckland.
Daniels, Roy. 1977. Minor Poets, 1880–1920. In *Literary History of Canada: Canadian Literature in English, Volume One*, edited by Cark F. Klinck, 438–446. Second edition. Toronto: University of Toronto Press.
Das, Harihar. 1921. *The Life and Letters of Toru Dutt*. London: Oxford University Press.
Davenport, Rodney, and Christopher Saunders. 2000. *South Africa: A Modern History*. Fifth edition. London: Macmillan.
Davis, C.O.B. 1855. *Maori Mementos: Being a Series of Addresses, Presented by the Native People to His Excellency Sir George Grey, KCB, FRS, Governor and High Commissioner of the Cape of Good Hope, and the late Governor of New Zealand; with Introductory Remarks and Explanatory Notes, to Which Is Added a Small Collection of Laments, etc*. Auckland: Williamson and Wilson.
de Kock, Leon. 1996. *Civilising Barbarians: Missionary Narrative and African Textual Response in Nineteenth-Century South Africa*. Johannesburg: University of Witwatersrand Press and Lovedale Press.
———. 2001. Sitting for the Civilisation Test: The Making(s) of a Civil Imaginary in Colonial South Africa. *Poetics Today* 22(2): 392–412.
Dean, Misao. 2013. *Inheriting a Canoe Paddle: The Canoe in Discourses of English-Canadian Nationalism*. Toronto: University of Toronto Press.
———. 1994. Susanna Moodie. In *Encyclopedia of Post-Colonial Literatures in English*, edited by E. Benson and L.W. Conolly, 1037. London: Routledge.
Derozio Henry. 2008. *Derozio, Poet of India*. Edited by Rosinka Chaudhuri. New Dehli: Oxford University Press.
Diamond, Elin. 1996. *Performance and Cultural Politics*. London: Routledge.
*Dictionary of New Zealand Biography*. http://www.dnzb.govt.nz
Domett, Alfred. 1872. *Ranolf and Amohia: A South-Sea Day-Dream*. London: Smith, Elder.
———. 1953. *The Diary of Alfred Domett, 1872–1885*. Edited by E.A. Horsman. London: Oxford University Press.
Drummond, William Henry. 1897. *The Habitant and Other French-Canadian Poems*. New York: G.P. Putnam and Sons.
Du Bois, W.E.B. 1903. *The Souls of Black Folk*. Chicago: A.C. McClurg.

Duff, Alexander. 1837. *New Era of the English Language and English Literature in India or, an Exposition of the Late Governor General of India's Last Act, Relative to the Promotion of European Literature and Science, Through the Medium of the English Language, Amongst the Natives of that Populous and Extensive Province of the British Empire*. Edinburgh: John Johnstone.

*The Dutt Family Album*. London: Longmans, Green and Co, 1870.

Dutt, Govin Chunder. 1878. Preface. Toru Dutt, *A Sheaf Gleaned in French Fields*. Second edition. Bhowanipore: Saptahik Sambad Press.

Dutt, Romesh Chunder ('Arydae'). 1877. *The Literature of Bengal; Being an Attempt to Trace the Progress of the National Mind in Its Various Aspects as Reflected in the Nation's Literature from the Earliest Times to the Present Day with Copious Extracts from the Best Writers*. Calcutta: I.C Bose.

———. 1900. Translator's Epilogue. In *The Ramayana and the Mahabharata*, edited by Romesh C. Dutt, 323–333. London: Dent.

Dutt, Toru. 1882. *Ancient Ballads and Legends of Hindustan*. London: Kegan Paul.

———. August 1874–July 1875. An Eurasian Poet. *The Bengal Magazine*, 3: 189.

———. 2005. *The Diary of Mademoiselle D'Arvers* [1879]. Trans. N. Kamala. New Delhi: Penguin India.

———. 1876. *A Sheaf Gleaned in French Fields*. Bhowanipore: Saptahik Sambad Press.

Eddy, Mary O. 1939. *Ballads and Songs from Ohio*. New York: J.J. Augustin.

Ellis, Markman. 1996. *The Politics of Sensibility: Race, Gender and Commerce in the Sentimental Novel*. Cambridge: Cambridge University Press.

Ellis, Peter Berresford. 1987. *H. Rider Haggard: A Voice from the Infinite*. London: Routledge and Kegan Paul.

Equiano, Olaudah. 1789. *The Interesting Narrative of the Life of Olaudah Equiano, or Gustavus Vassa, the African, Written by Himself*. London: Printed for the Author.

———. 2004. *The Interesting Narrative of the Life of Olaudah Equiano*. Edited by Angela Costanzo. Peterborough, CA: Broadview.

Erikson, Bruce. 2013. *Canoe Nation: Nature, Race, and the Making of a Canadian Icon*. Vancouver: U.B.C. Press.

Fanon, Franz. 1961. *The Wretched of the Earth*. Trans. Constance Farrington. Harmondsworth: Penguin.

Ferguson, Moira. 1992. *Subject to Others: British Women Writers and Colonial Slavery, 1670–1834*. London: Routledge.

Frame, Alex. 2002. *Grey and Iwikau: A Journey Into Custom (Kerei Raua Ko Iwikau Te Haerenga me Nga Tikanga)*. Wellington: Victoria University Press.

Francis, Daniel. 2010. *National Dreams: Myth, Memory, and Canadian History*. Vancouver: Arsenal Pulp Press.

Gerson, Carole, and Veronica Strong-Boag. 2000. *Paddling Her Own Canoe: The Times and Texts of E. Pauline Johnson, Tekahionwake*. Toronto: Toronto University Press.

Gandhi, Leela. 2006. *Affective Communities: Anticolonial Thought, Fin de Siècle Radicalism, and the Politics of Friendship*. Durham: Duke University Press.
Gandhi, Mahatma. 1927. *An Autobiography; or, The Story of My Experiments with Truth*. Trans. Mahadev Desai. Ahmedabad: Navajivan Publishing.
Ghose, Manmohan. 1926. *Songs of Love and Death*. Oxford: Basil Blackwell.
Gosse, Edmund. 1912. Introduction. In Sarojini Naidu, *The Bird of Time: Songs of Life, Death and the Spring*, 1–8. London: Heinemann.
Gosse, Edmund W. 1882. Introductory Memoir. In Toru Dutt, *Ancient Ballads and Legends of Hindustan*, vii–xxvii. London: Kegan Paul.
Gould, Philip. 2003. *Barbaric Traffic: Commerce and Antislavery in the Eighteenth-Century Atlantic World*. Cambridge, MA: Harvard University Press.
———. 2007. The Rise, Development, and Circulation of the Slave Narrative. *The Cambridge Companion to the African American Slave Narrative*, edited by Audrey Fisch, 11–27. Cambridge: Cambridge University Press.
Gray, Charlotte. 2002. *Flint and Feather: The Life and Times of E. Pauline Johnson, Tekahionwake*. Toronto: Harper Collins.
Gray, Stephen. 1977. Plaatje's Shakespeare. *English in Africa* 4(1): 1–6.
Grey, George. 1853. *Ko Nga Moteatea, Me Nga Hakirara o Nga Maori; or, Poems, Traditions and Chaunts of the Maories*. Wellington: Robert Stokes.
———. 1855. *Polynesian Mythology and Ancient Traditional History of the New Zealand Race, as Furnished by Their Priests and Chiefs*. London: John Murray.
Haggard, H. Rider. 1892. *Nada the Lily*. London: Longmans, Green.
Hall, Catherine. 2002. *Civilising Subjects: Metropole and Colony in the English Imagination, 1830–1867*. Chicago: University of Chicago Press.
Head, Lyndsay. 2002. Kupu Pai, Kupu Kino: Good and Bad Words in Maori Political Writing. In *Rere Atu, Taku Manu! Discovering History, Language and Politics in the Maori-Language Newspapers*, edited by Jenifer Curnow, Ngapare Hopa and Jane McCrae, 134–152. Auckland: Auckland University Press.
Heke, H., and Ngata, A.T. 1908. *Souvenir of the Maori Congress, July 1908: Scenes from the Past with Maori Versions of Popular English Songs*. Wellington: Whitcombe and Tombs.
Hight, James, and Alice M.F. Candy. 1927. *A Short History of Canterbury College (University of New Zealand) with a Register and Graduates and Associates of the College*. Christchurch: Whitcombe and Tombs.
Hollander, John. 1981. *The Figure of Echo: A Mode of Allusion in Milton and After*. Berkeley: University of California Press.
Hope, Laurence (pseud. of Adela Florence Nicolson). 1901. *The Garden of Kama and Other Love Lyrics from India*. London: William Heinemann.
Hulme, Peter. 1996. *Colonial Encounters: Europe and the Native Caribbean, 1492–1797*. London: Methuen.

*Indian Response to Poetry in English: A Festschrift for V.K. Gokak*. Edited by M.K. Naik et al. Madras: Macmillan, 1970.
Jackson, George Holbrook. 1913. *The 1890s: A Review of Art and Ideas at the Close of the Nineteenth Century*. London: Grant Richards.
Jackson, Michael. 1975. Literacy, Communication and Social Change. In *Conflict and Compromise: Essays on the Maori since Colonisation*, edited by I. H. Kawharu, 27–54. Wellington: A.H. and A.W. Reed.
Jackson Kerr, Donald. 2006. *Amassing Treasure for all Times: Sir George Grey, Colonial Bookman and Collector*. Delaware: Oak Knoll Press; Dunedin: Otago University Press.
Jea, John. n.d.1811?. *The Life, History, and Unparalleled Sufferings of John Jea, the African Preacher; Compiled and Written by Himself*. Portsea, England: Printed by the author.
Johnson, David. *Shakespeare and South Africa*. Oxford: Clarendon, 1996.
Johnson, Pauline. 1892. A Strong Race Opinion: On the Indian Girl in Modern Fiction. *Sunday Globe*, 22 May.
Johnson, E. Pauline, Tekahionwake. 2002. *Collected Poems and Selected Prose*. Edited by. Carole Gerson and Veronica Strong-Boag. Toronto: Toronto University Press.
———. 1997. *Legends of Vancouver* (1911). Intro. Robin Laurence. Vancouver: Douglas and McIntyre.
Johnston, Sheila M.F. 1997. *Buckskin and Broadcloth: A Celebration of E. Pauline Johnson-Tekahionwake, 1861–1913*. Toronto: Natural Heritage Books.
Justice, Daniel Heath. 2011. Current Trans/national Criticism in Indigenous Literary Studies. *American Indian Quarterly* 35(3): 334–352.
Kahn, Coppélia. 2001. Remembering Shakespeare Imperially: The 1916 Tercentenary. *Shakespeare Quarterly* 52(4): 456–478.
Kaiser, Bettina. 2008. Collegiate Debating Societies in New Zealand: The Role of Discourse in an Inter-Colonial Setting, 1878–1902. PhD Thesis, University of Canterbury.
Karetu, Timoti. 2002. Maori Print Culture: The Newspapers. In *Rere Atu, Taku Manu! Discovering History, Language and Politics in the Maori-Language Newspapers*, edited by Jenifer Curnow, Ngapare Hopa and Jane McCrae, 1–16. Auckland: Auckland University Press.
Laqueur, Thomas. 1976. *Religion and Respectability: Sunday Schools and Working Class Culture, 1780–1850*. New Haven: Yale University Press.
Leask, Nigel. 1996. Towards an Anglo-Indian Poetry? The Colonial Muse in the Writings of John Leyden, Thomas Medwin and Charles D'Oyly. In *Writing India, 1757–1990*, edited by Bart Moore-Gilbert, 52–83. Manchester: Manchester University Press.
Leete, Frederic Deland. 1912. *Christian Brotherhoods*. Cincinnati: Jennings and Graham.

Leighton, Mary Elizabeth. 1998. Performing Pauline Johnson: Representations of 'the Indian Poetess' in the Periodical Press, 1892–95. *Essays on Canadian Writing* 65: 141–164.
Lester, Alan. 2006. Imperial Circuits and Networks: Geographies of the British Empire. *History Compass*, 4(1): 124–141.
Lighthall, William Douw. 1889. Introduction. *Songs of the Great Dominion: Voices from the Forests and Waters, the Settlements and Cities of Canada*. London: Walter Scott.
Longfellow, Henry Wadsworth. 1911. *The Song of Hiawatha*. London: Harrap.
Lopenzina, Drew. 2012. *Red Ink: Native Americans Picking Up the Pen in the Colonial Period*. Albany: State University of New York Press.
Loughnan, R.A. 1902. *Royalty in New Zealand: The Visit of their Royal Highnesses the Duke and Duchess of Cornwall and York to New Zealand, 10th–27th June 1901: A Descriptive Narrative*. Wellington: Government Printing Office.
Low, Gail Ching-Liang. 1996. *Black Skins, White Masks: Representation and Colonialism*. London: Routledge.
Lukens, Margo. 2002. 'A Being of a New World': The Ambiguity of Mixed Blood in Pauline Johnson's 'My Mother'. *MELUS: Multi-Ethnic Literature of the United States* 27(3): 43–58.
Lyon, George W. 1990. Pauline Johnson: A Reconsideration. *Studies in Canadian Literature* 15(2): 136–159.
Lyons, Martyn. 1999. New Readers in the Nineteenth Century. *A History of Reading in the West*, edited by Guglielmo Cavallo and Roger Chartier. Trans. Linda Cochrane, 340–342. Amherst: University of Massachusetts Press.
Mackay, Isabel Ecclestone. 1913. Pauline Johnson: A Reminiscence. *Canadian Magazine* 41: 273–278.
Macmillan Brown, John. 1974. *Memoirs*. Christchurch: Canterbury University Press.
———. 1908. *Modern Education: Its Defects and their Remedies*. Christchurch: The Lyttleton Times.
Malabari, Behramji Merwanji. 1876. *The Indian Muse in English Garb*. Bombay: The Reporters Press.
Marcus, George E. 1986. Contemporary Problems of Ethnography in the Modern World System. *Writing Culture: The Poetics and Politics of Ethnology*, edited by James Clifford and George E. Marcus, 165–193. Berkeley: University of California Press.
Marrant, John. 1813. *A Narrative of the life of John Marrant of New York in North America; Giving an Account of His Conversion When Only 14 Years of Age*. Halifax: J. Nicholson.
Marx, Edward. 1999. Decadent Exoticism and the Woman Poet. In *Women and British Aestheticism*, edited by Talia Schaffer and Kathy Alexis Psomiades, 139–157. Charlottesville: University Press of Virginia.

May, Cedrick. 2008. *Evangelism and Resistance in the Black Atlantic, 1760–1835.* Athens, GA: University of Georgia Press.
McBride, Dwight A. 2007. *Impossible Witnesses: Truth, Abolitionism, and Slave Testimony.* New York: New York University Press.
McClintock, Anne. 1995. *Imperial Leather: Race, Gender and Sexuality in the Colonial Contest.* New York: Routledge.
McClung, Nellie L. 1945. *The Stream Runs Fast: My Own Story.* Toronto: Thomas Allen.
McEvoy, Bernard. 1911. Preface. In *Legends of Vancouver*, Vancouver and Victoria, B.C.: David Spenser.
McRae, Jane. 2007. 'Ki nga pito e wha o te ao nei (To the four corners of this world)': Maori Publishing and Writing for Nineteenth-Century Maori-Language Newspapers. In *Agents of Change? Print and Culture Studies After Elizabeth L. Eisenstein*, edited by Sabrina Alcorn Baron, Eric N. Lindquist and Eleanor F. Shevlin, 287–300. Amhert and Boston: University of Massachusetts Press.
———. 1998. Maori Literature: A Survey. *The Oxford History of New Zealand Literature*, edited by Terry Sturm, 1–32. Rev. edition. Auckland: Oxford University Press.
McRaye, Walter. 1947. *Pauline Johnson and her Friends.* Toronto: Ryerson Press.
———. 1929?. *Town Hall Tonight.* Intro. Lorne Pierce. Toronto: Ryerson Press.
Meiring, Jane. 1968. *Thomas Pringle: His Life and Times.* Cape Town: A.A. Balkema.
Mielke, Laura L. 2012. Introduction. In *Native Acts: Indian Performance, 1603–1832*, edited by Joshua David Bellin and Laura L. Mielke, 1–26. Lincoln: University of Nebraska Press.
Miller, Thomas P. 1997. *The Formation of College English: Rhetoric and Belles Letters in the British Cultural Provinces.* Pittsburgh: University of Pittsburgh Press.
Moodie (née Strickland), Susanna. 1985. *Letters of a Lifetime.* Edited by Carl Ballstadt, Elizabeth Hopkins and Michael Peterman. Toronto: Toronto University Press.
———. 1991. *Voyages: Short Narratives of Susanna Moodie.* Edited by John Thurston. Ottawa: University of Ottawa Press, 1991.
———. 1996. *The Work of Words: The Writing of Susanna Strickland Moodie.* Edited by John Thurston. Montreal and Kingston: McGill-Queen's University Press.
More, Hannah. 1816. *Poems.* London: T. Cadell and W. Davies.
Morra, Linda M. 2014. *Unarrested Archives: Case Studies in Twentieth-Century Canadian Women's Authorship.* Toronto: University of Toronto Press.
Morris, Patricia. 1980. The Early Black South African Newspaper and the Development of the Nove. *Journal of Commonwealth Literature* 15(15): 15–29.

Mukherjee, Meenakshi. 2000. *The Perishable Empire: Essays on Indian Writing in English*. New Delhi: Oxford University Press.

Munro, John M. 1969. The Poet and the Nightingale: Some Unpublished Letters from Sarojini Naidu to Arthur Symons. *Calcutta Review*, 1(September): 135–146.

Naidu, Sarojini. 1912. *The Bird of Time: Songs of Life, Death, and the Spring*. London: Heinemann.

———. 1905. *The Golden Threshold*. London: William Heinemann.

———. 1996. *Selected Letters, 1890s to 1940s*. Edited by Makarand Paranjape. New Delhi: Kali for Women.

Ngata, Apirana [sic] Turupu. 1893. *The Past and Future of the Maori*. Christchurch: *The Press* Office.

———. 1894. A Scene from the Past. *Auckland Star*, 25 October, p. 2.

Ngũgĩ wa Thiong'o. 1986. *Decolonising the Mind: The Politics of Language in African Literature*. London: James Currey.

Okereke, Augustine. 1998. The Performance and the Text: Parameters for Understanding Oral Literary Performance. *Across the Lines: Intertexuality and Transcultural Communication in the New Literatures in English*, edited by Wolfgang Kloss, 39–50. Amsterdam: Rodopi.

Owens, Louis. 1993. 'Ecstatic Strategies': Gerald Vizenor's *Darkness in Saint Louis Bearheart*. *Narrative Chance: Postmodern Discourse on Native American Indian Literatures*. Edited by Gerald Vizenor. Norman: University of Oklahoma Press.

Paterson, Lachy. 2006. *Colonial Discourses: Nuipepa Māori, 1855–1863*. Dunedin: Otago University Press.

Peterson, Bhekizizwe. 2008. Sol Plaatje's *Native Life in South Africa*: Melancholy Narratives, Petitioning Selves and the Ethics of Suffering. *Journal of Commonwealth Literature* 43(1): 79–95.

Peyer, Bernd C. 1997. *The Tutor'd Mind: Indian Missionary Writers in Ante-Bellum America*. Amherst: University of Massachusetts Press.

Plaatje, Solomon T. 1978. *Mhudi* [1930]. Edited by Stephen Gray. Oxford: Heinemann.

———. 1982. *Native Life in South Africa Before and Since the European War and the Boer Rebellion* [1916]. Johannesburg: Raven's Press.

———. 1996. *Selected Writings*. Edited by Brian Willan. Johannesburg: Witwatersrand University Press.

Pope, Alexander. 1968. *Poems*. Edited by John Butt. London: Methuen.

Pratt, Mary Louise. 1992. *Imperial Eyes: Travel Writing and Transculturation*. London: Routledge.

Prince, Mary. 1831. *The History of Mary Prince, a West Indian Slave, Related by Herself; with a Supplement by the Editor; to which is added, the Narrative of Louis Asa-Asa, a Captured African*. London: F. Westley and A.H. Davis.

Pringle, Thomas. 1834. *African Sketches*. London: Edward Moxon.

———. 1828. *Ephemerides; or, Occasional Poems written in Scotland and South Africa*. London: Smith, Elder.

———. 1835. *Narrative of a Residence in South Africa*. New edition. London: Edward Moxon.

———. 1838. *The Poetical Works of Thomas Pringle, with a Sketch of his Life by Leitch Ritchie*. London: Edward Moxon.

Pringle, Thomas. 2000. Preface. In *The History of Mary Prince, a West Indian Slave, Related by Herself* [1831], edited by Sarah Salih, 3. London: Penguin.

Quirk, Linda. 2006. Skyward Floating Feather: A Publishing History of E. Pauline Johnson's *Flint and Feather*. *Papers of the Bibliographical Society of Canada*, 44(1) (2006): 69–106.

Ramsay, James. 1784. *An Essay on the Treatment and Conversion of African Slaves in the British Sugar Colonies*. London: James Phillips.

Rattray, R.H. 1834. Introductory Lines. *The Bengal Annual: A Literary Keepsake for 1832*. Edited by David Lester Richardson. Calcutta: Samuel Smith and Co.

*Report of the Third Conference of the Te Aute College Students' Association.* Gisborne: *Poverty Bay Herald*, 1898.

Reeves, William Pember. 1898. *New Zealand and other Poems*. London: Grant Richards.

Rex, Cathy. 2006. Survivance and Fluidity: George Copway's *The Life, History, and Travels of Kah-Ge-ga-gah-bowh*. *Studies in American Indian Literatures* 18(2): 1–33.

Richards, Thomas. 1993. *The Imperial Archive: Knowledge and the Fantasy of Empire*. London: Verso.

Richardson, David Lester. 1840. *Selections from the British Poets from the Time of Chaucer to the Present Day with Biographical and Critical Notes by David Lester Richardson, Principal of the Hindu College*. Calcutta: Baptist Mission Press.

Roach, Joseph. 1996. *Cities of the Dead: Circum-Atlantic Performance*. New York: Columbia University Press.

*Robert Browning and Alfred Domett*. Edited by Frederick Kenyon. London: Smith, Elder, 1906.

Robin, Libby. 2007. *How a Continent Created a Nation*. Sydney: University of New South Wales Press.

Rogers, Shef. 1998. Crusoe among the Maori: Translation and Colonial Acculturation in Victorian New Zealand. *Book History* 1(1): 182–195.

Rose, Jonathan. 2001. *The Intellectual Life of the British Working Classes*. New Haven, CT: Yale University Press.

Ross, Kirstie. 2008. *Going Bush: New Zealanders and Nature in the Twentieth Century*. Auckland: Auckland University Press.

Rymhs, Deena. 2001. But the Shadow of her Story: Narrative Unsettlement, Self-inscription and Translation in Pauline Johnson's *Legends of Vancouver*. *Studies in American Indian Literatures* 13(4): 51–78.

Salih, Sara. 2004. *The History of Mary Prince*, the Black Subject and the Black Canon. *Discourses of Slavery and Abolition: Britain and its Colonies, 1760–1838*, edited by Brycchan Carey, Markman Ellis and Sara Salih, 123–138. London: Palgrave.

Sarkowsky, Katja. 2003. Writing (and) Art – Native American/ First Nations' Art and Literature: Beyond Resistance and Reconciliation. *Resistance and Reconciliation: Writing in the Commonwealth*, edited by Bruce Bennett, Susan Cowan, Jacqueline Lo, Satendra Nandan and Jen Webb, 90–101. Canberra: ACLALS: Association for Commonwealth Literature and Language Studies.

Schoolcraft, Henry Rowe. 1843. *Alhalla, or the Lord of Talladega, a Tale of the Creek War, with some Selected Miscellanies, Chiefly of an Early Date*. New York: Wiley and Putnam.

Schouten, Erica. 2005. 'The Encyclopaedic God-Professor': John Macmillan Brown and the Discipline of English in Colonial New Zealand. *Journal of New Zealand Literature* 23(1): 109–123.

Schalkwyk, David, and Lerothodi Lapula. 2000. Solomon Plaatje, William Shakespeare and the Translations of Culture. *Pretexts: Literary and Cultural Studies*, 9(1): 9–26.

Schweninger, Lee. 1999. Radicalism and Liberation in Native American Literature. In *Post-Colonial Literatures: Expanding the Canon*, edited by Deborah L. Madsen, 206–217. London: Pluto.

Shaw, Damian. 1998. Thomas Pringle's 'Bushmen': Images in Flesh and Blood. *English in Africa* 25(2) (October): 37–61.

Shelley, Mary. *Frankenstein; or, The New Prometheus*. London: Lackington, Hughes, Mavor, and Jones, 1818.

Shenstone, William. 1780. *The Poetical Works of Will* [sic] *Shenstone in Three Volumes with a Life of the Author and a Description of the Leasowes*. London: Joseph Wenman.

Shuffelton, Frank. 2001. On Her Own Footing: Phillis Wheatley in Freedom. In *Genius in Bondage: Literature of the Early Black Atlantic*, edited by Vincent Carretta and Philip Gould, 175–189. Lexington: University Press of Kentucky.

Sims, George R. 1879. *The Dagonet Ballads*. London: E.J. Francis.

Smith, Linda Tuhiwai. 1999. *Decolonizing Methodologies: Research and Indigenous Peoples* London: Zed Books/Dunedin: Otago University Press.

Stafford, D.M. 2005. *Te Arawa: A History of the Arawa People* [1967]. Auckland: Reed.

Stafford, Jane. 2004. Immeasurable Abysses and Living Books: Oral Literature and Victorian Poetics in Alfred Domett's *Ranolf and Amohia*. *Bulletin of the Bibliographical Society of Australia and New Zealand, Special Issue* 28(1, 2): 161–171.

Stafford, Jane, and Mark Williams. 2009. Indian Mysteries and Comic Stunts: The Royal Tour and the Theatre of Empire. *Journal of Commonwealth Literature* 44(2) (June): 87–105.

———. 2006. *Maoriland: New Zealand Literature, 1872–1914.* Wellington: Victoria University Press.

St Clair, William. 2004. *The Reading Nation in the Romantic Period.* Cambridge: Cambridge University Press.

Starfield, Jane. 1991. The Lore and the Proverbs: Sol Plaatje as Historian. Unpublished paper delivered at the African Studies Institute, University of Witwatersrand, 26 August.

Stephens, Meic. 2004. Morris, Sir Lewis (1833–1907). *Oxford Dictionary of National Biography.* Oxford University Press, September. http://www.oxforddnb.com

Stone, William L. 1841. *The Life and Times of Red Jacket, or Sa-Go-Ye-Wat-Ha; being the Sequel to the History of the Six Nations.* New York and London: Wiley and Putnam.

Strickland, Susanna ('now Mrs Moodie'). 1831. *Enthusiasm; and other Poems.* London: Smith, Elder.

Strickland, S. 1831. *Negro Slavery described by a Negro; being the Narrative of Ashton Warner, a Native of St Vincents; with an Appendix containing the Testimony of Four Christian Ministers Recently Returned from the Colonies on the System of Slavery as It Now Exists.* London: Samuel Maunder.

*The Study of Liturgy.* Edited by Cheslyn Jones, Geoffrey Wainwright, and Edward Yarnold. London: Society for the Promotion of Christian Knowledge, 1978.

Symons, A.J. 1904. *Studies in Prose and Verse.* London: J.M. Dent.

———. 1899. *The Symbolist Movement in Literature.* London: Heinemann.

Symons, Arthur. 1905. Introduction. In Sarojini Naidu, *The Golden Threshold*, 9–23. London: William Heinemann.

———. 1977. *The Memoirs of Arthur Symons: Life and Arts in the 1890s.* Edited by Karl Beckson. University Park: Pennsylvania State University Press.

———. 1896. *Silhouettes.* Rev. edition. London: Leonard Smithers.

Tagore, Rabindranath. 1918. Foreword. In *The Bengali Book of English Verse*, selected and arranged by Theodore Douglas Dunn, xv–xxvii. Bombay: Longmans, Green and Co.

Taylor, Gary. 1990. *Reinventing Shakespeare: A Cultural History from the Restoration to the Present.* London: Hogarth Press.

*This Strange Adventure: An Anthology of Poems in English by Indians, 1828–1946.* Edited by Fredoon Kabraji. London: New India Publishing Co, 1947.

Thomas, Sue. 2011. New Information on Mary Prince in London. *Notes and Queries* 58(1): 82–85.

———. 2005. Pringle v. Cadell and Wood v. Pringle: The Libel Trials Over *The History of Mary Prince. Journal of Commonwealth Literature* 40(1): 113–135.

Thwaite, Ann. 1984. *Edmund Gosse: A Literary Landscape, 1849–1928.* London: Secker and Warburg.

Traill, Catherine Parr. 1989. *The Backwoods of Canada* (1836). Toronto: McClelland and Stewart.
Trimmer, Mrs [Sarah]. 1810. *The Charity School Spelling Book: Part One, Containing the Alphabet, Spelling Lessons, and Short Stories of Good and Bad Boys, in Words of One Syllable Only; and Short Stories of Good and Bad Girls, in Words of One Syllable Only.* New edition. London: F.C. and J. Rivington.
Trumpener, Katie. 1997. *Bardic Nationalism: The Romantic Novel and the British Empire.* Princeton: Princeton University Press.
*The Vishnu Purana.* 1840. Trans. Horace Hyman Wilson. London: John Murray.
Viswanathan, Gauri. 1990. *Masks of Conquest: Literary Study and British Rule in India.* London: Faber.
Vizenor, Gerald. 1978. *Darkness in Saint Louis Bearheart.* St Paul, MN: Truck Press.
Voss, A.E. 1994. Sol Plaatje, the Eighteenth Century, and South African Cultural Memory. *English in Africa* 21(1/2) (July): 59–75.
Walker, Ranginui. 2001. *He Tipua: The Life and Times of Sir Apirana Ngata.* Auckland: Penguin.
Watson, J.R. 1999. *The English Hymn: A Critical and Historical Study.* Oxford: Clarendon Press.
Wheeler, Michael. 1979. *The Art of Allusion in Victorian Fiction.* London: Macmillan.
Whitlock, Gillian. 2000. *The Intimate Empire: Reading Women's Autobiography.* London: Cassell.
———. 2001. Volatile Subjects: The History of Mary Prince. In *Genius in Bondage: Literature of the Early Black Atlantic*, edited by Vincent Carretta and Philip Gould, 72–86. Lexington: University Press of Kentucky.
Willan, Brian. 1982. An African in Kimberley: Sol T. Plaatje, 1894–1898. In *Industrialisation and Social Change in South Africa: African Class Formation, Culture, and Consciousness, 1870–1930*, edited by Shula Marks and Richard Rathbone, 238–258. New York: Longman.
———. 1984. *Sol Plaatje: South African Nationalist, 1876–1932.* Berkley: University of California Press.
Williams, Mark. 1998. Literary Scholarship, Criticism and Theory. *The Oxford History of New Zealand Literature*, edited by Terry Sturm, 695–736. Rev. edition. Auckland: Oxford University Press.
Woolf, Rosemary. 1986. *Art and Doctrine: Essays on Medieval Literature.* Edited by Heather O'Donoghue. London: Hambleton.
Wordsworth, William. 1895. *Poetical Works.* London: Henry Froude.
———. 1974. Preface to *Lyrical Ballads* (1800). *Prose Works, volume 1*, edited by W.J.B. Owen and Jane Worthington Smyser, 118–159. Oxford: Clarendon Press.

Yeats, W.B. 1926. *Autobiographies: Reveries over Childhood and Youth and the Trembling of the Veil.* London: Macmillan.
———. 1986. *Collected Letters, Volume 1, 1865–1895.* Edited by John Kelly and Eric Domville. Oxford: Oxford University Press.
———. 1997. *The Collected Works, Volume 1: Poems.* Edited by Richard J. Finneran. Second edition. New York: Scribner, 1997.

# INDEX

**A**

Aboriginal languages, 186
Adams, Arthur
  'The Brave Days to Be', 196–197
Addison, Joseph, 30, 36
African Methodist Episcopal Church, 69
African National Congress (South African Native National Congress), 10, 15, 61, 69, 85
Alcott, Amos Bronson, 74
Allen, Chadwick, 7, 42, 52, 145, 179
Allusion, literary, 6, 65
Anderson, Benedict, 65, 146
Anglican Church, 143, 198
Anglo-Saxon, 7, 14, 45, 203, 204
  *See also* Old English
Anishinaabe, 11
Antigua, 108, 109, 128, 130, 134, 135, 136
*Anti-Slavery Reporter, The*, 123, 134
Anti-Slavery Society, 10, 16, 18, 108, 116, 118, 119, 126, 128, 132, 133, 142
  *See also* Slavery
Arawa, 190–192
Aristotle, 77
Armstrong, Isobel, 10

Arnold, Edwin, 50, 53, 75, 221
  *Light of Asia*, 75
Arnold, Matthew, 12, 14, 197
  Arnoldian, 200
  'Dover Beach', 53
Asa-Asa, Louis, 111–113, 121
  *See also* Strickland, Susanna
Attwell, David, 11, 13, 17, 219
*Auckland Star*, 207, 215
Aurelius, Marcus, 77
Austen, Jane, 132
  *Northanger Abbey*, 132
Australia, 186, 187

**B**

Bader, Clarisse, 37
Ballantyne, Tony, 77
Balzac, Honoré de, 77
Baptist Mission Press, 25
Baralong, 87–96
Bathgate, Alexander, 168, 169
Beaumont, Francis, 26
Beckson, Karl, 48
Beecher, Henry Ward
  *Life Thoughts*, 68
'Belle lettres', 203
Bengal, 7, 8, 10, 26–28, 33, 37, 39, 41, 53, 80

Bengali Renaissance, 7, 34
*Bengal Magazine, The*, 28, 37, 38, 55
*Beowulf*, 203
    See also 'The Lay of the Last Survivor'
Bermuda
    Brackish Pond, 108, 125, 129, 139
Bethune School, 36
Bible
    Book of Kings, 68
    Proverbs, 68
    Song of Songs, 67, 94
Binney, Judith, 209, 215
Binyon, Laurence, 51, 217, 220
*Birth of a Nation, see* Griffith, D.W.
Blackham, John, 62
*Blackwood's Magazine*, 18, 121, 137, 142
Blake, William, 66
Boehmer, Elleke, 63, 69
Bohanan, Otto L., 69, 76
    'The Awakening', 76
*Bohn, Henry George*, 75
    *Dictionary of Quotations from the English Poets*, 75
*Book of Homage to Shakespeare, A*, 79, 80
Botha, Louis (General), 61
Boy Scouts (American branch), *see* Seton, Ernest Thompson
Brackish Pond, *see* Bermuda
Brahmo Samaj movement, 36
Brantford Collegiate Institute, 15
Brinch, Boyrereau
    *The Blind African Slave, or Memoirs of Boyrereau Brinch, Nick-named Jeffrey Brace*, 117
    See also Benjamin F. Prentiss
'British-Indian Poetry', 26, 29, 31, 32, 218
Brotherhood Movement, 62, 66
Browning, Elizabeth Barrett, 14, 41, 175

Browning, Robert, 185, 194
Brown, John Macmillan
    appointment to Canterbury chair, 200
    curriculum and teaching philosophy, 200
    *Limanora: the Island of Progress*, 200
    *Riallaro: the Archipelago of Exiles*, 200
Bryant, Rev. William C., 147, 148
Buck, Peter (Te Rangi Hiroa), 197
Buffalo
    Graveyard, 148, 149
    Historical Society, 148–150
    interment of Red Jacket, 149
Bunyan, John, 66, 96
Burns, Robert
    'Man's inhumanity to man', 74
Burton, Antoinette, 16, 46
Byrd, Jodi A., 9
Byron, George, Lord, 36, 175, 199
    'Farewell to England', 36
    'Prisoner of Chillon', 199

C

Calcutta, 7, 10, 25, 28, 29, 31, 32, 37, 38, 44, 53
Campbell, Major, 26, 29
Campbell, Thomas
    'The Mother', 36
Campbell, W.W., 151
Canada, 1, 7, 10, 12, 17, 110, 118, 151, 158, 159, 162, 165, 167, 168, 222
Canoe (canoeing), 158, 165, 166, 171, 172, 193, 219
Canterbury College, 7, 200, 203, 206
Capilano, Chief Joe (Sahp-luk), 10, 18, 167–176
Capilano, Mary Agnes (Líxwelut), 167

INDEX   245

Cariou, Warren, 12, 15
Carman, Bliss, 151
Carretta, Vincent, 117
Castillo, Susan, 16
Catlin, George, 156, 175, 221
Cawthorne, W.A.
  *The Legend of Kuperree; or, the Red Kangaroo*, 220
Cayuga, 147, 149
Celt (celtic), 47, 188, 218
Celtic Revival, 47, 218
Chapman, Thomas and Ann, 191
Chattopadhyaya, Sarojini, *see* Naidu, Sarojini
Chaucer, Geoffrey, 25, 32
Chaudhuri, Rosinka, 32
Chrisman, Laura, 62, 67, 95
Christchurch, 7, 17, 198
Christianity, 2–5, 13, 15, 18, 19, 33, 43, 62, 64, 66, 70, 109, 123, 139, 162, 201
Christian Socialist Brotherhood, 15
Clarke, Marcus, 35, 166
Clifford, James, 11, 16, 86
Cobbett, William
  *Rural Rides*, 63
Colenso, Harriette, 62
Coleridge, Samuel Taylor, 138, 146
Collis-Buthelezi, Victoria, 80
Colonial Office, 61
Congregationalism, 62, 68, 110, 120, 143
Congress Party, 15
Conversion (conversion narrative), 2–6, 19, 32, 33, 36, 43, 53, 110, 113, 120–122, 147, 149, 162
Coppin, Levi Jenkins, 69
Copway, George
  lectures on Red-Jacket, 148, 149
  *The Life, History, and Travels of Kah-Ge-Ga-Gah-Bowh*, 19, 162

'Once more I see my fathers' land', 1, 5, 6
Cotton, Charles, 75
Coull, Dr, 133
Coupland, R. Harding, 194, 195
Cousins, James, 218
Couzens, Tim, 85, 88, 93–96, 105
Cowper, William
  'The Task', 72, 73, 96, 126, 129
'Cradle of the World, The', 17
*Crisis: a Record of the Darker Races, The*, 76, 101
Cugoano, Ottobah
  *The Narrative of the Enslavement of Ottobah Cugoano, a Native of Africa*, 116
Curnow, Allen, 52
Curnow, Jenifer, 191, 192
Curtin, Rev. Mr, 122
Cust, Lionel, 80


D
*Daily Province Magazine*, 166
*Daily Southern Cross*, 198
Darwin (Darwinian), 35, 200
Davidson, John, 45
Dean, Misao, 118
Defoe, Daniel, 63
  *Journal of the Plague Year*, 63
DeKock, Leon, 9, 12
De la Mare, Walter, 51
De Lisle, Leconte, 37
*Democrat, The* (Ann Arbour), 162
Derozio, Henry
  'Ode: from the Persian of Hafiz, freely translated', 29, 55
  'To India–My Native Land', 29, 55
Desrochers, Robert Jr, 119
Dickens, Charles, 63
Dickensian, 152

*Dictionary of National Biography, The*, 75
Dixon, Thomas J Jr., *The Clansman*, 84
Domett, Alfred, *Ranolf and Amohia*, 185, 186, 188, 207
Drummond, William Henry, 152, 161
Dubois, W.E.B., *The Souls of Black Folk*, 77, 101
Duff, Alexander, 30
Dumas, Alexandre, 77
Dunn, Theodore Douglas, *The Bengali Book of English Verse*, 15, 220
Dutch Reformed Church, 70
Dutt, Abju, 44
Dutt, Aru, 34, 37
*Dutt Family Album, The*, 31, 34
Dutt, Govin, 31
Dutt, Greece, 31
Dutt, Hur Chunder, 31
Dutt, Omesh, 31
Dutt, Romesh Chunder, 8
  *The Literature of Bengal*, 18
Dutt, Toru
  Edmund Gosse's reviews of, 16
  works; *Ancient Ballads and Legends of Hindustan*, 34, 38, 42–43; *Journal de Mademoiselle D'Arvers*, 37; 'Our Casuarina Tree', 53; *A Sheaf Gleaned in French Fields*, 34, 37, 38, 44; 'Sita', 43–44, 52
Dying race, myth of, *see* Proleptic elegy

**E**
Ellis, Markman, 127–128
Emerson, Ralph Waldo, 50, 221
Empire, British, 6, 7, 80, 188
*Encylopaedia of Canada, The*, 151
Epigraph, 31, 54, 65, 67–70, 74–79, 83

Equiano, Olaudah
  *The Interesting Narrative of the Life of OlaudahEquiano, or GustavusVassa, the African, Written by Himself*, 116, 117
Ethiopianism, 69

**F**
Fairburn, John, 107
Fanon, Franz, 176
Federal Sherman Institute, 200
Ferguson, Moira, 118, 143
*Fin de siécle*, 17, 45, 47, 52, 222
Flecker, James Elroy, 51, 220
Fletcher, John, 26
Forsyth, Mrs, 136
Fox, Charles James, 74
Frame, Alex, 192
Fugitive Slave Act, 68

**G**
Gandhi, Leela, 8–9
Gayley, Charles Mills, 80
Ghose, Manmohan, 9, 14, 51, 217, 220
Ghosh, Kasiprashad (Prasad, Kashi), 29, 32
Gladstone, Herbert (Lord), 61
*Glasgow Courier*, 134
*Globe, Sunday*, 155
*Globe, Toronto*, 151, 157, 222
Goldsmith, Oliver
  'The Deserted Village', 73
Gollancz, Israel, *see* A Book of Homage to Shakespeare
Gordon Shaw Opera Company, 152
Gosse, Edmund
  'At Homes', 47
  friendship with Sarojini Naidu, 30, 53
  reviews of Toru Dutt, 16

Gould, Philip, 113, 119, 126
Gray, Stephen, 93–96, 105
Gray, Thomas, 14
Grey, Sir George
  *Polynesian Mythology*, preface 1855, 186, 192, 194, 197; preface 1885, 186, 192, 194, 197
Griffith, D.W., *Birth of a Nation*, 84
Gronniosaw, James Albert Ukawsaw
  *A Narrative of the Most Remarkable Particulars in the Life of James Albert UkawsawGronniosaw, an African Prince, as Related by Himself*, 117
*Guardian, The*, 219

**H**
'Habitant' poetry, 152, 224
Hadfield, Octavius, 189, 195
Haggard, H. Rider
  *Nada the Lily*, 85
Hall, Catherine, 107, 109
Harcourt, Lewis Vernon (Lord), 61
Harte, Bret, 221
Hatton Garden, 129
Head, Lindsay, 190, 207
Hearn, Lafcadio, 51, 220
Heavysege, Charles, 151
Heinemann African Writers Series, 93
Heinemann, William, 51, 52
Higley, Brewster M., 'My Western Home', 91
Hindu College, 15, 25, 29, 31, 33, 36
*Hindu Intelligencer*, 29
'Hope, Laurence', pseudonym of Adela Nicholson
  *The Garden of Kama and other Love Lyrics from India*, 50
Hulme, Peter, 12
Hyderabad, 17, 150
Hymns, 4, 5, 9, 66, 68–72, 96, 123

**I**
Indigenous literary criticism, 9

**J**
Jackson, George Holbrook, 47
Jackson, Michael, 190
Jea, John
  *The Life, History, and Unparalleled Sufferings of John Jea, the African Preacher*, 117
Jespersen, Otto, 81
Johnson, David, 63
Johnson, E. Pauline (Tekehionwake)
  costume, 147, 153, 154, 157
  obituary, 151
  stage performances, 157, 158
  works; 'A Cry from an Indian Wife', 158; 'A Squamish Legend of Napoleon', 173; 'As Red Men Die', 161; 'A Strong Race Opinion', 155, 161, 175; 'Bass Lake (Muskoka)', 164, 165; *Canadian Born*, 158; 'The Cattle Thief', 157, 158, 160, 161; 'The Corn Husker', 161; The Death Cry', 161; *Flint and Feather*, 158, 159; 'The Grey Archway', 168, 170, 173; 'The Indian Corn Planter', 161; *Legends of Vancouver*, 10, 13, 166, 167, 174, 175, 222; 'The Lost Island', 170, 171; 'The Lost Salmon Run', 172, 173; 'The Lure in Stanley Park', 169; 'Outdoor Pastimes for Women', 158, 165; 'The Pilot of the Plains', 161; 'The Recluse', 167, 169, 171, 173; 'The Re-interment of Red-Jacket', 149; 'The Sea Serpent', 172–174; 'The Song My Paddle Sings', 165, 166;

Johnson, E. Pauline (Tekehionwake) (*cont.*)
  'The Squamish Twins', 167; 'Star Lake (Muskoka)', 164–165; 'The Two Sisters', 167–168, 172; 'The Two Sisters: the Lions', 167–168; The *White Wampum*, 158
Johnson, Evelyn, 154
Jones, Cheslyn, 70
Jones, Daniel, 67
Justice, Daniel Heath, 9

**K**
KaMancinza, Bambatha, 79
Karetu, Timoti, 206, 207
Keats, John, 14, 33, 175
Kelly, John Liddell
  *Heather and Fern: Songs of Scotland and Maoriland*, 21
  'Sonnet: In Maoriland', 21
Kerr, Donald Jackson, 192
Ke-sha-mon-e-doo, 2, 3
Kipling, Rudyard; Kiplingesque, 14, 15
*Koranta ea Becoana*, 67
Kufferath, Maurice
  '1914: Chant Funebre', 76

**L**
Ladies' Society of Birmingham for the Relief of British Negro Slaves, 133
Lampman, Archibald, 151, 152
Lang, Andrew
  *Myth, Ritual and Religion*, 47
Lapula, Lerothodi, 82
'Lay of the Last Survivor', *see Beowulf*
Lee, Sydney, 80
*Leicester Chronicle*, 134
Leighton, Mary Elizabeth, 157
Lester, Alan, 19
Lighthall, W.D., 154

London, 10, 16, 17, 31–33, 37, 38, 45, 51, 52, 62, 64, 67, 70, 73, 76, 80, 92, 109, 125, 128, 134, 167, 168, 170, 171, 186, 218, 219
Longfellow, Henry Wadsworth, 7, 153–155, 161, 175
  *Hiawatha*, 7, 154, 155, 175
Lopenzina, Drew, 8, 89
Loughnan, R.A., 215
Lovedale Press, 93
Lowell, James Russell
  'Brotherhood Song of Liberty', 71
  'Stanzas on Freedom', 69
Low, Gail Ching-Liang, 91
Luckie, Ida B, 76–77
  'Retribution', 76, 101
Lyall, Alfred, 50, 221
Lyon, George W., 174
Lyons, Martyn, 65
Lyttleton, Lord, 200

**M**
Macaulay, Thomas Babington
  'Hampden', 199
  'Minute on Education', 25
  'The Armada', 199
*Mahabharata*, 38–40
Mair, Charles, 154, 161
Malabari, Behramji, 30
Manicktollah Street, 7, 44, 53
Manning, Mr, 134
Mâori
  newspapers, 190, 203
Maoriland, 185, 196
Maritz, Manie, 107, 108, 137–139
Marossi, 107, 108, 137–139
Marrant, John
  *A Narrative of the life of John Marrant of New York in North America; Giving an*

# INDEX   249

*Account of his Conversion when only 14 years of age*, 113
Martin, Lady, 190
Martin, Mary, 37, 38, 70
Martin, William, 195
Marx, Edward, 222
Matabele, 85, 88, 90–96
Matanuku, TeRangi, 189
Maunsell, Robert, 195
Mayhew, Henry
  *London Labour and the London Poor*, 63
McClintock, Anne, 86
McClung, Nellie
  *The Stream Runs Fast*, 157
McDonald, James, 197, 198
McKenney, *see* McKinney
McKinney, Colonel(McKenney), 5, 11
McRae, Jane, 190, 191
McRaye, Walter, 152, 153, 157
Mechanics' Institutes, 195
Medievalism, 31, 40, 196
Memory, 12, 13, 42, 43, 53, 58, 68, 79, 87, 89, 93, 123, 149, 161, 163, 168, 169, 197, 202–205, 210, 222
Methodist, 4–7, 69, 120, 157
Meynell, Alice, 51
Mielke, Laura L., 16
Milton, John, 25, 30, 32, 37, 66, 175
Missionary
  Berlin Missionary Society, 63
  Church Missionary Society, 188, 191, 198
  *Missionary Herald*, 148
Mitford, Mary Russell, 120
Modernism, 14, 71, 72
Modernity, 12, 17, 35, 43, 53, 67, 159, 171, 176, 189, 196, 205, 223
Mohawk, 7, 10, 15, 17, 147, 149, 150, 152, 161, 162, 219

Molteno, Betty, 62
*Monthly Review, The*, 116
Moodie and Sankey, 62
Moodie, John Wedderburn Dunbar, 110
Moodie, Susanna, *see* Strickland, Susanna
Moore, Tom
  *Lalla Rookh*, 221
Moravian Church, 109, 134
Moravian ladies (Mrs Richter, Mrs Olufsen, and Mrs Sauter), 123
More, Hannah, 109, 119, 126
  'The Black Slave Trade', 140, 144
Māori
  Kingitanga, or Māori King, movement, 196
  language, 187, 206, 207
  mythology, 188
*Morning Chronicle*, 137, 146
Morra, Linda M., 158
Morris, Lewis, 75
Morris, Patricia, 64, 203
Morris [Richard] and Sceat [Walter W.], Specimens of Early English, 203
*Mother's Magazine*, 175
M'Queen, Mr, 133
Mukherjee, Meenakshi, 38, 222, 223

**N**

Naidu, Sarojini, *née* Sarojini Chattopadhyaya
  *The Bird of Time*, 51
  *The Golden Threshold*, 51
  'Indian Dancers', 49
National Association for the Advancement of Colored People (NAACP), 76, 77, 84
Native Ladies' Institution (Calcutta), 38

Native Ladies' Normal School (the Banga Mahila Bidyalaya), 36
Native Schools (New Zealand); Native Schools Act, 198, 206
Natives' Land Act (South Africa), 61, 66, 74
*Negro's Memorial, or, Abolitionist's Catechism, The*, 141
Newspapers, 6, 13, 30, 61, 67, 76, 84, 158, 162, 167, 169, 180, 190, 197, 198, 206, 208, 221
Newton, John
*Thoughts upon the Slave Trade*, 120–121
New Woman, the, 92, 156, 158
New Zealand, 7, 10–12, 26, 52, 64, 80, 163, 166, 168, 185–187, 191, 194, 195, 197, 198, 200, 201, 207–209, 222
*New Zealand Herald*, 187
New Zealand Institute, 195
Ngata, Apirana
 'A Scene from the Past', 7, 204, 205, 207, 209, 221
 'The Past and Future of the Maori', 198, 200, 204, 205
Ngata, Paratene, 200, 209
Nicholson, Adela, *see* 'Laurence Hope'
Northwest Rebellion, 158, 159
Novel, the
 gothic, 19, 132
 of sentiment, 19, 127, 128

## O

Ojibwa, 'War Song', 5, 11, 17
Old English, 202, 203
 *See also* Anglo-Saxon
Oneida, 147, 149
Onondaga, 147, 149

Orbell, Margaret, 193
Orientalism, 35, 50–52, 220
Orwell, George, 63
Ossian (Ossianic), 197
*Otago Daily Times*, 198
*Otago Witness*, 197, 198

## P

Palgrave's *Golden Treasury*, 30
*Pall Mall Gazette, The*, 50
Parker, Ely S., 148
Parkman, Francis, 155, 156, 175
Pater, Walter, 52
Performance (performativity), 10, 16, 17, 19, 40, 44–46, 52, 70, 81, 127, 129, 152, 153, 157–160, 162, 172, 173, 205, 210, 218, 222, 223
Peyer, Bernd, 3
Phillips, Mr, 130–134, 136, 137
Pirikawau, 189
Plaatje, Solomon T (Sol)
 'A South African's Homage', 80, 83
 early education, 15, 29, 63–64
 employment by the Post Office, 64
 in Kimberley, 63, 64, 67, 81, 82
 in London, 10, 17, 62–64
 *Mhudi: An Epic of South African Native Life a Hundred Years Ago*, 85
 *Native Life in South Africa Before and Since the European War and the Boer Rebellion*, 61–67, 69–76, 83
Pleasant Sunday Afternoon Societies, 62
Polynesian Society, 195
Pomare, Maui, 199
Pope, Alexander
 'An Essay on Man', 4
Pound, Ezra, 51
Prasad, Kashi, *see* Ghosh, Kasiprashad
Pratt, Mary Louise, 95

*Press*, Christchurch, 17, 198
Prince, Mary
　arrival in London, 76, 108–109
　birth, 112
　*The History of Mary Prince, a West Indian Slave, Related by Herself*, 17, 107–139
　movement, 107, 109
　relationship with Pringle, 10, 16, 18, 19, 107–111, 118, 119, 121, 122, 130–139
　relationship with Strickland, 10, 16, 18, 107–110, 119–121, 123, 129, 131–139
Pringle, Margaret, 107, 123
Pringle, Thomas
　Anti-Slavery Society, 16, 108, 119, 128
　relationship with Prince, 10, 16, 18, 19, 107–111, 118, 119, 121, 122, 130–139
　relationship with Strickland, 10, 18, 19, 110–113, 117–121, 123, 127–139
　in South Africa, 107, 137, 143
　works; 'The Bechuana Boy', 108, 137–139; 'The Bushman', 108; 'To Oppression', 108; 'To Sir Walter Scott', 107
Proleptic elegy (myth of dying race), 10, 11, 221
Proverbs, 75, 81, 88, 187, 192, 194

## Q

Quagga Press, 93
*Quarterly Review*, 121
Quashi, *see* James Ramsay

## R

Radcliffe, Ann, 65
Ramayana, 38, 39, 43

Ramsay, James
　*Essay on the Treatment and Conversion of African Slaves in the British Sugar Colonies*, 113
Rand, Theodore Harding
　*Treasury of Canadian Verse*, 152
Red Jacket, Chief
　burial (grave), 147, 148, 150
　'The Re-interment of Red-Jacket', 150
Reeves, William Pember, 80
　'The Passing of the Forest', 163
Remington, Frederic, 154
Rex, Cathy, 5
Richardson, David Lester
　*Selections from the British Poets*, 2
Richardson, John
　*Wacousta*, 7, 175
Richards, Thomas, 14, 27, 89
Riel, Louis, 158
Roach, Joseph, 17
Roberts, C.G.D., 151
Roberts, Emma, 28, 29, 32
Rogers, Shef, 206
Romanticism, Romantics, 3, 53, 72, 120
Ropiha, TeRiwau, 189
Rose, Jonathan, 67, 81
Rossetti, Christina
　'Goblin Market', 41
Ross, Robbie, 51
Ross, Ronald, 83
Rousseau, Jean-Jacques, 108
*Ruin, The*, 204

## S

Saintsbury, George, 75
Salih, Sara, 116, 119, 131, 134
Sanskrit, 30, 33, 38, 39, 43, 47, 203
*Saturday Review*, 218

*Savoy, The*, 50
Schalkwyk, David, 82
Schoolcraft, Henry Rowe
    'Alhalla, or the Lord of Talladega: a Tale of the Creek War', 155
    'Geehale: An Indian Lament', 6
Schouten, Erica, 203
Schriener, Olive, 92
Scott, Duncan Campbell, 152
Scott, Sir Walter, 107–108
    *Ivanhoe*, 7
*Seafarer, The*, 202
Seneca, 147–149
Sen, Keshub Chunder, 36
Seton, Ernest Thompson
    correspondence with Pauline Johnson, 154
    Woodcraft Indians; American Boy Scouts, 154
Settler nationalism, 7
Shakespeare, William
    *Merchant of Venice, The*, 79
    *Romeo and Juliet*, 77–78, 82
    tercentenary of death, 79
    *Titus Andronicus*, 78
Shelley, Mary
    *Frankenstein*, 133
Shelley, Percy Bysshe, 27, 45, 133, 166
Shenstone, William
    'He Compares His Humble Fortune with the Distress of Others', 113–114
Sims, G. R., 221
Six Nations' Reserve, 7
Slave narrative, 17, 18, 111, 115–121, 132, 133, 138
Slavery, 4, 17, 73, 108, 116, 119, 121, 125–127, 130, 131, 132, 134, 136, 222
    *See also* Anti-Slavery Society
Smily, Owen, 152, 153
Smith, G. C. Moore, 83
Smith, Linda Tuhiwai, 9
Smith, S. Percy, 197, 199
Society of Friends, 134
Solomon, Georgiana, 62, 84
Somerset, Lord Charles, 107
South Africa, 9, 10, 13, 61–67, 69–80, 83–87, 107, 137, 189, 217
South African Native National Congress (African National Congress), 10, 15, 61, 69, 85
Southey, Robert, 26
Stafford, Don, 190–192
Starfield, Jane, 75
St Clair, William, 66, 72
Stephens, George, 100
Stone, William L., 147–148
Strickland, Susanna; Moodie, Susanna (Mrs)
    amanuensis to Mary Prince, 18, 120, 122
    'Appeal to the Free', 128
    *History of Mary Prince, The*, 17, 107–139
    *Narrative of Louis Asa-Asa, A Captured African*, 111
    poetry, 19
    *Roughing it in the Bush*, 110
    *Slavery described by a Negro; being the Narrative of Ashton Warner, a Native of St Vincent's*, 111, 112
    'Trifles from the Burthen of Life', 118, 123
Sweet, Henry
    *Anglo-Saxon Primer*, 203
    *Anglo-Saxon Reader in Prose and Verse*, 203
Swinburne, Algernon, 35, 218
Symbolist poetry, 48
Symons, Arthur, 14, 16, 35, 45–51

friendship with Sarojini Naidu, 10, 15–17, 25–53, 220, 222
'Javanese Dancers', 49
*Studies in Prose and Verse*, 47
Synge, J.M., 218


T

Tagore, Rabindranath, 50, 220
  Foreword to *Bengali Book of English Verse*, 50, 220
Te Aute College, 15, 164, 198
Te Aute College Students' Association, 199
Te Heu Heu, Iwikau, 192
Tekehionwake, *see* Johnson, E. Pauline
Te Kooti Arikirangi Te Turuki, 196, 209
Tennyson, Alfred, Lord, 14, 45, 66, 96, 153, 175, 185, 197, 218
Te Rangikaheke, Wiremu Maihi (William Marsh), 10, 13, 16, 18, 185–210
*Te Wananga*, 190
Theosophy, 47
Thiong'o, Ngũgĩwa
  *Decolonising the Mind: the Politics of Language in African Literature*, 83
Thornton, James, 15
Thurston, John, 119
Thwaite, Anne, 35
*Times Literary Supplement, The*, 217
*Times, The*, 18, 51
Traill, Catherine Parr, née Strickland, 168
Translation, 3–5, 13, 34, 38–39, 42–44, 66–67, 73, 82, 89, 113, 114, 172, 176, 185–187, 194, 196, 198, 203, 205, 208, 220, 223
Trimmer, Sarah (Mrs)

*The CharitySchool Spelling Book*, 122–124
Trumpener, Kate, 94
Tswana, oral traditions, 89, 189–190, 221
Turk and Caicos Islands, 108
Tuscarora, 147, 149


U

'Ubi sunt' motif, 202, 204
*Umteleliwa Bantu*, 84–85
University
  Canterbury College, New Zealand, 7, 200, 203, 206
  dialectical or debating societies, 195, 200
  English literature, teaching of, 6–7, 19, 203
  London University, 62, 67, 70
  School of African and Oriental Studies, 62


V

Vancouver, 10, 13, 151, 166, 167, 169–171, 175, 222
Vedanta, 47
Victoria, Queen, 191, 198
Vikings, 192
*Vishnu Purana*, 38, 42
Viswanathan, Gauri, 8, 25
Vizenor, Gerald
  *Darkness in Saint Louis Bearheart*, 11, 21
Voortrekke (Voortrekkers), 79, 96
Voss, A.E., 71–72


W

*Wanderer, The*, 202
Ward, William, 62

Warner, Ashton, 111–112, 116, 121, 122, 131, 132
  See also Susanna Strickland
*Washington Post, The*, 147, 149
Watson, William, 45
*Weekly Register* (Antigua), 134
Werner, Alice, 28, 62, 80
Wesley, Charles
  'O for a thousand tongues to sing', 5
West Indies, 99, 121, 122, 131, 134, 137
Wheeler, Michael, 65, 95
White, John, 195
Whitlock, Gillian, 130, 136, 145
Wholers, J.F.H., 195
Wilde, Oscar, 14
Willan, Brian, 64, 67, 98
Wolf, Friedrich, 185
Woodcraft Indians, *see* Seton, Ernest Thompson
Wood, Mr John and Mrs, 18, 109, 122, 132–136, 139, 154
Woolf, Rosemary, 204
Wordsworth, William
  'Daffodils', 27
  *Lyrical Ballads*, Preface, 27, 115
  'Ode to Duty', 36
  'Westminster Bridge', 27
  'Yew-trees', 53
Wrentham Congregational Chapel, 120

X
Xhosa, 82

Y
Yeats, John Butler, 46
Yeats, W.B.
  *Crossways*, 4
  friendship with Edmund Gosse, 35, 36, 45, 46, 47, 51
  *The Rose*, 47, 98, 99, 103
  *The Wanderings of Oisin*, 47
Young Maori Party, 199

Z
Zangwill, Israel, 80, 102